Praise for

THE DOORS YOU CAN OPEN

"Through rigorous research and compelling storytelling, Rosalind Chow revolutionizes our understanding of how careers advance. She demonstrates that the path to leadership runs through helping others rise—and that speaking up for those with less influence can create organizations that are more equitable and more effective."

—Daniel H. Pink, #1 *New York Times*–bestselling author of *Drive*

"*The Doors You Can Open* is a powerful exploration of sponsorship and its potential to transform professional relationships. Drawing from her personal experiences and research, Chow highlights how sponsorship can break down social barriers, offering practical strategies to help others succeed. This book is a must-read for leaders and anyone looking to elevate those around them and foster meaningful change in the workplace."

—Dr. Marshall Goldsmith, *New York Times*–bestselling author of *What Got You Here Won't Get You There*

"*The Doors You Can Open* has a beautiful message: we all have the power to help each other as sponsors by spreading praise and advocating for people we admire. This gem is packed with useful, research-based advice about how to give and get effective sponsorship. Chow's warm and witty writing voice makes it a joy to read."

—Robert I. Sutton, *New York Times*–bestselling author of *The No Asshole Rule*

"Groundbreaking and inspiring, *The Doors You Can Open* has transformed how I think about that dirty word: networking. I highly recommend it for anyone striving for more authentic relationships and greater success."

—Dolly Chugh, author of *The Person You Mean to Be*

"With a generous and skillful blend of storytelling, research, and practical advice, *The Doors You Can Open* transforms sponsorship into an embodied practice that every clear-eyed professional should add to their skillset. When you think of *the* book on sponsorship, it should be this one."

—Lily Zheng, author of *DEI Deconstructed*

"*The Doors You Can Open*'s insightful synthesis of groundbreaking research, gripping real-world stories, and compelling personal narratives opens the door to profound new possibilities. Chow shows how subtle changes in how we approach the world can dramatically alter the life outcomes of those around us, and our own. Building off her impactful research on power and status, she demonstrates why solving problems is a more effective method for navigating social networks than leveraging value. *The Doors You Can Open* will not only help you become a more committed sponsor but will lead you to create a life full of deeper connections."

—Adam Galinsky, author of *Friend and Foe*

"Packed with powerful insights, *The Doors You Can Open* is a must-read for anyone striving to uplift others in their careers. Drawing on her expertise in power and status, Chow seamlessly blends stories and science to offer practical guidance for becoming a more effective networker, influencer, and sponsor."

—Katy Milkman, author of *How to Change*

"*The Doors You Can Open* is a smart and engaging book that argues for a new style of networking. Chow's concept of sponsorship is grounded in the idea that senior advisors should be more than just mentors who shape juniors in their image. Instead, they should shape how *others* see those juniors, opening doors that might otherwise remain closed. Chow weaves research and advice together beautifully, explaining why sponsorship works and how to be a sponsor in practice. An excellent read."

—Adam Alter, *New York Times*–bestselling author of *Irresistible*

"*The Doors You Can Open* is a compelling call to action for anyone in a position of power who seeks to make a difference in the careers of others. By grounding her advice in both scientific evidence and real-world examples, she shows how sponsorship can reshape workplace cultures and open doors to success for those who need it most. This book is an essential tool for leaders committed to advancing diversity, equity, and inclusion in meaningful ways."

—Linda Babcock, author of *Women Don't Ask*

"Chow has spent her career studying how to break barriers, and her book is filled with engaging stories, compelling evidence, and actionable advice."

—Adam Grant, #1 *New York Times*–bestselling
author of *Think Again*

"*The Doors You Can Open* has been a valuable addition to our sponsorship efforts. Her powerful personal anecdotes and rigorous, evidence-based framework lend their weight to a common refrain I share with our leaders: anyone can be a sponsor! I strongly recommend this book to leaders at all stages of their sponsorship journeys to learn more about how to effectively act as a sponsor."

—Miriam Warren, Chief Diversity Officer, Yelp

THE
DOORS
YOU CAN
OPEN

THE
DOORS
YOU CAN
OPEN

A New Way to Network, Build Trust, and Use Your Influence to Create a More Inclusive Workplace

ROSALIND CHOW

PUBLICAFFAIRS
New York

PublicAffairs
Hachette Book Group
1290 Avenue of the Americas, New York, NY 10104
www.publicaffairsbooks.com
@Public_Affairs

Printed in the United States of America

First Edition: April 2025

Published by PublicAffairs, an imprint of Hachette Book Group, Inc.
The PublicAffairs name and logo is a registered trademark of the
Hachette Book Group.

The Hachette Speakers Bureau provides a wide range of authors for
speaking events. To find out more, go to www.hachettespeakersbureau.com
or email HachetteSpeakers@hbgusa.com.

PublicAffairs books may be purchased in bulk for business, educational,
or promotional use. For more information, please contact your local bookseller or the
Hachette Book Group Special Markets Department at special.markets@hbgusa.com.

The publisher is not responsible for websites (or their content) that are not
owned by the publisher.

Print book interior design by Bart Dawson.

Library of Congress Cataloging-in-Publication Data

Names: Chow, Rosalind, author.
Title: The doors you can open : a new way to network, build trust,
and use your influence to create a more inclusive workplace / Rosalind Chow.
Description: New York, NY : PublicAffairs, [2025] |
Includes bibliographical references and index.
Identifiers: LCCN 2024044796 | ISBN 9781541702752 (hardcover) |
ISBN 9781541702776 (epub)
Subjects: LCSH: Social networks. | Social interaction. | Organizational behavior.
Classification: LCC HM741 .C48 2025 | DDC 302.3/5—dc23/eng/20241121
LC record available at https://lccn.loc.gov/2024044796

ISBNs: 9781541702752 (hardcover), 9781541702776 (ebook)

LSC-C

Printing 1, 2025

For Lia and Simon and the
next generation of door-openers

CONTENTS

INTRODUCTION

A s soon as the Miami Marlins' new general manager was
announced in November 2020, the response was immense.
The *Washington Post* breathlessly described the new GM this way:
"There may have been no more qualified general manager candidate
in baseball than the one the Miami Marlins just hired to lead their
baseball operations department. The résumé was extensive. Respect
around the game, universal. And the news, which came Friday
morning, was historic." Other headlines were equally dramatic: "A
Baseball First, at Last," trumpeted the *New York Times*.

The target of this enthusiastic reporting? Kim Ng (pronounced
"Ang"), the first female general manager and second Asian American ever to lead a Major League Baseball (MLB) team. In fact, Ng
is the first-ever female GM not only in professional baseball, but
among all four of the major American men's sports.

Almost as soon as her new role was announced, people began to
ask why it had taken so long. "If you look at her résumé, she would
have been on the fast track to becoming an MLB general manager,"
said former Mets pitcher Ron Darling. "She was on the slow track,
quite frankly, because she was an Asian woman." Darling wasn't the
only one to raise this point. "I felt from 15 years ago that she was
always the best candidate for the job, and for whatever reason, people weren't prepared to make that move," said Dan Evans, the former
GM of the Dodgers and one of Ng's many supporters. What Evans

was referring to was the fact that, up to that point, Ng had been interviewed and passed over multiple times for a GM position. By one count, she had interviewed more than ten times for the role. It had gotten to the point that Ng once joked, "Always a bridesmaid," when asked to comment on having been passed over yet again.

Given this backdrop, perhaps it is not surprising that the first forty-five minutes of questions from reporters during Ng's first press conference as the Marlins' general manager were not about her strategy for leading the Marlins, but rather about her perseverance through years of being overlooked for the GM position. Indeed, an entire book could be written about the factors that hold people back, about why doors so often do not open for people even when they have been standing right in front of them and knocking for some time.

This is not that book. This book is about the people who notice that someone is outside and mobilize other people to open the door.

Kim Ng's door-opener was Baseball Hall of Famer, New York Yankees legend, and Miami Marlins' co-CEO and part-owner Derek Jeter. As Jeter described on *The Today Show*, "Kim was the first person I called," he said. "She was the *only* person I called."

Kim Ng finally got the job she wanted and deserved because Derek Jeter sponsored her.

SPONSORS OPEN DOORS BY MAKING *OTHER* PEOPLE WANT TO OPEN DOORS

When I first started working on this book, my husband, Jeff, was my primary cheerleader. Whenever friends asked us how life was, I would respond with the usual vagueness. "We're good; everything's fine!" But Jeff would announce proudly, "She's just being modest. She's working on a book!" Of course, the next question would invariably be "What's the book about?"

"It's about sponsorship!" I would chirp, putting on a bright smile, but carefully watching their faces. About half of the people would furrow their brows in response, asking, "Sponsorship? What's that?" The eyes of the other half would light up and they would ask, "Oh, that's like mentorship, right?"

Most people don't know what sponsorship is, and the people who think they know what it is think that sponsorship is the same as mentorship.

Maybe you're part of that 50 percent who have never heard the term. That's understandable; unless you're in the business world, most people think of sponsorship as the financial backing an athlete gets from a company, like Nike sponsoring Tiger Woods.

Or maybe you're part of the group who's heard of sponsorship but have always thought of it as being the same as mentorship. That's understandable too; for a long time, the two terms have been conflated, or sponsorship was seen as a form of mentorship.

Here's a simple saying to help us get clarity before we begin: "Mentors talk *to* you; sponsors talk *about* you."

The main difference between mentorship and sponsorship is who is acted upon. When we mentor people, we are trying to change *them*. Think of an influential adult with whom you had a relationship when you were a child. Maybe you had a trusted person who listened to you when you had trouble at school or at home and gave you guidance on how to move forward. Perhaps you had a teacher who provided you the nudge you needed when you weren't sure if you would enjoy a new activity, and due to their encouragement, you discovered a love for dance or art or history. Or a manager who nurtured you in your first job and gave you impactful feedback when you felt completely in over your head. This kind of support— coaching, feedback, advice, encouragement—all falls under the category of mentorship. When we mentor people, we are trying, subtly or not so subtly, to affect their behavior, their attitudes, or their skills and abilities.

Now think of a person who perhaps advocated for you to receive accommodations when you were having difficulties at school or at home. Maybe you had a teacher or two write recommendation letters for you when you applied to college. Perhaps you had a coach or orchestra teacher who made sure you were on the field or on the stage when a talent scout was present, making it so that the scout was able to see you perform. Or a manager who defended you in closed-door meetings, perhaps changing the narrative about why a project was not as successful as hoped. This kind of support—advocacy, visibility, protection—is sponsorship. When we sponsor people, we are trying, subtly or not so subtly, to affect how *other people* (whom I'll be calling the audience or target for the rest of the book) behave toward or think about our protégés.

Mentors act on mentees. Their task is to make mentees better, to make mentees ready and attractive candidates for great opportunities. But, as we see with Kim Ng's story, just because a mentee is excellent does not mean that people are necessarily willing to take a chance on them. A mentee whom a mentor has helped to craft into an exceptional candidate can still be left out in the cold. This is where sponsors come in. Sponsors act on audiences. Their task is to make audiences notice their protégé, to think well of them, to want to open the door and invite the protégé to come right on in.

If Jeter had mentored Ng, he might have given her tips on how to ace her interview or tell her what skills she needed to further develop before she would be considered seriously for a GM position. But the only time Jeter spoke with Ng before her interview with the Marlins was to ask her if she was open to applying for the position. Once he knew that she was willing to be considered, he persuaded a group of concerned decision-makers to see Ng differently, to see her as the obvious choice—the *only* choice—to hire. He sponsored her.

If you're anything like me, you read the above and thought to yourself, "Wow, I wish I had a Derek Jeter in my life." I mean, who wouldn't want a powerful sponsor advocating for us? But the desire that so many of us have for finding sponsors obscures the fact that we, too, can be sponsors.

Now before you think to yourself, "But I'm no Derek Jeter! Sponsors are people with power, people who make the decisions. I don't have control over anything or anyone," know this: anyone can sponsor, because our ability to sponsor and our effectiveness as sponsors rest on whom we know and who trusts us. Even though most of us don't have the power to hire someone to be the GM of a Major League Baseball team, we can still be sponsors because almost everyone knows other people who trust them. This means that almost everyone can use sponsorship to convert that trust into changed relationships between the people we want to help and the people who trust us.

HOW I GOT HERE

In 2018, Leanne Meyer, then a director in executive education at the Tepper School of Business (where I work), emailed me to share that they had started working with a new client, The Advanced Leadership Initiative (now Institute). TALI had commissioned Tepper Executive Education to find them a faculty member who would build a new custom program for Black professionals. The program would be the flagship program for the organization, and Leanne wanted to know if I would be willing to lead it.

I was confused. Why me? First, not to state the obvious, but I'm not Black. I'm Asian. Didn't it seem inappropriate for an Asian person to be chosen to lead a program for Black professionals? But setting that aside, I had never led, never mind played a significant role in, an executive education program before. And now, Leanne was asking me to spearhead a new program; wouldn't it make more sense to reach out to a more seasoned faculty member first?

But after speaking with Leanne in more detail, I learned a few things. First, at that time, Tepper did not have a single Black faculty member, making me, one of a handful of non-White faculty, the next-best option (yikes). I also learned that this initiative was brand new and somewhat experimental, and funding was not at all assured. Finally, and most important, Leanne told me the leaders of TALI wanted the program to have an explicit focus on sponsorship. Aha, I thought. Now I get it.

Sponsorship was something I had been researching for several years by that point and had become the focus of my work. And the fact that this program was nascent and running on a shoestring made any potential missteps I might make as a novice faculty director less visible. Leanne had, in essence, pitched me the perfect stretch assignment. Having nothing to lose, I proposed something much more ambitious than I would have suggested otherwise.

To my surprise, the leaders at TALI, all of whom were Black, liked the concept and gave Leanne the go-ahead to move forward with me as faculty director. Leanne introduced me to Evan Frazier, the cofounder of TALI, who I later learned was friends with Leanne outside of TALI business. Leanne must have done a good job selling me—sponsoring me—to Evan because there was never a time when I felt that Evan questioned whether I was the right person to lead this new program. That was not the case with the other TALI cofounder, Greg Spencer. Greg's reception was...chilly. I could tell by the way he appraised me and spoke about the program that he had significant reservations about my suitability.

I didn't blame him. I had zero corporate experience and was someone who didn't and would never have the lived experience of a Black person in the United States. All the doubts that Greg had I had too.

But what Greg, Evan, and Leanne didn't know was that before I started studying sponsorship, I had studied the topics of power, status, and social hierarchies (all of which are relevant to sponsorship, as we'll soon see). One of the fundamental themes of my research is understanding the ways that people manage knowing that they are participants in unequal systems. Much of this work has been done by looking at people's experiences of and responses to racial hierarchies, specifically White Americans' beliefs and attitudes about their racial group's dominance in the American racial hierarchy. Several of my papers explore White Americans' discomfort with being a member of a group that is privileged. Other papers have demonstrated that this discomfort can motivate White Americans to dismantle power differentials between racial groups. Yet more have explored how White Americans' discomfort can lead to behavior that reinforces existing power differences. By the time Leanne reached out to me about the TALI program, I had been studying the psychological underpinnings of social inequality for more than a decade.

When you've been studying something for that long, and especially when you've been studying something as depressing and demoralizing as social inequality, you get tired of it. I wanted to be done with writing about the intractability of social inequality. I wanted to focus on potential solutions, on things people can do to truly move the needle. My need to do something different, something constructive, is how I came to sponsorship. I wanted to understand how people in positions of power can raise up others, particularly those from lower power groups, rather than hoard visibility, resources, and opportunities for themselves.

In short, I was (and am) an expert in racial inequality *and* an expert in sponsorship. And aside from not being Black, there wasn't a single other person at Tepper, or at Carnegie Mellon more broadly, who would have been better suited to lead a program that was designed to affirm the lived experiences of Black professionals and to facilitate relationships between the program participants and corporate leaders in positions of power.

The program we built together—the Executive Leadership Academy (ELA)—has been, by all accounts, a resounding success. As its prominence has risen (it now has a national version), so too has mine. Corporations outside of Pittsburgh heard about it and wanted versions of their own. I now teach in or direct several other programs in addition to this original program, almost all of which have the objective of accelerating the careers of people from marginalized communities. But the ELA will always have a special place in my heart, because beyond the professional satisfaction from having helped to build something successful, I have been changed by the relationships I've had the fortune to build through it.

One of the relationships I am most grateful for is with none other than skeptic number 1, Greg Spencer, whom I am now pleased to call friend, mentor, and sponsor. Even though I am no longer the faculty director for the ELA, I still teach in the program about sponsorship and its inner workings (much of the content of which we'll be covering in this book). In the most recent session I taught for the ELA, I was introduced without mention of my involvement in the creation of the program. I decided not to say anything about it, but Greg later shared with the group that I was the original faculty director who had designed much of the curriculum. The change in the participants' attitude toward me was palpable. It's not that they had been unreceptive previously, but they were much warmer after Greg's announcement. One of the participants later playfully chided me, "Why were you being so humble? You helped make this program! You should have told us!" I replied, "Sure, I could have. But would it have made the same impression?" He stopped and thought and then said, "So that's what you mean when you say that sponsorship is powerful."

Information is so much more impactful when it comes from

someone you trust. In this context, Greg was more trustworthy than I was, because with this group of Black professionals, he was an insider. For him to vouch for my bona fides was so much more effective than anything I could have said or done.

THE RISKS OF SPONSORSHIP

While the saying "Mentors talk to you; sponsors talk about you" highlights the difference of who is acted upon, it doesn't address another key difference between mentorship and sponsorship: the level of risk taken on by sponsors. The high-profile nature of Derek Jeter's sponsorship of Kim Ng has irrevocably tied his legacy and reputation to hers. Nor is Ng's career purely her own; how well she does as the GM of the Marlins also has implications for Jeter's reputation.

Actually, how well she *did*.

Fans of baseball will likely know that Kim Ng's story doesn't have a happy ending (yet). Jeter left the Marlins in 2022 over disagreements with his co-owner's business approach to the team. Jeter's departure meant that Ng lost a key supporter, but it also meant that she gained more latitude in the Marlins' hiring decisions. Her trades that season are widely credited with helping the Marlins reach the playoffs for the first time in decades. Even so, at the end of the season, the owner of the Marlins informed her that he would be hiring a president of baseball operations, effectively demoting Ng to second in command. In response, she opted not to renew her contract and remains unaffiliated with a team as of this writing.

Ng's story is a complicated one that we will return to later in the book. Here, however, I want to focus on the flip side of sponsorship: the impact that sponsorship can have on sponsors. When people engage in sponsorship, they "lend" their reputation to the protégé. What this means is that the sponsor's and protégé's reputations become inextricably intertwined. Ng's success has reflected well on Jeter. But if Ng had done poorly, Jeter's credibility could have been damaged. His future ability to sway other groups to hire his preferred protégés could have been weakened.

The more visibly and explicitly a sponsor advocates for a protégé, the more reputational damage they can incur if the protégé should fail.

Mentorship isn't as risky for mentors as sponsorship is for sponsors, and that's part of why we don't see sponsorship occurring as much as mentorship. But this all begs the question: If sponsorship is so risky, why would anyone choose to do it?

Simple: high risk, high reward.

Many people assume that the payout of sponsorship accrues only to the protégé, when in fact sponsors can benefit a great deal as well. When we elevate others who subsequently live up to our attestations, we are elevated in turn. Derek Jeter didn't just give Kim Ng the opportunity of a lifetime; in elevating her, his profile was also raised. Baseball commissioner Rob Manfred has praised Jeter for his steadfast commitment to diversity and inclusion, calling Jeter a "highly respected voice on our diversity and competition committees" and pointing out his willingness to hire women into top roles (in addition to hiring Ng, Jeter brought in Caroline O'Connor to the Marlins, and she was later promoted to president of business operations, the second woman to rise to this position in Major League Baseball).

In effect, Ng was not the only beneficiary of Jeter's sponsorship. Jeter was too. So it goes with sponsorship in general: protégés and sponsors alike benefit from sponsorship. The mutual social elevation that comes from successful sponsorship is why, when people ask me how they can find a sponsor, I tell them they are thinking about it all wrong.

If you want others to sponsor you, be a sponsor. When we elevate others, people will want to elevate *us*.

THE REWARDS OF SPONSORSHIP

Being a sponsor was key to my being "discovered" by Nicole Torres, a cohost of the popular *Harvard Business Review* (HBR) podcast *Women at Work*. Up to that point, my research had a decidedly academic bent; no one outside of the ivory tower was likely to care about or pay attention to my work. But the work I was doing on sponsorship was not work I wanted to be hidden away in esoteric academic journals. I wanted it to be out in the wild, where it could have a greater impact. So I was thrilled when some of the work was accepted by a small academic conference at Harvard Business School. I knew it would be a great opportunity for the research to have wider visibility.

It had been, if I might say so myself, one of my better presentations. I could tell the audience was with me and thought the research was cool. I was flying high. But I hadn't done the work alone. My coauthor, then doctoral candidate Elizabeth Campbell, was a huge part of it. While the core ideas behind the research were mine, Elizabeth was the one who had collected the data and analyzed them. She had been working on the research as closely as I had, and I wanted to ensure that she would get that recognition, even though I was the one giving the talk. So at the end of the presentation, I made an impassioned request that any school looking to hire a new faculty member in the next few years should seriously consider hiring Elizabeth.

As it turns out, my sponsorship of Elizabeth is what captured Nicole's attention; I had shown that I wanted to be a sponsor more than I was looking to be sponsored. She saw that I walked the talk. She was sufficiently impressed that she had the podcast producer invite me to participate in an episode on sponsorship.

Being on the *Women at Work* podcast allowed me to meet Amy Gallo, an editor at *HBR*, who later interviewed me for her book *Getting Along*. After the interview, I asked Amy about book writing and shared that I was thinking about writing one. Amy strongly encouraged me to take the plunge and do it. She also asked me to send her a pitch for an article, which resulted in an *HBR* piece, "Don't Just Mentor Women and People of Color. Sponsor Them."

Sponsoring Elizabeth is how I caught the attention of Nicole Torres, who then introduced me (a form of sponsorship) to Amy Gallo, who then sponsored my work to the editors of *HBR* and offered to introduce me to book agents and publishers. Being a sponsor got me sponsors.

USING SPONSORSHIP TO RETHINK NETWORKING

The idea that we should sponsor others to get ahead is an inversion of the usual logic of how to advance in life. That logic goes: Identify who in your network has the resources you need. Initiate contact—network—with people who have the resources you need and build relationships with them, so that when you need access to those resources in the future, your contacts will share them with you. Seeing relationships in this way is why so many of us are hell-bent on finding sponsors; we see ourselves as lacking the visibility we need, and so we are desperate to try to find people who will elevate us.

When you're in a position of needing something that only someone else can provide—in this case, visibility—you are in a low(er) power position. In this way, networking in its usual incarnation emphasizes differences between those with power and those without. Those with power—resources—use networking as an opportunity to trade resources. But those who lack power aren't seen as good networking partners, which often means that they don't get a lot of attention. After all, if the point of networking is to find people with the resources we need, connecting with people who lack those resources is functionally a waste of our time.

Sadly, there are groups of people who are assumed to be less valuable as network partners. Women are often perceived to have networks of lower "value," in that they aren't expected to be connected to other well-connected people (this is not, in fact, true). The thing is, if someone holds the view that other people are only "worth" networking with if they can provide something of value, like introducing them to important people, then they are unlikely to pay attention to or spend time building a relationship with someone they assume to lack value in this way. Perhaps that is why researchers have found that even though men and women engage in the same amount of networking, to whom they reach out and who accepts their outreach differ. Specifically, men are more likely to reach out to and to accept outreach requests from other men than they are to women, resulting in men having less gender diversity in their networks than do women. But because men tend to be in positions where they make decisions about promotions or raises, these network differences are then associated with gender inequality.

This kind of automatic evaluation of social worth is harmful, not just for the people who are presumed to be valueless, but also for society more broadly, because the collective is unable to fully identify and benefit from the talents of all its members. After all, if women's networks are just as valuable as men's, leaving women out means that the resources they have in their networks are less likely to be effectively utilized.

I want to offer a different approach to networks and relationships, one that reconsiders how we assess value and worth. Instead of focusing on what we ourselves can give or get from others (which highlights whether we or they have power or not), we can focus on what—who—we can help others to find. In this version of networking, the value we provide is based not on who we are or what we can do, but on our ability to solicit information from people so that we can connect them with others who would benefit from knowing them. In this world, our value comes from our ability and willingness to connect other people—using our social capital for collective good.

We can open doors for other people. We can be sponsors.

HOW TO USE THIS BOOK

This book is structured as follows. First, we'll explore how and why our current approach to social networking undergirds the persistence of social inequality and contrast it with an approach that reconceives the purpose of networking to be about ensuring that the group is aware of its collective resources. Then we'll look at the first stage of sponsorship: whom we choose to sponsor. Whom we choose to sponsor depends on who is available to us and whom we notice. Next, we'll consider how the revised version of networking might change whom we engage with and how we engage with them, such that we increase the likelihood that we will obtain the type of information that fosters mutual trust in relationships. With that greater trust and higher-quality information, we will be more effective sponsors, the strategies of which will constitute the latter chapters of the book.

Understanding the nuances of sponsorship has the potential to empower you and make you aware of the immense impact you have on others and, in turn, yourself. But if you are willing, I'd like us to take sponsorship one step further. Yes, this book will help you to see sponsorship in a new and more precise way. But I also hope that it will open your eyes to how sponsorship is not equitably distributed, in terms of both whom we are willing to sponsor and how we are willing to sponsor them. The sad fact of the matter is that two people with the exact same achievements do not always get the same sponsorship and, then, the same outcomes. Our psychology makes it so that we are more likely to know certain people, notice certain people, and trust certain people. None of these factors are correlated with people's ability and merit. That's a shame, not just for them, but for us collectively.

Consider a world where Derek Jeter had not sponsored Kim Ng. It's likely that it would be a place where people might continue to question the place of women in professional sports. When the Dodgers passed over Ng for the general manager position in 2005, the *New York Times* wrote, "By passing over Ng, [the Dodgers] missed out on [making] history." Imagine that: as early as 2005, baseball enthusiasts already recognized Ng as being a worthy contender for a GM role. But she didn't achieve that role until 2020, when Jeter sponsored her and showed the world that there are no rooms where women shouldn't go. Indeed, part of the reason Ng persevered for as long as she did is that she knew that her success was tied to something bigger than herself. Even though she suspected that some of her interviews for the GM position were not "real" interviews—by interviewing her, teams could claim to have considered a woman for the role—she felt that she had to go on. "[There] had to be somebody who kept that notion of a woman running a club alive," Ng has said. "It's pretty crushing when you get turned down . . . but I thought it was necessary." Now that she's been in the GM role, she's hopeful for how her success will affect others. She believes it has opened teams' eyes. "[Teams] are increasing the pool of women in more entry-level positions. . . . [W]e've seen more women coaches at the minor league level than ever before, women who are scouts, women on our medical staffs. . . . [W]e're starting to really multiply."

Derek Jeter's sponsorship of Kim Ng had (and has) impacts that go beyond those incurred by him, Ng, and the Marlins, all of which were positive. His sponsorship also influenced the larger narrative around who belongs. It has led to an expansion of people's willingness to consider who is qualified. Who is valuable. In this way, Jeter and Ng's story demonstrates how sponsors—particularly those with power—can use their visibility to not only elevate specific individuals, but also elevate important issues that add collective value for more than just the people involved in any single sponsorship decision. Sponsorship is a way for us to shape the social landscape around us. And while most of us may not be in positions as powerful as Derek Jeter's or in situations where we can engage in the highly visible forms of sponsorship that he has undertaken, what you'll see is that those are not the only ways to sponsor.

All of us can be sponsors and, in so doing, effect change. This is the singular message of this book. You, me, WE have an incredible power: the power to change people's relationships with one another—and through those relationships the social world in which we live—through sponsorship.

1 | HOW TO NETWORK LIKE A SPONSOR

I can always tell when it's recruiting season on campus because half my students don't show up to class.

College recruitment events are a coordinated effort between colleges and companies, and it's a lot of work for all parties involved. Companies send staff to the college, where they spend one or two days at a career fair, giving out corporate swag (I am in possession of an inordinate amount of logoed thermos mugs, totes, and battery banks) and interviewing potential candidates. The school supplies the space for the event and logistical support. To me, career fairs seem like a giant headache, but they're probably worth it for the companies. They're almost certainly worth it for the colleges. Career fairs help companies generate a large pool of qualified applicants. And these events presumably increase the odds that students will become gainfully employed after graduation, which impacts a college's rankings. Career fairs are, in a way, a sponsorship event writ large; colleges sponsor their students to recruiters. Should a suitable match be made, the colleges can report higher postgraduation employment numbers, students get jobs, and companies get qualified new hires. Win-win-win.

Rationally, I understand why career fairs make sense. Even so, for a long time, I detested (and to some degree still detest) them. By design, they reflect our societal bias toward extroverts. And in my more cynical moments, I see them as a form of institutionalized hazing due to the amount of stress they put on students.

I remember one faculty recruiting event at Harvard Business School the year I was on the academic job market. At these events, job candidates are invited to mingle with HBS faculty, usually in a fancy hotel's ballroom and plied with good food. But it's hard to enjoy the experience, because in most academic fields, there are always many more job candidates than there are faculty or faculty openings. For every open position, a school might receive a hundred or more applications. When a desired resource, like a job, is that scarce, it makes people do all sorts of crazy things.

The year I went, the second the doors opened, a sea of job candidates rushed the room. Like a school of hungry piranhas, they collectively scanned the room, looking for HBS faculty to approach. In this case, the faculty were over by the hors d'oeuvres table, where they were summarily mobbed by job candidates, each trying to insert themselves into the conversation with a witty comment, hoping to impress. Candidates recited their elevator pitches. They claimed all sorts of flexibility: they were willing to move anywhere, teach any course, collaborate with anyone on any topic. The volume of the frenzy steadily increased.

I watched all of this from a corner, furiously stuffing food in my mouth, hoping to discourage people from approaching me. From my corner, I judged them. I judged my fellow students for groveling. I judged them for "playing the game." I judged the faculty for being willing participants in what I considered to be a degrading experience for job candidates.

But if I'm being honest, I was also disappointed in myself for not having the courage or mental fortitude to do the thing research shows is one of the strongest predictors of getting a job: networking.

My distaste for networking stems from the fact that I see it as a sorting mechanism, an exercise where we evaluate people based on whether they have resources we want. Having done this assessment, we then put our attention and efforts into cultivating relationships only with those we have deemed to have value, in the hopes that we will someday be able to utilize that value. I mean, what is a job fair but a place where recruiters look for valuable candidates and candidates compete to convince recruiters of their value? Networking in this way is fundamentally about value identification, extraction, and exchange.

Now, I acknowledge that nobody really recommends thinking about networking in this way anymore. When was the last time you heard someone say, "Go out and use people!"? But the reality is that it's hard to remove that cold evaluation from networking. Fundamentally, people looking to optimize their networks must evaluate the resources available to them. At the heart of this perspective is the notion that people are resources to be used.

The problem with sorting people based on our perception of their potential value to us is that we are often wrong. We make snap judgments on the basis of who someone is and how they look—stereotypes—rather than on what they are actually capable of. If our ability to discern who has value is inherently flawed, so is the way we network.

HBR's most popular article on networking, "Managing Yourself: A Smarter Way to Network," advises readers to assess their existing networks for the types of resources their connections currently provide to them. There are six kinds of resources that people can provide: information, political support and influence, personal development, personal support, a sense of purpose, and accountability for work-life balance. "It is important to have people who provide each kind of resource in your network," the authors write. "Categorizing your relationships will give you a clearer idea of whether your network is extending your abilities or keeping you stuck."

So right out of the gate, the authors are saying that the best networks are the ones that help us get resources.

Having assessed the resources available in your network, the authors instruct you to see if there are relationships you should "back away from." These are relationships that "sap you of energy or promote unhealthful behaviors." This is a piece of advice I agree with. However, I find the next step less useful: you are to look to see if your relationships provide too many of the same benefits. If too many of your connections provide redundant resources, the recommendation is to "de-layer" your network by selectively culling your contacts, so you can focus more time and energy on more valuable relationships.

"More valuable relationships" are those with people who can fill resource gaps. To determine who these people might be, you are to write down three professional or personal goals and then identify people who can help with the achievement of these goals. Perhaps existing contacts can provide these resources that you just haven't capitalized on yet. If not, then you should find new contacts who can provide the resources that your current network lacks.

I don't know about you, but writing all of that makes me feel icky. I don't want to go through life treating my relationships as though they are battery banks where once I've used up one person's energy/resources, I toss them and move on to the next. Yet some of the most common networking advice essentially boils down to the idea that the point of networking is for people to extract value from their connections, making sure that they are using their connections to their fullest potential.

If the point of social relationships is to be as efficient as possible in whom we spend time with and to maximize the likelihood we have access to the resources we need, then this approach makes sense. But it objectifies us. We aren't being told to see other people as people. We are being told to see them as tools to be used. To be fair, the authors include a few admonitions to "look for ways to give back to [your] contacts." However, fundamentally, the approach here is still the same as it ever was: to classify people as having more or less value and to prioritize the ones who have the resources we want.

This is a cold and calculating way to approach social relationships.

Now, it's unlikely that we will ever be able to completely extinguish the act of assessing people on the perceived value they might bring. After all, part of the reason stereotypes exist is to help us navigate an increasingly complex social world, in which the sheer amount of information we have access to far exceeds our ability to thoughtfully consider each and every person we engage with. Even so, I want to propose a more humane approach toward networking, one that isn't about sorting people on the basis of their potential value to us.

Like the classic networking for resource-extraction approach above, networking for sponsorship is also an inventory exercise. However, what is being inventoried is different. Whereas the standard networking approach involves inventorying our networks for who has the resources we need, a networking-for-sponsorship approach mentally catalogs *who knows what and who needs what.*

"Taking inventory" and "taking stock" are terms usually used in retail, in which retailers keep track of what products they have. That way, when a customer wants something, the retailers know if they have it and where to find it. In a similar way, networking as a sponsor requires that you know what problems people in your network have (customers) and whom you know who can solve those problems (desired products). So the goal of networking is to have as complete an understanding as possible about the people who need help and the people who can help them. Networking for sponsorship is fundamentally about identifying and making fruitful connections.

Now, I admit that seeing people in our networks as customers and products is not that different from seeing people as tools to be used. But I want to stress that the approaches are different in that the taking of inventory does not involve evaluating people on their potential benefit to us. It merely asks us to act as knowledge managers for the collective. We can keep track of who in the network has what resources and who has what needs. Having this information makes us better at facilitating mutually beneficial relationships *for other people.*

In this approach, mutual benefit is not just nice to have. Mutual benefit is the point.

This reframes networking from "What can this person do for me?" to "Whose problem can I help solve?" This isn't to say that we won't benefit from this kind of networking—we absolutely will. But the point is to stop looking to extract value from our relationships and start looking to add value that benefits the collective.

THE VALUE OF GOSSIP AND WHY "WHO YOU KNOW" MATTERS

Most of us have heard the adage "It's not what you know; it's who you know." The simple interpretation of this saying is that social capital (the resources we possess through our social relationships) is more consequential for success than human capital (the internal resources we possess, like skills, intelligence, and formal training). And while that may be true (evidence certainly suggests that success is at least a combination of both, not just one or the other), this interpretation misses much of the nuance that makes social networks so valuable (and challenging to study!).

A focus on "who you know" obscures *why* who you know matters. Who you know necessarily impacts *what* you know. So a more accurate—and, yes, awkward—turn of phrase might be "It's not who you know, but what who you know knows."

I'll use myself as an example of how this works. I'll be the first to admit that I'm not very up-to-date on the latest news in the organizational behavior world. As a result, I am heavily reliant on friends who are better connected than I am to the people who are movers and shakers in that circuit. One of those friends is a woman named Gabe. Gabe is an immensely agreeable person who seems to be friends with everyone. This means that people are willing to tell Gabe what's going on in their departments or with colleagues in the field. She always has the latest on who is on the job market, who is moving schools, or who has a questionable reputation.

In the traditional networking-for-extraction approach, Gabe is more valuable as a connection than I am because she has more resources—information, connections—than I do. She can parlay that resource (information) into trading for other resources (additional information), effectively increasing the informational resources she holds. In a networking-for-sponsorship approach, Gabe is similarly more valuable as a connection than I am, but for slightly different reasons. She has access to a large inventory of people with a wider variety of both people with problems and other people with skill sets who could solve those problems. In effect, Gabe is better positioned to make mutually beneficial connections than I am—probably than most of us are!

Who you know impacts your inventory, which impacts your ability to sponsor effectively.

———————

Perhaps a less charitable moniker for what Gabe does is "gossip." Here I want to make a case for why gossip can (but not always!) be a good thing. Whatever your feelings are about gossip—I, for one, get extremely anxious at the thought of other people talking about me—the reality is that gossip serves important social functions. Gossip is really about trust. It's helpful to know who you can trust, who can be relied upon, who is more likely to be generous to others. It is through gossip—and the reputations that they build—that we as a collective can enforce group norms; it allows us to praise good group members and to punish bad ones.

Gossip can be about all sorts of topics, but if you are really paying attention, what you'll tend to find is that it more often conveys information about who is untrustworthy and who is a bad group member. Someone was indicted for tax fraud? Someone cheated on their partner? We'll gossip about that. Someone showed up at a party and left without paying for their share of the bill? Someone took credit for a project but didn't actually contribute to the work? Gossip. When we gossip about someone, it's usually to talk about how they have done something that violates our sense of what is appropriate behavior.

In one study, researchers tracked the gossip within a sorority house on a university campus. Each sorority sister was given a list of the names of the other sorority sisters and asked to indicate how well they knew and liked each sister. Then they were also asked to indicate how much each sorority sister was gossiped about and what their general reputation was. The researchers found that the sorority sisters who were most often named as the subject of gossip were the ones with controversial reputations. Targets of gossip were rated as being more well known but less well liked, as deserving less status, and as having less admirable reputations.

I don't know about you, but I would hate to be identified as someone other people talk about. And this is actually one way that gossip is good: The fear of being gossiped about keeps a lot of us in line. Another reason it can be good is that gossip can save us from making regrettable decisions based on a lack of information. Gossip might lead us to turn down a job offer to work with an abusive supervisor. Gossip can help uncover job opportunities that we might not have known about otherwise. So, while it never feels good to be the topic of gossip—especially when the gossip may not be factually correct—imagine a world *without* gossip. A world like that might be more equal and liberating, but it would also be far more taxing and costly to navigate.

As sponsors, what we want to trade in is good gossip. We'll talk more about what this means in Chapter 8, but the short version is this: when we say nice things about other people, people see that we both notice what's positive about other people and are willing to say nice things about other people. Both of these increase people liking us, further increasing the impact of our sponsorship.

SPONSORSHIP MEANS GIVING UP POWER

Because Gabe is close to many important people that I am not close with, Gabe acts as a "broker" for me—someone in a network who straddles two different individuals or groups that are otherwise not connected. People who are "in the know" are those who, through their connections, receive new information and, critically, *control who they will share that information with*. Their ability to control who has access to information constitutes a form of power. I depend on Gabe for access to information about our field and have very little privileged information to exchange. So, in our particular relationship, she holds more power than I do.

Another way to think about the power of brokerage is the metaphor of a bridge. Imagine you have two friend groups, one of which is composed of people who went to college with you and another of which is composed of your friends from work. If there's no other overlap in those groups besides you, then you are the bridge (broker). As that bridge, you have the power to choose whether to share information across the two groups or to keep information to yourself. Let's say that you and your friend Pat are both looking for new jobs. You find out that your friend from work Sam is looking to hire. The position is one that both you and Pat would find appealing. As a broker, you now have a choice: Do you tell Pat about this potential job opening? Or do you keep it to yourself so that you don't have to compete with Pat for the role?

That you have unilateral control over this decision is indicative of the power you hold through your position as a social bridge. And power, for some individuals, is the entire point of networking: to ensure that they are consistently the first to receive information and hold the ability to control who has access to that information so they can get ahead. Indeed, the research consistently finds that people who can act as brokers benefit in many different ways. They are more likely to be hired, get bigger raises, and have faster times to promotion.

Now, one way to capitalize on the power that comes with brokerage is to hoard it. The other is to give up control over the resource and to share it with others. Let's imagine that while you are enticed by Sam's open position, you know that Pat is really a better fit for the role. You decide to help Pat get the role. Here, again, you have some choices. You could tell Pat about the job opening and encourage them to apply (which would count as mentorship). A more impactful option, however, would be for you to introduce—sponsor—Pat to your work colleague Sam. Note that if you choose to sponsor Pat to Sam, you are, functionally, giving up the power that you held by being their sole connector. Your power, in this case, doesn't just come from knowing about the open position; it also comes from your ability to decide whether to connect Pat and Sam.

In effect, sponsorship is an act of giving up power. And if power is the currency we most care about, then none of us should be sponsors. But, as we will discuss throughout the book, being a sponsor has benefits for sponsors as well as protégés. The question, then, is why? If having power is good, then why would giving it up through sponsorship be good for sponsors?

Because even though sponsorship involves giving up power, it gets us *status*.

THE DIFFERENCE BETWEEN POWER AND STATUS

As with mentorship and sponsorship, most people see power and status as interchangeable. One reason people don't readily distinguish between them is that they often go hand in hand; famous people are often rich, and rich people are often famous. But there are people who are famous who aren't über-rich, like the Reverend Martin Luther King Jr. or Mister Rogers. And there are people who are rich but not famous, such as Françoise Bettencourt Meyers, the world's wealthiest woman and granddaughter of the founder of L'Oréal. I bet many of you have never even heard of her.

Another reason power and status are often lumped together is that their outcomes are often similar; we use power or status (or both) to get others to do what we want. The powerful exert their influence through coercion, and those with status exert their influence through compliance. We do things for powerful people because we *have* to (they can give us things we want or withhold things we need); we do things for high-status people because we *want* to. We are kind because Mister Rogers tells us to be kind. We care about social justice because Dr. King told us that we should. Neither of them held or holds power over us, but they can influence our behavior all the same.

But let's say you had to choose one or the other. Would you rather have power? Or status? There is growing social scientific evidence that suggests that if there's one to avoid, it's probably power, because power often changes people for the worse. Power refers to having control over others' access to resources (like compensation or a hierarchical position), and one implication of having control is the ability to focus purely on what you want without regard for consequences. This can lead people with power to objectify others, seeing them not as individuals, but as objects to be used to help achieve the power holder's goals. It also means that if people aren't relevant to the powerful person's goals, they effectively become invisible to the powerful person.

Power changes how we see and approach the world such that we are concerned, first and foremost, with maximizing what is good for us, typically without regard for what is good for others. A focus on attaining power undergirds the value-extraction orientation to networking.

In contrast, status refers to the respect and admiration with which we are held in the eyes of others (like popularity). The fact that having status depends on the actions and beliefs of others means that it is inherently relational; status is earned, often given to those who are seen as putting the needs of the group over their own. The logic here is that because our collective survival used to be based on individuals' willingness to place the group's welfare above their own—to hunt together and share the kill, to plant together and share the harvest—humans reward group-oriented behavior by "giving" status to those who contribute to the group.

Status, similar to power, also changes people, but its impact is different. Having status makes us more, not less, attentive to others' needs. And status undergirds the sponsorship orientation toward networking. This is why I advocate for people who want to find sponsors to *be sponsors first*. Sponsoring other people is a way to show our willingness to forgo our own interests—we are giving up the power we hold as brokers to help others in our social circles. In return, we are given status, which makes others want to reciprocate our good deeds in turn.

Nice people can indeed finish first, and sponsorship is one of the ways that happens.

CASE IN POINT: HEIDI ROIZEN

It's hard to be a business school professor and not talk about Heidi Roizen. Roizen was one of Silicon Valley's first female CEOs, having cofounded a software company called T/Maker in 1982, which she sold in 1994 to Deluxe Corporation. She then worked from 1996 to 1997 at Apple with Steve Jobs, where she was responsible for building and maintaining relationships between Apple and its development partners, such as Microsoft, Intuit, and Adobe. In 1999, she became a venture capitalist, first serving as a managing director of Softbank Venture Capital before moving on to a different firm as a partner. Roizen is perhaps most well known these days for being the subject of a popular case study used in business schools around the world. It details how she built her career through extensive networking. She is famous for hosting exclusive parties, where she would invite the titans of tech and other "interesting" people over for informal dinners at her home.

The case is primarily used to illustrate the power of networking. However, interest in Roizen exploded after a professor at Columbia University, Francis Flynn, ran a study using his master of business administration (MBA) students. Flynn had the students read Roizen's case but with a critical twist: he assigned some students to read about Heidi Roizen and others to read the same story, but about someone named Howard Roizen. He then asked them to rate how much they perceived Roizen to be competent and likable and how much they would want to work with Roizen. Perhaps unsurprisingly, there were big differences in how the students saw Heidi versus Howard. They acknowledged that although Heidi was just as competent as Howard, they liked her less. They were also less inclined to work with Heidi than they were with Howard, seeing Heidi as being overly aggressive. In this way, the case became an illustration of how people's perceptions of the same behavior can differ depending on gender. When Howard exercised his power to connect otherwise disconnected people, that was seen as being helpful. When Heidi did the same, that was seen as being manipulative.

Echoing these findings, other researchers asked MBA students to map their own networks and the networks of their peers and rate each other on competence and warmth, just as Flynn had his MBA students rate super-networker Heidi or Howard. And, just as Flynn's MBA students rated Heidi Roizen as being less warm and likable than Howard Roizen, the researchers found that female students who were seen as potential super-networkers—to have a lot of brokerage opportunities in their network—were also perceived to be less warm than, but just as competent as, male students with similar networking opportunities.

I want to stress here that these ratings are based not even on how much the female students actually broker, but on students' *perceptions* of their female peers' *opportunities* to broker. Simply being in a position of potential power, even without exercising it, was enough to reduce people's liking of a woman. Heaven forbid, then, that a woman actually *uses* her power. Indeed, when women negotiate a job offer and have other job opportunities waiting in the wings (ostensibly giving them greater power in a negotiation), those negotiations are more likely to end with an impasse than if the job candidate is a man. Meaning, even though having good outside options usually helps people to get what they want, when women are in this position, *people would rather walk away from a potentially mutually beneficial agreement than give women what they want.*

While these studies didn't factor in race, we can assume there would be similar results for a man or woman of color. This is the danger of networking as a woman or anyone who is socially pro-scribed from having and exercising power. If networking is about control over resources, then only some people are supposed to do it and benefit from it. This reality, then, is another reason I dislike net-working; when networking is about navigating access to resources—exercising power—it works better for those who already have power than those who don't.

Roizen's story illustrates two separate but equally import-ant points. Yes, it highlights the extreme gender disparity when it comes to who can have and use power. But it's also a story about the value of sponsorship, because even though hypothetical Heidi Roizen wasn't particularly well liked by the MBA students, real-life Heidi Roizen is quite well liked by all who know her.

According to Roizen, her approach to networking is not at all about extracting value from her relationships. Rather, network-ing is about what she can give. She looks for interesting people who are doing interesting things and who share her values. One friend describes her as someone who "simply likes to get to know and be friends with good-quality, talented people—that's her primary moti-vation." Another friend says, "Part of Heidi's skill is that she truly understands the meaning and value of a win-win relationship. . . . Heidi knows her role is to be the 'door'…through which people make connections." Indeed, Roizen has a policy that she doesn't make introductions unless it's a win-win for the person who wants the introduction and the person to whom she might be making the introduction. For this reason, Adam Grant calls Roizen, in his book *Give and Take*, an "Otherish" giver, a person who gives when it's good for the recipient *and* good for themselves.

I have a different name for her: sponsor.

Roizen uses her infamous dinner parties to sponsor people, to create or augment positive relationships between people who might otherwise be unaware of or have only passing knowledge of one another. Because she has already screened her invitees based on how interesting they are or for being good people, the people at her parties can start their conversations knowing that the individuals with whom they are speaking are likely to be people who are worth paying attention to. Roizen's parties add collective value by ensuring that these relationships are planted in the warmth of a greenhouse, instead of starting in the cold.

Roizen's success (and popularity) comes from networking with the intention of elevating other people in her community. She networks to find opportunities to sponsor. The people who benefit from her sponsorship then reward her efforts with status. And with that status, Roizen is able to exert influence over others and achieve her goals. In this way, Roizen gets what she wants, but not because people feel like they have to do what she wants. They *want* to.

Being a sponsor is rewarded with status, and having status is how nice people can finish first.

STATUS HELPS *EVERYONE* WIN

Rewarding people with status is one way that the collective tries to put a damper on our selfish tendencies. It is a reward that aligns individuals' incentives with the group's needs; doing what is good for the group can also be good for the self. Even so, not everyone is deterred from prioritizing their self-interest at the expense of the group. This can show up as choosing *not* to sponsor. And if sponsors add collective value, those who withhold sponsorship *reduce* collective value.

I am reminded of my good friend Patrick, who had an extremely difficult time graduating from his doctoral program. Most doctoral students graduate with their PhDs in six or so years; Patrick didn't graduate until after eight. When he began his doctoral studies, he was extremely happy and satisfied with his experience. He had a good relationship with his adviser, and he was making great progress on his projects. But as the years went by, he started to notice problems. His adviser would assign him to more and more projects, but she also wouldn't allow him to finish the projects he was already on. She would find something wrong with how he had done the analyses, or she would want him to collect more data. When doctoral students can't finish projects, they can't publish papers, and if they don't publish papers, they can't get jobs after graduating. Patrick started to worry about whether he would ever graduate, let alone find a job.

Finally, Patrick realized that his adviser had no intention of letting him graduate. The reality was, he was a great graduate student—reliable, motivated, and capable—and she relied on him to do all sorts of work. Once he graduated, she wouldn't be able to get half the things he did for her done. Once he realized this, Patrick reported his adviser for abusing her authority, and after a tense year of negotiations, the department ultimately let him graduate. However, his adviser was never officially sanctioned for her behavior. Patrick was left disillusioned with academia and decided not to continue with his research. In his case, the academic field lost out on the potential contributions of a highly qualified scholar because he was too valuable to his adviser. Patrick was a victim of talent hoarding.

Talent hoarding refers to a situation where leaders implicitly or explicitly discourage high-performing employees from being promoted because they don't want team performance and their own evaluations to suffer. However, the personal benefits that leaders might have from not letting high performers advance are costly for everyone else. Their selfishness deprives the worker and the company both because the high performer could have had a promotion, a raise, or other benefits from working in a position that is more challenging and fulfilling, and the company suffers from an artificial shortage of high-performing internal candidates who could have been helping the company even more if they had been promoted to an appropriate position. Win-lose-lose.

Talent hoarding is the hallmark of a power-hungry leader, someone who is focused on maximizing their own outcomes, at the expense of pretty much everyone else.

Contrast the talent-hoarding approach to an approach where leaders use their relationships to elevate others, the sponsorship approach. It is true that when managers successfully promote their subordinates to other parts of the company, their teams experience an initial dip in performance. However, this "hit" is more than off-set by the benefits the manager and team obtain over time from the increase in high-quality applicants who want to replace the promoted worker.

Sponsorship is the hallmark of a status-oriented leader, someone who is focused on ensuring that everyone else benefits. They create collective value: the company wins by having high-quality internal talent pools, the manager wins by having more high-quality applicants, and the promoted subordinate wins by getting a raise, public recognition for good work, and opportunities for further development. Win-win-**win**.

Another way that the status boosts that come from sponsoring benefit the collective is that granting people status can reduce their bias. Research finds that people who provide recommendations—a form of sponsorship—on Yelp are often biased, in that Yelpers tend to rate restaurants where they are served by a woman lower than restaurants where they are served by a man. However, once reviewers attain "elite" status, an exclusive honor bestowed yearly upon the "best" Yelpers in a given city, their rating behavior changes such that they no longer rate restaurants differently depending on the gender of their server. The researchers call this the "disciplining" effect of status; when given status, people know that they are being watched and that there are higher expectations for their behavior. They then endeavor to live up to those expectations by focusing less on non-quality-related aspects, such as server gender.

In contrast, power tends to increase people's tendencies toward bias. Why? Recall that powerful individuals tend to approach the world in terms of achieving their own goals, which leads them to see other people as objects to be used in service of attaining those goals. Seeing other people as objects also means that powerful people tend not to differentiate between people because they simply aren't paying attention. When we don't pay attention, we rely on cognitive shortcuts. Using cognitive shortcuts when dealing with people means we rely on stereotypes. Hence, research has linked having power with greater stereotyping and bias.

Seeking status through sponsorship is a way for everyone to win.

ASK AND YOU SHALL RECEIVE

You've probably seen Kyle Webster's work without knowing it. He's an international award-winning illustrator whose work has graced the pages of the *New Yorker, Time*, the *New York Times*, the *Wall Street Journal*, and many more. But he is arguably most well known for his digital brush sets, which enable graphic designers to generate images that look like they were painted on natural media, such as watercolor or gouache. Webster decided to sell his brush sets on somewhat of a lark; he saw another illustrator selling their brushes and thought, why not? To his surprise, his Kylebrush sets were exceptionally popular, so much so that in 2017, Adobe approached Webster about purchasing his company and adding his brushes to their Photoshop Creative Cloud suite of tools.

Adobe's interest in purchasing his company was Webster's dream come true. In fact, he may have sparked their interest by stating forthrightly in an interview that "if Adobe made me a truly fair and respectable offer, I would gladly discuss selling the whole thing." But after his initial excitement at their interest, Webster quickly realized he was out of his depth. He had no idea how much his company was worth or what additional term deals he should ask for. Being a solopreneur in the creative industry, Webster was fiercely independent, and he was inclined to push forward on his own, trusting in his ability to figure things out. Except in this case, Webster didn't have time to figure things out; Adobe had given him only a short window to decide, and he needed to figure things out *now*. If Webster's willingness to sell Kylebrush was predicated on Adobe's making a fair and respectable offer, and Webster couldn't figure out what constituted a fair and respectable offer, the deal was going to fall through. Webster despaired of having his dream so close, only to have it slip away. So he decided to set aside his pride and ego and reluctantly asked his network for help.

The problem: Webster didn't know anyone who had the experience and expertise that he needed; all his friends were, just like he was, illustrators and designers. None of them, as far as he was aware, had ever negotiated the terms of a sale of a business to a multinational corporation. Thankfully, that didn't stop him from reaching out to his network. He went to his friends and asked them if *they* knew anyone who might fit the bill. As Webster puts it, "[We] all have different networks, usually comprised of people with varying professions that are not necessarily related to our own; our connections might not always benefit us directly, but they could be of enormous value to somebody else. Your friend, the graphic designer, might have a cousin who is a trademark lawyer, an orthodontist, or an astronaut—**you don't know until you ask.**"

Webster's network held more resources than he knew. One of his illustrator friends, James Yang, had an agent who had negotiated some very large deals for Yang with very large clients. Moreover, this agent, David Goldman, worked with associates whose job was to generate valuations for businesses looking to be acquired. To his delight, Webster found exactly the person he needed within only a few days. "I knew, after only one conversation, that [Goldman] could take me across the finish line, because his knowledge and experience were exactly what was missing from the equation. Together, we had the right combination of skills to make my dream a reality."

Who were the winners in this situation? Obviously, Webster and his agent, Goldman. But that misses a number of other people who also benefited from Webster's success. How much happier do you think Yang is, knowing that he helped his friend Webster to succeed? How much more money has Adobe made, now that they provide exclusive access to brushes that illustrators cannot use on any other platform? And how much better is the illustrator world for having broad access to Webster's brushes, now that they are automatically offered through Photoshop? This was a deal that had many winners. This was a deal that created immense collective value.*

It wouldn't have happened if Webster hadn't asked for help, which allowed his friend Yang to act as a sponsor.

Webster didn't build his network with the intention of using his friends in this way, and he nearly missed out on having his dream come true because he wasn't aware of the resources in his network. He also nearly missed out because he almost didn't make his network aware of his need for certain resources. Not being aware of what resources his friends had and not being willing to ask them for the kinds of resources he needed made it so that Webster almost missed out on the value-creating power of sponsorship.

For sponsorship to happen, we need to be more willing to come clean about our challenges. Yet most of us resist sharing this type of information because we don't want to come across as not knowing, not having, not being in control. Why? Again, it comes back to

---

* To be clear, not everyone was happy about Adobe's purchase of Kylebrushes because not all illustrators use Adobe Photoshop. However, quantifying the loss to artists who don't use Photoshop but want to use Kylebrushes against the gain to artists who use Photoshop and would otherwise not have known about Kylebrushes goes beyond the scope of this book.

seeing social relationships as being vehicles for resource extraction. When networking is about assessing who is valuable and who isn't, we want to ensure that people see us as valuable. This means that we are inclined to seek and share information in a way that emphasizes only one side of ourselves: the good side, the happy and self-sufficient side. We want to be as attractive as possible as exchange partners, and that means signaling that we have resources that others should want.

A single-minded focus on being seen as someone who has resources that others might want misses the notion that *there is value in having problems others can solve.*

As we reconsider how we network and whether to become a sponsor, we must also reconsider how we often feel about sharing our failures or struggles with others. Struggling with something or needing help should not automatically be seen as a deficit. Failure is a core part of learning. We need help when we are stretching beyond what we know or are comfortable with, and being willing to ask for help should be seen as a sign of strength and emotional maturity, not as a sign of weakness. After all, if we have unfulfilled aspirations, it's often because we have big dreams. And if we never share about our unfulfilled aspirations, we might never get the help we need. Would Derek Jeter have known to sponsor Kim Ng for the Marlins' GM position if she hadn't made it very clear that she wanted to be a GM?

Networking doesn't have to be about evaluating other people on whether they have value. It doesn't have to be about strategically deciding who is worth our time and who isn't, leading those of us who fear that we will be seen as lacking value—like job seekers—to opt out of networking. Instead, let's think about networking as a way to expand our understanding of what resources and problems exist in our communities so that we can more effectively act as match-makers and problem solvers for ourselves and for others. In this way, networking is not about power seeking and power hoarding. It is about creating, expanding, and sharing collective value.

2 | A MATTER OF TRUST

Anyone who is of a particular age and not in a committed relationship is probably familiar with the following questions: "When are you getting married?" "Have you found someone yet?"

Or, as my parents once put it to me, "You're not getting any younger."

On a whim, David Weinlick began to tell his friends and family that he knew exactly when he was going to get married: June 13, 1998, which was three years in the future. Until then, they should stop asking him about it. The problem: he didn't have a serious partner. Two years later, in 1997, he still didn't have one.

As the ordained date drew closer, Weinlick's friend Steve Fletcher made a crazy suggestion. Fletcher had just returned from a political convention and threw out the idea that Weinlick should find his life partner through a democratic process, where the candidate with the most votes wins. In this case, the candidates would be women competing to marry Weinlick, and the voters would be Weinlick's close friends and family. Weinlick himself would not have any choice in the matter; whoever his friends and family chose for him was going to be the woman he married on June 13, 1998. Was David in? Incredibly, he signed on to the plan.

Fletcher, now Weinlick's "campaign manager," sprang into action. He brought on campaign staff, made up of Weinlick's friends and family, to support the "Campaign to Elect a Mrs. David Weinlick." They sent out press releases. They made a TV commercial and placed ads in newspapers. A website was created. The effort was noticed by *The Today Show*, and the hosts talked about David's quest and showed the ad on air. After the spot on *The Today Show*, Weinlick's phone began ringing nonstop.

Many people were skeptical of the partner-selection process and the potential marriage's longevity. Weinlick's own father said, "I am not particularly happy with this event, which I think makes light of something, which to me, should be taken more seriously." Weinlick acknowledged the risks, saying, "I understand why people would think it would fail." But he also believed that the notion that romance was necessary for marriage needed to be challenged. Weinlick said, "I think love develops. It's not just there."

Hundreds of women applied to marry Weinlick. Not all were serious contenders, but Weinlick's campaign spoke to all of them, trying to narrow the field. Finally, on June 13, 1998, twenty-five finalists arrived at the Mall of America, where they campaigned for the support of Weinlick's friends and family. A group of fifty-five voters cast their ballots at three o'clock, and one Elizabeth Runze was the runaway winner due to her pragmatic stance toward marriage. She told the voters that she believed that trust and respect are the keys to a good marriage, not necessarily love and romance. "I think it's a fabulous idea. I believe in it. I think it will work," she said before the votes were counted. "All the building of the relationship will come after marriage."

An hour later, after the bride-to-be was fitted into a wedding gown, Elizabeth Runze and David Weinlick stepped up to the altar set up in the massive Mall of America rotunda and were married. It was the second time they had seen each other, the first being a week prior when Runze picked up a candidate survey and spoke with Weinlick for about five minutes. But even if they didn't know much about each other, they did know that they shared one key belief in common: that the success of a marriage depended on mutual understanding and commitment. As Runze's mother said, "She's very serious about it. She's very committed to the idea and so is he. They'll probably be married [for] 67 years."

They didn't last sixty-seven years, but they did make it close to twenty, only to have their love story cut short when David died of colon cancer in 2018. Despite this sad ending, Elizabeth says she would do it again in a heartbeat. "If someone would have told me on the day of the wedding that you're going to marry this stranger and you're going to have this awesome relationship and fantastic love but it's going to end when he's 48, do you still want to do it? I'd say yeah."

Although unconventional in its execution, the Weinlicks' plan benefited from something that many other couples have similarly benefited from: the sponsorship of friends and family. In the Introduction, I talked about how one key difference between sponsorship and mentorship is who acts on whom. Mentors act on mentees by making the mentees better. In this case, David's friends and family could have tried to change David—to mentor David—if they thought that his lack of success in relationships was due to some deficiency in him. But that's not what they thought was the problem. To them, David was great. He just needed to be seen by the right person. Their strategy, then, was to make him more socially visible. If they could just make women aware of how great David was and that he was looking for a companion, he would have a better chance of fulfilling his goal of finding a life partner. In this way, David's friends and family acted as sponsors. They made an audience (eligible women) aware of a protégé (David) and his many positive qualities. They also changed an audience's (David's) impression of or relationship with a protégé (Elizabeth). After all, what is getting married other than a legally binding positive change in relationship?

Countless couples meet by being set up on blind dates or at parties hosted by mutual friends. David merely made this process public and explicit. He hadn't managed to find a life partner on his own, so he enlisted the help of his friends who he believed had the resources and know-how to find her. Critically, David trusted his friends and family to know him well enough to pick the right person for him, so much so that he vowed to marry the woman they picked for him, sight unseen. Similarly, Elizabeth trusted his friends and family to be sincere in their efforts to find David the right person and to know him well enough to be a good judge of whether she would be a good match. Their mutual trust in David's friends and family paid off "with the greatest love story of my life," according to Elizabeth.

In other words, this is a situation that highlights how power is helpful, but not necessary, for people to be sponsors. Despite being Elizabeth's sponsors to David and vice versa, David's friends and family didn't have any real power over David or Elizabeth, at least not in the standard way that most people think about power. What they *did* have was trust: David's trust in them, their trust in their own ability to identify the best match for David, and Elizabeth's trust in their identification of her as that best match.

The key to effective sponsorship is trust.

———

For the past several years, companies have hired me to help them with their sponsorship programs. I've found that most company-instituted programs tend to follow this script:

1. Identify the people that the company would like to participate as protégés.
2. Solicit the names of people who are willing to serve as sponsors or identify the people the company would like to participate as sponsors.
3. Pair up sponsors and protégés, using whatever system seems to make sense. Sometimes it's totally random.
4. Host a kickoff session to celebrate the start of the sponsorship journey.
5. Wait and pray for positive results.

Obviously, this is not a recipe for success. Now, I don't blame program managers for taking this approach. It requires the lowest cost in terms of both time and money; if leadership doesn't choose to allocate sufficient resources to support a stellar sponsorship program, this is an approach that at least checks the boxes. But that's about as much as it does, because like most things in life, how much you get out of something tends to depend on how much you put in.

I hear the stories: sponsors or protégés (or both) don't follow through with the program guidelines and either never schedule or cancel meetings with each other. Or sponsors and protégés meet, but the conversations are so painfully awkward as to persuade both people to swear off participating in similar programs going forward. In a few cases, where both parties are eager to make the relationship work, they get lucky and end up having helpful conversations. But none of these could be considered truly fruitful sponsorship relationships.

What's missing? By now, you know: trust—specifically, sponsors' trust in their protégés.

I was asked to help advise the launch of a high-profile sponsorship program for a large health-care company in which members of the national executive team were assigned to sponsor rising leaders in the company. I asked my contacts at the company if all the executive sponsors were equally supportive of the effort. Well, my contacts said hesitantly, most of the sponsors are. They all understand in theory why it's important. But they aren't all on board with *doing* it.

Shortly after that conversation, I saw what this resistance looked like firsthand when we sent out the protégé-pairing assignments to the sponsors. Although we had been having difficulty getting some sponsors to respond to our requests in preparing for the launch of the program, this communication garnered an instant response, with one sponsor expressing concern about how the program would work. They wrote, "To credibly advocate on someone's behalf, I would need to know them, their work, and their reputation." The sponsor went on to say that while they would be more than happy to mentor their assigned protégé, they felt that it would violate their standards of integrity if they were to advocate for someone they didn't know. In effect, they were saying, I won't sponsor someone I don't trust.

Were I in the sponsor's position, I might have the same reservations. I wouldn't want to sponsor someone I don't know. What could I say about them that would be sincere and genuine? I'm happy to help people, but I'm not going to put my relationships on the line for someone I barely know. It's much safer to just give them the gift of my time, to provide mentorship. Perhaps, after having mentored someone for some time, I might be willing to sponsor them. But not before.

This is as good a place as any to address one of the most common questions I get about sponsorship and mentorship: Can someone be a mentor *and* a sponsor to the same person? Absolutely! Mentors are often sponsors, and sponsors are often mentors. When I work with doctoral students, I mentor them (by training them how to be rigorous social scientists) and sponsor them (by introducing them to people in my network and nominating them for awards). But I don't usually start out with both. My willingness to mentor students usually depends on their level of motivation; if they are motivated enough to ask me to work with them, I'm generally happy to do so. If the performance that I observe while mentoring them convinces me that they have the potential to be a capable researcher, I'll think about ways to sponsor them as well. But not everyone I mentor is sponsorship worthy. That doesn't mean that I don't like them, care about them, or want the best for them. But when it comes to putting my own reputation or relationships with other people—the audience—on the line, I use different standards. And that's okay.

The situation I described above isn't that different from the prototypical sponsorship "origin story." Most sponsorship relationships start as mentorship relationships. After working together, the mentor may be sufficiently impressed with the mentee that they become converts; they are figuratively converted into sponsors. But it doesn't have to happen that way. Sometimes, people witness such a strong performance from a protégé that they jump straight to sponsorship and skip the mentorship part. One of my sponsors, David Motley, is an example of this. David first met me when I was facilitating a session for the Executive Leadership Academy, the program I developed for the advancement of Black professionals in Pittsburgh. Afterward, he came up to introduce himself. He then gave me one of the biggest compliments I've ever received: "I've been to executive-leadership programs at the best universities, Harvard, Wharton, you name it. You are absolutely on par with the top teachers at those universities." Months later, he invited me to collaborate with him on a US Naval War College program for three-star admirals titled "World Class Performance: The Role of Leadership, Talent, and Process." David's initial impression of me was so strong, he didn't feel that mentorship was necessary. Having identified me as a worthy protégé, he chose to connect me to the opportunities that suited my strengths. When the US Naval War College had a problem—it needed someone to discuss organizational culture— David knew he had a solution in his inventory of contacts: me.

So yes, mentors are often sponsors and sponsors are often mentors, but *they are not the same.* Because mentorship and sponsorship act on different parties, they provide different benefits.

I don't want you to take this to mean that mentorship is less than or not as important as sponsorship. Mentorship can be incredibly powerful. Having a mentor can mean the difference between wanting to quit and staying in a job. Research has repeatedly shown that people with mentors are more satisfied and happier at work than those who don't have mentors. And your mentor doesn't have to be your boss. In fact, peer mentorship is particularly beneficial for the well-being of women and non-White minorities in male and White-dominated workplaces. I can personally attest to the importance of peer mentorship!

But just because they are both important does not mean that they are the same or have the same effects. How we experience our day-to-day lives on the job is affected by whether we have mentors or not. How high we climb in terms of our careers is affected by whether we have sponsors or not. That means that for people to thrive, they need both mentorship *and* sponsorship.

WHAT WE "SPEND" WHEN WE SPONSOR

In the same way that mentorship and sponsorship provide different benefits, they also call for the provision of different resources. Mentorship, for the most part, involves the provision of time. We spend time with our mentees when we meet with them to talk them through how to navigate tricky situations or when we give them feedback on their presentations. Sponsorship, on the other hand, involves the provision of social capital. We put our relationships and reputations on the line when we tell someone that they should give our protégé a chance.

David went out on a limb for me in involving me in the US Naval War College program. He had seen me teach only once or twice at that point, and it was not on material that was related to what the War College wanted in their program. His being willing to put my name forward therefore constituted a leap of faith. He chose to trust me. It was similarly a leap of faith for the program directors, who had never seen me teach before. They could rely only on their trust in David's assessment of my teaching. In this way, David implicitly asked the program directors to take the trust they had in him and transfer that trust to me.

Sponsorship is a form of trust transitivity; if you trust me, and I trust them, then you should trust them too.

When this works out—when our trust in our protégés is shown to be well deserved—sponsorship reinforces trust across *both* relationships: the trust between sponsor and protégé and the trust between sponsor and audience. The Naval War College program participants reacted positively to David's and my presentation, so much so that we have continued to be invited back in the years since. As the protégé in this situation, I have obviously benefited from this opportunity and am extremely grateful to David for sponsoring me. Our relationship is stronger for having worked together. David's relationship with the program directors has similarly benefited from this arrangement; should I ever be unable to coteach with him, I'm sure that the program directors will gladly trust his judgment on who might replace me. At the very least, I am certain he will continue to be asked to be involved in the program, and likely others like it, in the years to come. But beyond those of us involved directly in this exchange—David, me, and the program directors—the leaders in the program have benefited from our nonmilitary expertise. They consistently identify our session as being one of the most impactful in the program.

It doesn't always work out this way. Sometimes, protégés don't live up to expectations. Imagine that the first time David and I taught together had been a disaster. Clearly, I wouldn't have been asked to come back, but what about David? Would the Naval War

College have continued to involve him in the program? It's hard to know, but the very fact that this question could come up highlights the risk David was taking on in putting my name forward. When sponsors ask someone to take a chance on their protégé and the protégé ends up not working out, it's not just that this other person no longer believes in the protégé. They're also likely to no longer believe in—or at least will be less trusting of—the sponsor.

THE ROLE OF POWER IN SPONSORSHIP

Sponsorship risks our relationships in a way that mentorship does not. People who have power can absorb those risks to a greater degree than those with less power. That means that sponsorship is more likely to be given by those with power, power that can buffer them from the potential negative consequences of sponsorship. Given that resources are not equally distributed across social groups, this has implications for who gives sponsorship and the effectiveness of their sponsorship.

Findings from a 2008 survey conducted by Catalyst (a nonprofit focused on advancing the careers of women in corporations) found that men and women were about equally likely to report having an active mentoring relationship (58 percent of women and 55 percent of men). However, the returns to men and women for having a mentor were different; men who had mentors were paid $6,726 more in their first jobs than were men without a mentor. In contrast, the pay boost for women with mentors was only $661 more than women without a mentor. Perhaps most galling: men with mentors reported receiving $9,260 more in their first job than women with mentors, even when controlling for years of experience, industry, and global region.

Why were men's mentors so much more impactful than women's mentors? To examine this question further, the researchers looked at who was mentoring whom. They found that women were more likely to have female mentors (35 percent) than were men (11 percent). One might conclude that female mentors are not as effective as male mentors, but that's not actually the issue. Rather, it was that the mentors of women tended to be in lower-level positions than were the mentors of men. Specifically, men's mentors were more likely to be at the C-suite or senior executive level (62 percent of men versus 52 percent of women). When taking the positional power of the mentor into account, the mentor's gender no longer mattered; women who had high-level mentors (of any gender) were promoted at the same rate as men with high-level mentors (the bad news: despite having similar promotion rates, women's promotions still came with lower salary increases than men's promotions). The researchers concluded that the issue facing women is, in large part, the lower power of their sponsors rather than the lack of sponsorship per se.

As with most things in life, power matters. Being in a position of power—C-suite executives in a company, generals in the military, parents in families, teachers in classrooms—tends to come with access to more information than is granted to those with less power, giving them a higher-level view of what is going on. This means, then, that they also have more knowledge of the "problems" that others have, giving them more opportunities to engage in sponsorship. People with power can also use it to exert influence over others, making it so that their sponsorship can be more explicit and effective.

Power also matters because it can change the calculus around the risk of sponsorship, perceived or otherwise. In Chapter 1, we talked about how power refers to control over desired resources. Here, we need to add nuance to that statement: power refers to control over desired resources *that others cannot get elsewhere*. Anyone who has looked for a job will understand this notion intuitively. They might be a great candidate, but there are also other great candidates out there, making them substitutable to employers. Substitutable job candidates have little power when it comes to the hiring dynamic. The tables turn when a job candidate has multiple job offers. In this scenario, employers are as substitutable to the job seeker as the job seeker is to the employer. For this reason, the job seeker is in a much better position to negotiate for what they want.

When other people need you more than you need them, you are free to do what you want. If people don't like what you are doing, what's that to you? They don't control your access to things you care about and so can't threaten you. In this way, having power can protect people from negative consequences of their behavior, resulting in what I call "behavioral latitude," the freedom to do whatever the heck it is that they want. There are many studies showing that being put in a position of power—or even just the mind-set of power—increases the likelihood that people will behave in ways that are consistent with their own desires, consequences be damned. I will never forget a faculty meeting I attended as a junior professor in which a senior White male professor brazenly clipped his nails. Everyone could see bits of nail flying over the table and hear the clippers clicking. Was he oblivious or deliberately disrespectful? Only he knows the answer to that. Whatever his intent, his implicit message was clear: I don't care about what you think, nor do I need to care about what you think.

Steven, a physician-researcher, had a sponsor whose power enabled him to engage in unconstrained behavior and have access to more opportunities to sponsor. Like most physician-researchers, Steven first completed his medical residency before applying for a research fellowship. When he found out he had been accepted to work with a highly accomplished researcher in the field, Morton, he was ecstatic. However, upon arriving at his fellowship, Steven noticed a disconcerting pattern: whenever he told people that he would be working with Morton, they would grimace and say something along the lines of "Good luck with that." He soon discovered where this response was coming from; Morton was, as Steven put it to me, "very challenging to work with."

The issue was that Morton was so accomplished, he didn't particularly care (or need to care) about how his behavior impacted other people. His research brought in massive research grants to the university, so much so that higher-ups were willing to put up with his less than desirable interpersonal behavior. The money he was bringing in was not easily substitutable for the university. This meant that despite having a reputation for being aggressive and unprofessional, Morton didn't face any repercussions other than the distaste his colleagues seemed to have for him, which didn't seem to bother him very much anyway.

Power buffered Morton from the consequences of his antisocial behavior. And while it may not have endeared Morton to his colleagues, it certainly made him a formidable sponsor. Because of his stature in the field, Morton was constantly asked to give talks at other universities or at prestigious academic conferences. In other words, he had access to a lot more information about potential opportunities than the average faculty member. Not being much of a people-pleaser, he wasn't inclined to accept these invitations, but neither did he let those invitations go to waste. Instead, he used them to sponsor Steven. Specifically, Morton would decline the invitations but in responding with his regrets would tell the organizers to invite Steven instead, which they often did, giving Steven ample opportunities to showcase himself as a protégé worthy of Morton's sponsorship.

While power has been linked to a lot of not-so-great behavior, its effects need not always be bad. Not having to care what others think can make it so that sponsors think outside the box in terms of who they'll support. When the Marlins hired Ng, she had been passed over numerous times for the GM position. It was clear that decision-makers were aware of Ng and thought highly of her. They just couldn't get over the fact that in hiring her, a woman and an Asian American, they would be doing something different. For most people, different is risky. If they hired Ng and she ended up being a bad call, they would be blamed as much for choosing to make a risky hire as she would be for her poor performance. Jeter, perhaps feeling more secure in his standing as one of the world's greatest baseball players and co-owner of the team, may not have seen Ng as risky at all.

The chronic hesitation that other teams had to hiring Ng is not dissimilar to the reluctance that poor Black Americans have to referring their friends and family members for jobs, even when they know about job opportunities and that their friends and family are seeking jobs. Despite being in a position to sponsor, they don't. Their reluctance is noteworthy because most research finds that we tend to give our friends and family preference when it comes to opportunities like these. When asked why they don't help their friends and family, poor Black American interviewees reported that they didn't want their relationships and reputations to be tainted by making a bad recommendation to their managers.

Put differently, lacking power makes people more attentive to the risks involved in sponsoring others, effectively increasing their standards for trusting the protégé. The flip side of this is that having power has the opposite effect of making people more willing to take risks, either because they don't see the risks or because they don't believe that a mistake will be that costly. If hiring Kim Ng was seen as risky, then she needed someone who felt more assured of their power—Derek Jeter—to know what they wanted and be willing to put her forward.

Now, I'm not claiming that power always shields powerful sponsors entirely from the consequences of bad decisions. While the research suggests that having power makes risky decisions seem less risky, that doesn't mean that the decisions *aren't* risky. And in fact, since power blinds the powerful from seeing those risks, it can make them sponsor in ways that strongly tie their reputations to protégés that can have catastrophic downstream consequences if the protégé doesn't work out. A widely respected CEO of a major global company, Arwin, was described to me as "an icon." After successfully leading the company for many years, Arwin was introduced to a newly hired and relatively untested young woman, Arya, in whose career he immediately took a professional interest. Her career began to advance at an "extremely fast rate." But when Arya was promoted to the high-level position of country lead, she expressed to Arwin that she did not want the role; she wasn't as ambitious as Arwin wanted her to be, nor did she want to move to a new country. Arwin insisted on her taking the position. The day she was supposed to start her new position, Arya never showed up. She resigned on the plane ride over, and in the aftermath of Arya's abrupt exit, Arwin ended up resigning shortly thereafter.

Because we, as sponsors, don't have complete control over our protégés, sponsorship is a gamble. It would be disingenuous to state otherwise. However, power can serve as a buffer. It can buffer power holders from fully considering the risks involved in their choices. It can also buffer power holders from being penalized to the same degree as those with less power for engaging in problematic behavior and making bad decisions (although, as we see in Arwin's case above, power is not perfectly protective). All of this leads powerful sponsors to pay less attention to risks, instead allowing them to focus their attention on the many sponsorship opportunities available to them and on exerting their influence in the decision-making processes for those opportunities.

Power matters. It can free us from the restrictions that bind others, but that freedom can also lead us astray.

A SHORT INTERLUDE ON
POWER AS A POSITIVE

Up to this point, you may have concluded that I am not a huge fan of power. Not so! It's that I'm not a huge fan of how *some* people respond to having power.

Power is a magnifier of our preexisting tendencies and preferences. If someone is inherently self-oriented, then having power makes it possible for them to act on their already existing selfish tendencies. This effect underlies the saying that "power corrupts." One of the ways power corrupts is by making it more likely that people will see others as objects to be used, as we discussed previously. When I was the only woman working with several senior male faculty members on a subcommittee, I was asked to take notes of the conversation for the group. I'm sure that there are all sorts of other reasons I, out of all the people there, was seen as being the most capable at taking notes, but at least one reason is probably that in this situation, the men in the group had something that needed to be done that they didn't want to do themselves. As the least powerful person there, I was there to be useful (to be used?). In this way, the overarching story of power is that it leads people to be more oriented to achieving their goals. Often, this means that they see people as means to an end, not as individuals in and of themselves.

But power as magnification can work the other way as well. If someone is inherently more focused on others—group oriented—then power enables them to act on their impulses to help the group. Research shows that group-oriented power holders are *more* attentive to others, rather than less. Basically, magnification is agnostic as to what it is magnifying; power merely exaggerates whatever was already the case. Derek Jeter may have been less concerned about the potential risks associated with hiring Kim Ng due to the power he had as co-owner and CEO of the Marlins. But his power may have also made him more willing to act in ways consistent with his commitment to the diversification of baseball.

So no, I am not unequivocally against people having power. Power, like any tool, can be used for positive or negative purposes. What I want to push back on, however, is the idea that only powerful people can be sponsors. We can all be sponsors, because sponsorship relies on trust, and trust is more closely tied to status than it is to power.

WHEN IT COMES TO SPONSORSHIP, STATUS TRUMPS POWER

I want to go back to the example of CEO Arwin and his protégé Arya for a moment. If you recall, Arwin's sponsorship of Arya was highly effective . . . except he never bothered to check with Arya if what he was sponsoring her for was actually what she wanted. When Arwin pushed her into an international assignment, Arya had finally had enough and simply resigned on the plane ride over.

Arwin's sponsorship likely leveraged his power as CEO. That is, people agreed to Arya's promotions because they thought they had no choice in the matter. Indeed, the speed of Arya's ascent in the organization suggests that her advancement was the result of Arwin's use of power to move her along rather than her capabilities in winning over other decision-makers. In using his power so blatantly, Arwin may have been *more* liable for Arya's mistakes than if he hadn't used his power so overtly to advance his protégé. So, when Arya so spectacularly flamed out, Arwin's standing in the company suffered to the point that he felt he had to step down.

Note that when Arya failed to show up, Arwin didn't lose his power. He was still CEO. What he lost was *status.* The respect and admiration others may have had in him were lost when his decision-making and judgment had been shown to be wildly misguided. And because our effectiveness as sponsors is so strongly predicated on trust—the audience's trust in a sponsor—it's unlikely that he would have been able to sponsor credibly again in that role.

Despite the benefits of power, it is actually status that is the key to effective sponsorship. The respect and admiration that others have for us translate into trust. That trust is something we can leverage to change other people's beliefs and behaviors, even if we lack formal power over them. Consider: David Weinlick's friends did not have any sort of formal power over him or Elizabeth Runze. Yet they were instrumental in changing the relationship between the two of them. Children who come home and share how much fun they have been having at school change how we see their teachers. Junior-level employees who express gratitude for a supportive manager change how their peers see the manager. When we meet a new person at a friend's party, our friend has played a role in changing how we see this new person. Anything we do that creates connections or increases people's trust in one another is sponsorship, so all these examples involve sponsorship. However, none of the sponsors in these situations has power. They have status.*

Sponsors with status leverage the trust that the audience has in them to convince the audience to see their protégés the way they do. Our judgment of a peer's manager depends on the extent to which we trust the coworkers who tell us about how great it is to work for the manager. Our satisfaction with our children's teachers depends on the extent to which we believe our children when they say how wonderful their teachers are. To the extent that we are trusted by others, we can—and should!—be sponsors, transferring the trust we have in our protégés to the audience.

Trust is the great equalizer when it comes to sponsorship. Because sponsorship is fundamentally about trust—a sponsor's trust in a protégé, the audience's trust in a sponsor—this means

---

* We may not think of our children having status, but if status is respect and admiration, I'd argue that most of us actually do respect and admire our children. Growing up is hard! That they can so quickly learn how to navigate an increasingly complex world is, frankly, awe inspiring.

that although power can certainly impact who is sponsored, what they are sponsored for, and how explicitly they can be sponsored, power isn't the only path to being an effective sponsor. In fact, as we saw with Arwin, powerful sponsorship can backfire in spectacular ways. For this reason, I encourage people to focus more on managing their status. Anyone can sponsor, regardless of how much power they have, as long as their judgment is trusted.

We will talk more about this in Chapter 7, but the other reason status is so helpful when it comes to sponsorship is that it also serves as a mask. It makes our sponsorship stealthy. Covert. Undercover. When we sponsor, it's best if our audience doesn't notice it, because persuasion and influence attempts are most effective when they aren't seen as such. Having status obscures the likelihood that people see our sponsorship as its true form: a form of persuasion and influence.

If you are a parent of a teenager, you will immediately recognize the downside of using your power to get them to do what you want. The more you want your teenager to do something, the less they'll want to do it. To counter this effect, some parents use "reverse psychology," expressing a preference that is opposite to their true preference, hoping to use their teenager's oppositional tendencies to push them into wanting what the parents want. Savvy workers might do something similar with their managers. Maybe you have a solution for a problem you have encountered, but you know that your manager is more likely to support your solution if they think they came up with the idea. So you ask questions that lead them to the solution that just so happens to also be the one you prefer.

Choice: the perception of choice or lack of it is one determinant of how people will respond to our sponsorship. We are not, however, equal-opportunity rejecters of having our choices constrained; it matters *whom* the constraint comes from. Consider the teenager who reflexively rejects their parents' advice, but when that same advice comes from a respected peer, it suddenly seems compelling.

Or the beleaguered leadership-development director whose recommendations to the executive team aren't implemented, but once an external subject-matter expert, who may be seen as more legitimate or credible than the internal expert, is brought in and makes the same recommendations, the executive team becomes enthusiastic about the proposed changes.

Advice and information from a person with power can feel coercive. Their desire to influence us, to get us to do what *they* want, is obvious. Advice and information from a person with status, on the other hand, feel like . . . information. It's information we can trust, because people with status are the people who are on our side, who want what we want.

When it comes to sponsorship, status trumps power, because we trust those with status more than we trust those with power. And in the end, what matters for sponsorship is trust.

3 | SMALL-TOWN LIVING IN A BIG CITY

In a theoretical matchup, who has more social capital: George Clooney or Elon Musk?

In one corner, we have George Clooney, actor-philanthropist extraordinaire. He has been nominated for numerous Academy Awards for his work in movies such as *Michael Clayton, Up in the Air*, and *The Descendants*. He won an Oscar for Best Supporting Actor for *Syriana*. His most commercially successful movie was *Ocean's Eleven*, which he then reprised with *Ocean's Twelve* and *Thirteen*. Aside from his acting, writing, producing, and directing work, Clooney is also known for his humanitarian work. He is a "messenger of peace" for the United Nations and, along with Brad Pitt, Matt Damon, Don Cheadle, and others, cofounded Not on Our Watch, a nonprofit dedicated to drawing global attention to international crises and to ending mass atrocities. In fact, he and his wife, international human rights lawyer Amal Clooney, connected at least in part over their shared passion for humanitarian causes.

Aside from his A-list friends, Clooney's philanthropic work has led him to be connected with a wide array of individuals from other fields. He first met then-senator Barack Obama in 2006 at an event to raise awareness about the humanitarian crisis in Darfur. The two hit it off, and Clooney publicly supported Obama during his presidential campaigns. Shortly after Obama left office in 2017, his family was photographed spending time with the Clooneys at their private Italian villa. Clooney's philanthropic work has also put him in contact with high-net-worth philanthropists, such as Bill Gates and Jack Dorsey, former CEO of Twitter (now X). In 2020, he followed Gates and Dorsey in announcing a combined donation of $1 billion to charities addressing the coronavirus epidemic.

In the other corner, we have Elon Musk, one of the richest men in the world. While not an actor, he is arguably just as recognizable, if not more, than Clooney. Musk is famous for being a successful entrepreneur, having made his first millions by selling his company Zip2, the proceeds of which he used to found what would end up becoming PayPal, which was then sold to eBay in 2002 for many millions. Musk then used that money to found SpaceX, a company dedicated to spaceflight. Shortly after, he became an early investor in Tesla, later becoming its CEO and turning Tesla into one of the most recognizable electric-vehicle brands in the world. He also cofounded OpenAI, the company behind ChatGPT. He is perhaps currently most famous for his misadventures in purchasing and running Twitter.

Like Clooney, Musk has contacts in a wide variety of fields beyond his home base of the tech-entrepreneurship world. He too has some entertainment connections; he had cameos on *The Big Bang Theory* and the movie *Iron Man 2*. Musk has also been a guest host on *Saturday Night Live* and was an executive producer of the movie *Thank You for Smoking*. And like Clooney, Musk is involved in philanthropic work, although his giving, compared to the size of his wealth, puts him in the ignoble category of being one of the least charitable billionaires in the world.

Aside from the difference in the amount of money both men contribute to philanthropic causes, the types of causes they support are also different. Clooney's charitable work is focused mostly on humanitarian issues. In addition to his support for the nonprofit Not on Our Watch, Clooney organized a telethon to collect donations for Haiti after the 2010 earthquake there. In 2006, he went to Chad and Sudan with his father to film a documentary, *A Journey to Darfur*, with the intention of raising public awareness of the humanitarian crises there. In 2012, he organized a protest in front of the Sudanese embassy, during which he was arrested for civil disobedience (he had intended to be arrested when he organized the protest).

In contrast, Musk's charitable work is often tied to his business ventures. Alongside Peter Diamandis, Musk has pledged $100 million to XPRIZE, a competition designed to encourage the development of innovative solutions for carbon removal from the atmosphere (which he would presumably also invest in). He's given $55 million to the St. Jude Children's Research Hospital, which, on its surface, seems unrelated to his other endeavors. However, a closer look reveals that his donation was in response to a call by his friend Jared Isaacman, another billionaire tech entrepreneur, who purchased seats on a SpaceX flight to raise awareness and support for St. Jude Hospital. Musk has also donated $30 million to public schools and nonprofits in the Rio Grande Valley in South Texas, where SpaceX rockets are built.

Okay, so now you have the info to do the comparison: two immediately recognizable men, both wealthy, both involved in charitable work, and both with connections that span beyond their original social "homes": Musk in technology and Clooney in entertainment. Given this, let's consider the question again: Who has more social capital?

It depends on what it is that you are trying to accomplish.

George Clooney's network, although spanning across the entertainment, political, and humanitarian worlds, is what researchers call a dense, interconnected network. Most of the people in Clooney's world know one another (or of one another) and share the same values, making it so that they trust one another and can speak with one voice on topics related to their interests. As an example of how closely aligned the people in Clooney's social circles are, in 2022, Amal Clooney, Michelle Obama, and Melinda Gates launched a new initiative called "Get Her There," a global campaign dedicated to educating and empowering adolescent girls. In this way, Clooney's social capital can be seen as manifesting through his ability to quickly mobilize other influential individuals in his network to act in a coordinated way. His coordinated COVID-19 donation came in April 2020, nary a month after the world shut down. The speed with which this money was raised illustrates the power of dense, interconnected networks; dense networks are ideal for the efficient execution of tasks.

In contrast, Elon Musk's network is looser, more open. Even though all three of his companies—Tesla, SpaceX, and X/Twitter—touch on technology, the specific technology and the organizational visions involved are quite different. Tesla's quest is to move people away from gas-powered cars, SpaceX to send humans to Mars, and X/Twitter to facilitate communication between people. Aside from his three main companies, Musk also leads the Boring Company, a tunneling start-up, and Neuralink, a company working on brain-computer interface technology. What this means is that Musk's contacts are wide ranging and likely have different priorities. Differing priorities, in turn, can make coordination more difficult. So if the question is, who can get their social circles to move quickly on issues important to them, Clooney's dense network is probably more effective than Musk's.

On the other hand, the expansiveness of Musk's network means that he has access to a wider set of information than does Clooney. As an entrepreneur invested in innovation of many kinds, a wide-ranging network serves Musk well; having a toe in multiple ponds makes it so that Musk has knowledge of a variety of ideas that he can recombine in imaginative (and lucrative) ways. It also makes it so that whatever field he might want to go into next, it's likely that he'll already know at least one mover and shaker in that world who can help him get connected to the right people. Musk's network illustrates the power of open, weakly connected networks; open networks are ideal for the generation and spread of new ideas.

So as unsatisfying as it might seem, the answer to the original question is that, regardless of your personal opinions of either, both men have loads of social capital. It's just that their social capital stems from different strengths. Clooney's social-capital strength comes from his ability to quickly activate a close-knit set of similarly influential contacts who have a shared set of values. Musk's social-capital strength comes from his ability to access information and people from a broad spectrum of industries and fields.

Access and activation: these are the two foundational components to social capital that impact who we sponsor and how.

ACTIVATION: SMALL-TOWN SOCIAL CAPITAL

What is social capital, exactly? If you ask ten different people, you'd probably get ten different answers.

If I were trying to answer this question systematically, I would pose this question to thousands of people and then identify consistent themes in their answers. Here, I did the next best thing, which is to ask ChatGPT. Because ChatGPT's answers draw on a vast repository of data on how people have talked about social capital in many different contexts, it is, arguably, as representative a sample as

I might hope to get. My specific prompt was "Give me five different definitions of social capital that the average person might generate."

Here's what it came back with:

> Social capital is who you know, not what you know. It's like having a network of friends or acquaintances who can help you out when you need something.
>
> It's the trust and goodwill that people have for you in your community. You build it up by doing favors and being reliable, and you can "cash it in" when you need a hand.
>
> Social capital is your reputation. If people think you're smart, honest, or talented, that can open doors for you.
>
> It's about belonging to groups or communities where everyone helps each other out. Could be a church, a neighborhood, or even an online forum.
>
> Social capital is like the currency of relationships. You earn it by being a good friend, a trusted colleague, or a helpful neighbor, and you can spend it when you need support or opportunities.

Each of these definitions, whether uttered at a family dinner, over drinks with friends, or in a casual workplace chat, boils down to the same core concept: social capital is the value embedded in our relationships that can be leveraged for various social goods.

Here's what I want you to notice: all these definitions are about *activation*—the ability to utilize resources that others have. Even though the first definition mentions the importance of whom you know, its focus is about getting help from friends or acquaintances when you need something. Others mention "cashing in" on the trust others have in you, perhaps to get help, support, or opportunities from others. Here, ChatGPT is pulling from a long-standing, wide-spread sociological view that social capital is fundamentally about interpersonal trust. Basically, if we are to work efficiently together, it's easier to do so if we trust one another. Otherwise, we will feel compelled to expend time and energy double-checking one another's work or actions. This is why "trust but verify" is a misnomer. We don't verify the actions of the people we trust. The very act of verification erodes trust; when we verify, we essentially say that we don't trust.

If trust is the key to social capital, the natural next question is: How do people build trust with one another? Most of the time, trust comes from our direct experiences with someone. Think about the last time you made a new friend. You likely started small, perhaps meeting for short periods at a neutral location, such as a coffee shop or on a walk through the neighborhood. But as your comfort with this person grew, you might have started letting them in a bit deeper into your life. Maybe you introduced them to your spouse or partner. Maybe you invited them over to your house for dinner. The same goes for the people we sponsor at work. Few of us would immediately recommend a new colleague for something critical. Rather, we are likely to sit back and observe. How do they handle themselves? What is the quality of their work? Over time, after enough repeated observations, we might build enough trust in them to put their name forward for more important or difficult tasks and, importantly, to do such tasks without us feeling like we must constantly be there, looking over their shoulder.

Building trust takes time. Unfortunately, time is often in short supply. This is where social capital comes in; one way to quicken or bypass the trust-building process is to rely on the information contained in the social connections that bind us together, rather than on direct experience. If I haven't worked with you before, but we know someone else in common, then I might use that relationship as a proxy for building trust with you myself. I may be willing to do this because I can hold you accountable for bad behavior with the people we know in common. If we know people in common and if you betray my trust, I can alert our mutual friends and acquaintances to your poor behavior and you may end up ostracized from our shared community. Given this dynamic, merely knowing that we know people in common can serve as a stand-in for trust built through personal experience, making it so that we are more willing to trust new people with whom we share connections than new people who are completely unknown to our social circles.

Increased accountability is not the only reason we are more likely to trust people we know in common. Knowing whom people associate with also gives us information about the kind of person they are. Consider the adage "A [person] is known by the company [they] keep." We are "certified" by our social connections; our connections provide insight into the standards against which we are held. If the people we associate with are known to have high standards for inclusion into their group, people infer that we have passed those high standards and should therefore be held in similarly high esteem. Sadly, the converse is also true: "A [person] who lies down with dogs will get up with fleas." If your contacts are known to have questionable taste in friends, then your association with them does you no favors.

This dynamic is illustrated by an anecdote supposedly about the Baron de Rothschild, a member of one of the wealthiest families of the twentieth century. An acquaintance of Rothschild's had asked him for a loan, which he declined to provide. However, Rothschild offered instead to walk "arm in arm" across the trading floor of the Stock Exchange with the loan seeker. What Rothschild was banking on (pun intended) was that by publicly "claiming" an association with the acquaintance, his reputation for financial acuity would rub off on the acquaintance, increasing the likelihood that observers would be willing to extend the acquaintance a loan.

You can think of this as the "small-town" version of social capital, where social capital is the benefit that comes from not having to constantly monitor one another for trustworthiness. In this version of social capital, the communities that are tight-knit, where everyone knows everyone else, are those with the greatest amount of social capital. Everyone knows their place and their role, which makes coordinated group effort relatively conflict free. Clooney prides himself on having a close set of friends who are not movie stars. There are "nine guys [I've known for] twenty-five years; they're the guys I see every Sunday." This camaraderie enables Clooney to effectively coordinate elaborate social events on tight deadlines, as when he was able to, in the span of one day, gather his friends and arrive unannounced (but not unwelcomed!) at the funeral of one of the friend's fathers.

Notably, one side effect of relying on small-town social capital stems from the fact that the resources in the group are not infinite. When resources are finite, there needs to be clear delineation between those who are entitled to the group's resources and those who are not. This means that as an identified in-group member, you might be trusted and given more resources when needed, but you are also expected to do the same for others. So even if you don't know someone personally, there may be an expectation that you will trust them and share your resources with them if they identify themselves as part of the in-group.

The power of small-town social capital, then, is activation; we trust those with whom we are connected through our networks, increasing our willingness to share our resources and to cooperate with them. Small-town social capital is what George Clooney has. It is also the kind of social capital that Derek Jeter relied on when he began to rebuild the Marlins; almost all his hires, including Kim Ng, shared one characteristic: they had all worked at the Yankees at some point or another. Small-town social capital, where people (mostly rightfully) assume that everyone is pulling in the same direction, enables groups to be highly cohesive, efficient, and effective.

ACCESS: BIG-CITY SOCIAL CAPITAL

The other side of social capital is access to information and human capital through our social connections. While the "small-town" view of social capital emphasizes the coordination benefits that come from trust (activation), the "big-city" view of social capital emphasizes the benefits that come from having *access* to a lot of different information and people with different skills and abilities (human capital). This perspective on social capital is what drives much of the advice given about networking that we discussed in Chapter 1. Here, the idea is that people tend to inhabit different social circles, each with their own shared set of information, knowledge, and skills. People who can cross social boundaries—network bridges or brokers—are those who have access to the information and human capital resources contained in multiple groups. They can then use that access opportunistically, either by changing their actions to account for information that they have but others don't (think insider trading) or by combining the information from different social sets to create innovations that others cannot.

As an example of the innovative power of a wide-ranging network, consider Intellectual Ventures, an "insight" firm dedicated to the generation of ideas, patenting them, and then selling those patents to interested client companies. In effect, IV is a firm built around monetizing the kind of innovations that can occur when you bring together many kinds of people with many kinds of problems. Their strategy is simple: bring together the smartest minds in the world, have them talk, and see what happens.

In one invention session, IV brought together a group of physicians and a physicist. The physicist revealed that he had come across an article in the *New England Journal of Medicine* in which there was a throwaway line about the number of cancer cells in each milliliter of blood. The physicist was struck by how high the number was and reasoned that if there were truly that many cancer cells circulating in the bloodstream, it must mean that cancer cells are floating around in our bodies for a considerable amount of time before one manages to lodge itself somewhere and become a tumor. And if that was true, then one potential cure for cancer could be to implant a filter in cancer patients' blood vessels, essentially clearing the blood of cancer cells before any of them could metastasize. This was an insight made possible by taking information and a problem from one field (medicine) and using the skills and perspective from another field (physics) to propose solutions. According to Malcolm Gladwell, who wrote about this group, "If someone who knew how to make a filter had a conversation with someone who knew a lot about cancer and with someone who read the medical literature like a physicist, then maybe you could come up with a cancer treatment. . . . They had different backgrounds and temperaments and perspectives, and if you gave them something to think about that they did not ordinarily think about . . . you were guaranteed a fresh set of eyes."

Note that Intellectual Ventures doesn't produce products based on its innovative insights. It merely patents the ideas and then sells them to companies that might find such ideas useful. In this way, IV is a clear demonstration that bringing together new perspectives and generating new ideas can create valuable resources that others will pay for.

If small-town social capital operates via the resource of trust, big-city social capital operates via the resource of information or people.

USING SOCIAL CAPITAL AS A SPONSOR

In an ideal world, our networks would have both the depth of George Clooney's networks and the breadth of Elon Musk's. But if we had to choose between them, here are the trade-offs: The breadth of Musk's network makes it more likely that he'll meet people who are very different, both from him and from each other, than will Clooney. Moreover, Musk's diverse network means that he is more likely to be aware of unique opportunities that he can then sponsor his protégés for. Because his network is unlikely to overlap with the networks of those of his protégés, those who are looking to establish their reputations in new spaces will be helped the most. In this way, Musk's strengths as a sponsor stem from his access to many kinds of people, who have many different problems that his many different potential protégés can help solve.

Consider Musk's hiring of Linda Yaccarino as CEO of Twitter/X. At that time, Twitter was bleeding advertisers, leading to huge losses in revenue. Advertisers had noted the rise in hate speech on the platform and Musk's own problematic tweets. They did not want their products and brands to be shown alongside such content, nor did they want to be seen as supporting a company that enabled hate speech. Musk's problem, then, wasn't a technical one; it was a marketing one. Enter Yaccarino, an unknown in the world of technology, but a trusted player in the world of marketing. "If anyone can translate the Musk vision into advantages for marketers, she'll be able to do it," an advertising industry insider said when her appointment was announced. Their partnership can be seen as one of mutual sponsorship: Musk introduced Yaccarino to the technology world, lending her legitimacy in that industry. In return, Yaccarino lent Musk and Twitter her stamp of approval in the advertising industry (unfortunately, Musk continues to make problematic statements on X, often putting Yaccarino in the position of having to defend his personal stances rather than marketing new developments at X).

Big-city social capital expands the number of sponsorship opportunities available to sponsors. In contrast, Clooney's more insular network—everyone knows and trusts everyone else—means that the diversity of problems he can solve is more limited, as is the diversity of the people he knows who can solve them.

Recall, however, that effective sponsorship rests on trust. For a sponsor to make good matches between protégés and audiences, people need to trust the sponsor enough to be willing to share information about their problems and their dreams and goals. Knowing who needs what and who wants what is how sponsors can generate win-win-win matches. And if we agree that trust is foundational to sponsorship, then the social capital that increases trust—small-town social capital—is the type that will be more effective. So while Musk's expansive network might offer the potential for a more diverse set of sponsorship opportunities and protégés, it might simultaneously work against others' willingness to trust him with the information that would enable him to live up to that potential.*

Clooney, on the other hand, has shown himself to be deeply committed to a small(er) set of people and a more specific set of values. A member of the group of men with whom Clooney is close—the ones he calls "the boys"—recounted how Clooney invited them all over to dinner at his house. Upon their arrival, the guests were led to a table and on each chair, there was a black suitcase stuffed with reams of twenty-dollar bills. According to the friend, Clooney explained, "Listen, I want you guys to know how much you've meant to me and how much you mean to me in my life. I came to L.A., I slept on your couch. I'm so fortunate in my life to have all of you and I couldn't be where I am today without all of you." The men were shocked and surprised. One friend, a successful entrepreneur, refused the money, to which Clooney replied, "If [friend] doesn't take the million dollars, nobody gets it." Because not all the men were wealthy (one worked at a bar in the airport and struggled to support his family), they all ended up accepting the generous gift (some later donated the money to charity). That Clooney made his

---

* Granted, Musk is not the best example to use when discussing trustworthiness and poor behavior. First off, Musk's immense wealth shields him from many of the negative consequences of his erratic behavior. But second, he himself doesn't think people should trust him, saying, "Just because I tweet something does not mean people [should] believe it."

gift contingent on all the friends taking the money is emblematic of how small-city social capital works: it's one for all and all for one.

Clooney is also dedicated to speaking out about humanitarian causes, using his celebrity to elevate the visibility of the wars in Africa. Clooney went to the White House to personally appeal to then-president Obama for the United States to be more involved in Sudan, where a civil war had killed several hundred thousand people. Going beyond words, Clooney personally bankrolled a satellite (using his earnings from being the spokesperson for Nespresso) for the Satellite Sentinel Project, which uses the imagery gathered by the satellite to monitor the violence in Sudan. Clooney says, "I want war criminal[s] to have the same amount of attention that I get. I think that's fair."

At this point, I think most of us would agree that Clooney seems like an upstanding guy. We don't like him just because he's a charismatic and good-looking actor; we also like him because he treats his friends well and he has leveraged his social visibility to elevate others. As a result, when George Clooney decides to speak up on behalf of something or someone, people listen. In this way, Clooney exemplifies what we discussed in Chapter 2: we give status to those who put the needs of the group above the self.

Big-city social capital enables sponsors to see more doors that can be opened for their protégés through their access to more diversified information and people. Small-town social capital enables sponsors to activate other people by getting them to willingly open those doors for their protégés.

BALANCE IS KEY

In the end, what determines our social capital depends on our level of access to diverse resources and our ability to activate our relationships so that those resources are shared with us. Access can be thought of as big-city social capital; big cities tend to comprise a multitude of individuals who are often members of different social groups with whom we interact in superficial ways. Activation, on the other hand, can be thought of as small-town social capital; small towns are inhabited by people who tend to be similar to one another and know what's going on with everyone else. These interconnected relationships are fertile ground for trust, which enables people to coordinate effectively.

Kim Ng is someone who has a balance between big-city and small-town social capital. While Derek Jeter seems to rely more on small-town social capital in making his hiring choices (he has mostly hired only ex-Yankees), Ng has always shown a deliberate willingness to go after big-city social capital. After her first job with the White Sox, she left to work at the American Baseball League office as the director of waivers and records. Her move was driven by a desire to access a broader set of information. She says, "When you're with one club, you do things one particular way. When you go to the central office, or to a league, in my case, you get to learn how 13 or 14 other clubs conducted business." Once she identified a promising new way of doing things, she would implement it in her own teams, resulting in one scouting director calling her "a great plagiarizer." Despite sounding derogatory, what he meant was that Ng isn't hung up on sticking with tradition or a victim of "Not Invented Here" Syndrome. Willingness to incorporate what you learn from other groups is a hallmark of a big-city social capitalist.

Another reason Ng went to work at the American Baseball League was to gain access to people outside of the White Sox. She says, "At a club, you don't necessarily get that exposure to other executives; in reality, those other executives were my potential new bosses." Working at the league also meant that she could work with executives from the other teams without being in an adversarial role, which would have been the case if she had been representing a specific team. Her approach paid off, so much so that when Brian Cashman was promoted from assistant GM at the Yankees to GM, he hired Ng away from the league to fill his old position. Ng's deliberate move to spend time in the league offices made it so that she now has a network more like Elon Musk's, where she has access to diverse information and people.

Kim Ng has both small-town *and* big-city social capital. She has a deep bench of trust with those in the Yankees network and wide-ranging connections from her stints in the American League office (and later at Major League Baseball).* It's a unique combination that makes her a role model for the rest of us when it comes to balancing the two types of social capital. The versatility of her connections makes it so that when she needed creative ideas and information to make optimal decisions, she could draw on her big-city social capital of diverse connections across different baseball teams and specialties. And when she needed efficient coordination from her team, she could draw on her small-town social capital of strong interpersonal relationships. Those strong bonds of reciprocal trust—I trust you to do your part, and you trust me to do mine— allowed her team to work together effectively.

Whom we sponsor, whom we sponsor them to, and what we can sponsor them for all hinge on our big-city and small-town social capital. We can use our big-city social capital to access a diverse set of potential protégés and a diverse set of opportunities and problems to solve. Having identified a problem (someone with a need) and a solution (someone whose dreams could be fulfilled by solving

---

* For any non-baseball-following readers, you should know that there are actually two baseball leagues in the United States: the American League and the National League. The Major League Baseball organization oversees both the American and National Leagues.

the problem), we can then use our small-town social capital to make the match and increase the likelihood that the audience gives the opportunity to our protégé.

It pays to be a sponsor with social capital; the key is to have a balance of both types.

4 | WE DON'T KNOW WHO WE DON'T KNOW

When Jeff and I got married, we did so with the understanding that neither of us wanted to have children. It wasn't that we actively did not want children, but Jeff wasn't particularly drawn to them, and due to my small stature, I had long believed that giving birth might kill me. Not to mention, we were both pessimistic about the idea of forcing our hypothetical children to live in a world full of climate crises, ideological extremism, and inequality. But biology does its own thing, I suppose, and when Jeff first held his newborn nephew in his arms, he looked at me and said, "I want one."

Before we lost our childless independence, we decided to take two big bucket-list trips. We went to the Galápagos and Antarctica—the Galápagos because I love wildlife and wanted to see the famous endemic species living on the island and Antarctica because it's one of the places in the world that may not be there, at least in its current incarnation, in twenty years due to climate change. We started with the Galápagos.

To get to our cruise ship, we first flew into Quito, the capital of Ecuador. There, we were treated to a bus tour of historical Quito and a trip to the equator line. I took a careful look around as we got on and off the bus, scoping out the other passengers as potential tablemates. I didn't have particularly high hopes. After all, most people our age can't afford trips like this, let alone work jobs that would grant the amount of vacation time one would have to take. True to expectation, we didn't see many, if any, younger people on the tour. I'm also pretty sure I was the only non-White person there. No matter; this was entirely consistent with what Jeff and I had expected, and we were perfectly happy to keep to ourselves.

As we were waiting in line to board the ship, the other passengers asked us the usual questions: What do you do? Where are you from? When we told them that we live in Pittsburgh, people kept asking us if we were "with that other group from Pittsburgh." At this, we furtively looked around, trying to identify the appropriate party. We didn't see anyone, but there was, indeed, luggage waiting to be put on board the ship with Steelers paraphernalia on it.

Turns out, the family from Pittsburgh was staying in the cabins right next to ours and consisted of a husband and wife, Peter and Chelsea, who were about twenty years older than us, and their two adult children, Jennifer and John, who were about five years younger than us. We introduced ourselves as the "other Pittsburghers," and slowly, over the week, we found ourselves spending more and more time together, opting, more often than not, to sit with one another for meals and walking with each other during the shore excursions. We found we had many things in common. All of us were college graduates: Peter was a lawyer, Chelsea had a master's in public policy from Carnegie Mellon University, Jennifer had gone to CMU for undergrad, and John had just graduated from college. The family was Jewish, as is Jeff, and they were extremely curious about Jeff's secular approach to his Jewish background. Although we did not explicitly discuss politics, it was clear that we were aligned on many social issues. At the end of the cruise, we promised to stay in touch. After all, we lived in the same city.

Jeff and I didn't have high hopes, though; how many times have people promised to stay in touch after meeting on a trip and actually followed through? To our great surprise, nary two months after our trip, Peter and Chelsea invited us to their Passover seder, a Jewish celebration that is essentially a religious service centered around a dinner. The seder tends to be a treasured family affair, and it was meaningful that our new friends wanted to include us in their celebrations. In fact, when we arrived, we were touched to find ourselves the only nonfamily members there. So began a wonderful friendship in which Peter and Chelsea took us under their wings, becoming our surrogate Pittsburgh parents.

One thing that we immediately noticed about Peter and Chelsea was that whenever we were out to dinner with them, we would invariably run into people they knew. It occurred so frequently that it became a long-running joke with us. Notably, we didn't know many people in common, so Peter and Chelsea took it upon themselves to act as brokers and share their big-city social capital with us. Peter enthusiastically sponsored Jeff for the board of the Jewish Community Center (JCC), on which Jeff subsequently served for nearly seven years. Through that board service, Jeff forged relationships with other prominent people in the community, relationships that he has since leveraged when taking on a leadership role at a different nonprofit board. Being on the JCC board was also how Jeff met his now best friend, who then went on to sponsor me to join the board of yet another different not-for-profit.

We are immensely grateful for having gone on our Galápagos trip. The trip went further than merely exposing us to a remarkable and far-flung location; our social lives have been massively enriched as well. Some days, our meeting seems completely miraculous. What are the odds?

Except . . . what *are* the odds? Think about it this way: Who has the time and money to take such a trip? Who knows enough about the Galápagos to be interested in going there? Once you start to think about those who would want to go to the Galápagos and to cross-check that list against those who would have the means to do so, the likelihood that we would have met people that we would have become friends with goes up significantly. Put differently, selection biases in who would choose to and be able to afford to go on such a trip means that we were predestined to find at least one or two people with whom we would "click." Seen in this light, making lasting friends on a cruise to the Galápagos no longer seems quite so extraordinary. What *is* extraordinary is that we found friends who lived in the same city as we did.

Whom we can meet—have access to—is predicated on a combination of at least two factors: motivation and ability. Where do we *want* to go? Where *can* we go? Moreover, who we meet is similarly predicated on *others'* motivation and ability to gain access to the same spaces we go. Jeff and I had both the motivation and the ability to take a dream trip to the Galápagos. But that alone would not have been sufficient to ensure that we would have met our Pittsburgh parents. They, too, needed to have a similar motivation and ability to take the trip.

Whom we meet and choose to befriend is not entirely random. Where we spend our time determines who is available to us, and more often than not, the people who are available to us are similar to us. This is because the same motivations and resources that inform our decisions about where we go also inform their decisions about where they go. Combine these factors with how we decide whom to approach in our social environments, and what we'll find is that whom we have access to—whom we can sponsor and whom we can sponsor people to—is often not random either.

Given this, it becomes extremely important for us to consider whom we *don't* know.

So, whom don't you know?

YOUR TRUSTED TEN

Let's try an exercise called the Trusted Ten, which I frequently use when I teach executives about networks.*

Take out a piece of paper or open a spreadsheet on a computer. Create a table with eleven rows and ten columns (you might want to turn your paper so that it is in landscape orientation). Label the top left column "Name." In that column, I'd like you to write down the names of the people you trust the most (who are not family members). By "trust," I mean the people you wouldn't hesitate to reach out to if you had a problem and needed help. Don't fixate on the number of names you have; it's called the Trusted Ten, but the actual number doesn't matter.

Okay, so now you have your list of what I will call your Trusted Ten (or eight or five or fifteen). Now, label the tops of the other columns "Gender Identity," "Race/Ethnicity," "Age," "Sexual Orientation," "Occupation," "Education Level," "Marital Status," "Religion," and "Disability—Y/N." Go ahead and fill in the rest of the grid, so that for each person, you list their characteristics (and if a piece of paper or your computer is not readily available, you'll see that a sample spreadsheet has been provided at the back of the book for you).

---

* I did not create this exercise, and I have been unable to identify who the creator is. If you know, please get in touch with me so that I can give them proper credit!

Okay, now that you've filled this all in, take a good long look at your spreadsheet. What do you notice about the people in your Trusted Ten?

Here's what I see when I look at my Trusted Ten: out of the sixteen contacts I have listed, about 75 percent are White. Two are Black, one is Asian, and one is Latino. Nine are female; seven are male. All are heterosexual, and all are older than thirty-five years old. Around 60 percent have PhDs or the equivalent, and one has a law degree. A third of my Trusted Ten are fellow CMU employees, and about 70 percent work in higher education.

Now let's consider who I *don't* know. I don't have a single gender-nonconforming person on my list. Nor do I have close connections with anyone who identifies as homosexual. I don't have close friends who are substantially younger than myself, and I also have significant gaps in terms of the educational attainment of my Trusted Ten. Specifically, I don't know anyone without a secondary graduate degree. My network is also very limited in terms of occupational diversity. I don't have a single doctor in my Trusted Ten, which is worth remarking upon because the largest employer in Pittsburgh is the University of Pittsburgh Medical Center, which employs hundreds, if not thousands, of doctors. I also have only one MBA on my Trusted Ten, which is rather surprising considering that I work in a business school. Finally, I would be remiss if I didn't point out that only 25 percent of my Trusted Ten are non-White.

When I run the Trusted Ten exercise, there is usually a visceral "ah" from the crowd as they start to fill in the demographic columns. It quickly becomes obvious to them that their Trusted Ten tend to be similar to one another—homogenous—on at least one or two dimensions. Their Trusted Ten also tend to be similar to them—homophilous—on at least one or two dimensions. My network is both homogenous and homophilous in terms of educational attainment; I know a lot of people with PhDs, and I myself have a PhD. Women tend to have Trusted Tens with a lot of women;

White individuals tend to have Trusted Tens with a lot of White individuals. The inclusion of people who are similar to ourselves in our network is so common that homophily is considered a fundamental organizing principle of social networks.

To show you the strength of homophily, consider data extrapolated from the 2022 American Values Survey. In this survey, respondents were asked to do a similar sort of task to that of the Trusted Ten, except they were asked to list up to seven people with whom they regularly discussed "important matters." After identifying those individuals, they were asked to provide demographic information for each. Based on this survey, researchers from the Public Religion Research Institute were able to estimate the racial composition of the average American's network. They found that 90 percent of the friends of an average White American would also be White. In fact, about *two-thirds of all Whites in America do not have a single non-White friend.**

I'm going to let that one sink in for a moment.

Why do we end up primarily socializing with people who are like us? Sociologists point to two primary explanations: availability and approach. The dynamics underlying availability and approach are sufficiently different that we will tackle each in turn.

WHO IS AVAILABLE TO US?

Whom we know often depends on who is available—who is present—in the places we go.

---

* I am not saying that two-thirds of all White Americans do not know a single Black person. The survey specifically asks people to list those with whom they discuss important matters. Meaning, the people with whom they feel comfortable enough to talk about issues that they might need help with. What these data mean, then, is that two-thirds of all White Americans do not have a Black friend to whom they would turn to talk about things that trouble them.

The impact of availability can help to illustrate why there are so few Asians in my Trusted Ten. If my Trusted Ten followed the traditional rules of social networks, I should have many more Asians in my Trusted Ten. Instead, I have a preponderance of White people in my Trusted Ten. Why is that? Here is where it might be helpful to know that Pittsburgh is known as one of America's least racially diverse cities; over 84 percent of its population is White. Only 4 percent is Asian, and most of that is concentrated in the areas around the universities. The lack of racial diversity is so apparent that Jeff and I have a running gag: whenever we go anywhere beyond a one-mile radius of Carnegie Mellon, one of us will look around the room and often declare, "One of these is not like the others."

That explains, however, only my side of the equation. The other side has to do with the motivations and abilities of other Asians to live in Pittsburgh. Do they not live here because they can't? Or because they don't want to? I highly doubt that Asians don't live here because they can't afford to; after all, they are choosing to locate themselves in some of the most expensive cities and states in the country (California and New York)! So the likelier answer is that they are *choosing* not to live in Pittsburgh. After all, if you had a choice, would you rather live in a city where there are more people who look like you or in one where you develop a running joke with your partner about how you're the only one there who looks like you?

Asians aren't alone in this. A lot of people feel most comfortable when they are in spaces where there are more people like them. White Americans tend to live in neighborhoods that are predominantly White. Given that White people are constantly in spaces where there are few non-Whites, is it any wonder that their networks are so White?

But here, too, power plays a role. People with more resources have a greater ability to dictate where they spend their time than those with fewer resources. This means, then, that even if everyone has the motivation to spend time in spaces full of people similar to them, that doesn't mean that everyone has the ability to do so. Although Black Americans also tend to live in neighborhoods that are predominantly Black, there is significantly more racial diversity in Black-dominated neighborhoods than in White-dominated neighborhoods. Those with power not only choose to spend more time in the spaces where they feel comfortable, they can also use that power to erect barriers to entry so that those spaces stay comfortable for them. Non-Whites don't have that same level of ability; if a Black person wants to be a member of the corporate elite, they must go into White-dominated spaces to achieve that goal.

This is all to say, where we are motivated to and have the ability to spend our time, in large part, determines the types of people who are available to us. But these same dynamics are true for other people too; just like us, other people have different motivations and abilities that dictate where they will spend *their* time. Who is available to us—who goes where we go—is a combination of those two factors: where we want and can go and where others want and can go. Often, the configuration of those factors works together to increase the homophily and homogeneity of our Trusted Ten. This is especially true for people who are members of groups that tend to have more resources, which give them the ability to go to more and different spaces. Often, they will use that ability to go places that are harder for people different from them to access.

WHOM DO WE APPROACH?

You might recall that at the beginning of the chapter, I mentioned that there are two factors that determine who we know: who is available to us and whom we choose to approach (and who chooses to approach us). The discussion above was about availability. Here, I want to talk about what happens when we take availability as given. When you are stuck on a boat in the Galápagos, whom among the other passengers will you decide to approach? Who will approach you?

A few months ago, I was teaching a session on networking at another university. The morning of my session, I went to the communal dining room for breakfast. I was the first to arrive. The room was full of tables, and each table had a sign on it, indicating whether the table was intended for participants of the program in which I was teaching (a Black leaders program) or a different program. Since I was teaching in the Black leaders program, I sat down at one of the tables marked for that program.

As other people began to filter in, they began to exchange confused looks. The other program turned out to be composed of Asian participants, and they were confused as to why there was an Asian woman sitting at a table for the Black leaders program. Likewise, the Black program participants walked in and were confused as to why there was an Asian woman sitting at a table for the Black leaders program. Amused, I sat and waited to see what would happen. Would one of the Asian participants come over to tell me that I was sitting at the wrong table? Would they choose to disregard the signage and join me? Would one of the Black participants tell me that I was at the wrong table? Would they just start seating themselves at a new table?

Who—if anyone—would choose to approach me?

A smartly dressed Black woman took in the scenario. I saw her glance at one of the other empty tables designated for the Black leaders program and then at me. I could almost hear the gears turning in her head. What should she do? I think she could tell that I was watching, making it so that if she didn't join me, it was going to be obvious that she was choosing *not* to sit with me. Perhaps it was my imagination, but I swear I saw her give a little sigh of resignation. She then walked over to where I was seated and asked if she could join me. Of course! I said, I'm Rosalind Chow, and I'm going to be working with you today! Oh! she said, all smiles. I'm so excited for your session! As soon as she sat down, several other Black participants joined us, and we proceeded to have an energetic conversation about my background and what they had been learning in the program so far. The conversation was, in fact, so much fun that we were all almost late for the session, and several of my tablemates approached me afterward to say that they wished that they could have sat down and chatted with all the instructors from the program in the same way.

None of us would have had the joy of that conversation if I hadn't deliberately put myself into their space and *if they hadn't been willing to join me*. I made myself available; they (thankfully!) chose to approach.

The most common reason people don't approach others is that they are worried that the other person will reject them. All of us will find ourselves in situations where it's unclear how others will respond to us. Maybe it's your first day at work. Maybe you just moved into a new apartment and you run into the neighbors. Or maybe you're living some version of the ubiquitous "new kid at school has to choose a place to sit at lunch" trope. Meeting strangers for the first time can often feel like a gamble: Will they like me? Add race or gender into the mix, and some people will nope right out of that situation if they can. The unfortunate reality is that most of us want more diversity in our friendship circles but believe that people in other groups do not share that same desire. When asked about their interest in having more diverse friendships, White students reported that they are more interested in having Black friends than Black students are in having White friends. The opposite was true of Black students; they believed that they are more interested in having White friends than White students are interested in having Black friends. This mismatch in perception versus reality can make it so that people are (inaccurately) hesitant to approach one another, especially across differences such as race.

What's unfortunate is that although many of us don't approach others because we fear rejection, we don't likewise see that the other person might not approach us for the same reason. After all, if I don't approach you because I think you might reject me, it's also plausible that you don't approach me because you are worried I might reject you! This dynamic reminds me of a Dr. Seuss story called *What Was I Scared Of?* In it, there is a character who keeps running into a green pair of disembodied pants. They are so frightened by these encounters that they end up going to great lengths to hide themselves. But lo, they keep running into those pants, even in the most desolate of locations. In the end, they realize that the pants are just as scared of them as they are of the pants, which have similarly been hiding in all sorts of obscure locations to avoid the protagonist. After this realization, the two become good friends.

Make a move, people. People are more likely to be afraid of being rejected by you than they are to reject you!

In fact, there's a growing stream of research evidence that suggests that talking with strangers brings with it its own kind of happiness. Yet because so many of us believe that approaching others is a risky endeavor, we opt not to, and this means that we are all losing out on shared opportunities to generate joy. Social scientists worked with Chicago public transportation to run a "Talk to Me Day." On that day, they gave three separate groups of commuters on Chicago buses and trains different instructions: to strike up a conversation with the person sitting next to them, to sit quietly by themselves, or to do their normal routine (which is typically to keep to themselves). Those instructed to strike up a conversation with a stranger reported being significantly happier after their commute than those told to be solitary or to go about their daily routine.

Critically, our happiness isn't solely determined by the amount of dialogue we have with others; it matters with *whom* we have those dialogues. Other research shows that just as eating a variety of foods is healthier for us, variety in social interactions is too. Instead of talking only with your partner or close friends, make sure to get your daily dose of interactions with coworkers and strangers as well!

We tend to avoid approaching people who are different from us because we fear rejection. But when both sides are waiting for the other side to make the first move, we deprive ourselves—and others—of joy. Our unwillingness to approach other people is a missed opportunity to create collective value.

AS ALWAYS, POWER PLAYS A ROLE

Here, again, I want to raise the issue of power and how it impacts our networks. While it's true that White Americans might have greater access to other White Americans, it's also true that non-Whites also exert control over whom they know by changing whom they will choose to approach so that they, too, end up with more homophilous networks than what might be expected, given who is available. Researchers tracking the development of friendships in an elite MBA program found that even though non-White MBA students make up a small proportion of MBAs, within a few weeks of the beginning of the semester, non-White students had a *higher* proportion of same-race friends in their networks than did White students. But note that finding those same-race friends wasn't as easy for non-White students; while White students tended to create connections with other White students in their preassigned class sections, non-White students had to look *across* class sections to find other non-White students. Similarly, women in male-dominated companies also have more women in their networks than might be expected, given their smaller numbers. But they too have to work harder to find those contacts, by searching across firms to find other women.

This is why homophily is considered such a fundamental feature of social networks; even if there aren't many similar people available to us, we will seek out what small number of them we can to approach.

Why do those in the numerical minority feel compelled to engage in so much extra effort to find others who are like them? Part of the answer is that those in the numerical minority tend to have more negative experiences that are related to their identities. They therefore feel the need to do additional reconnaissance to better understand the social landscape. But they aren't going to ask just anyone about how "safe" a place is; they feel more comfortable obtaining this information from peers who have a similar lived experience to themselves. Job-seeking female MBA students spend just as much time networking with male alumni—who can provide them with general work- and career-related advice—as do male MBA students. However, female MBA students also reach out to more alumni overall than do male MBA students because they spend additional time connecting with female alumni in particular, in an effort to acquire information on internal gender dynamics within companies.

Other research shows that the same-gender networking that women engage in isn't just a "nice to have," but a "need to have." The most successful male MBA students are those who are connected to other well-connected peers. In other words, they have big-city social capital. In fact, this is one of the most significant predictors of male students' job placements. Female MBA students, however, need to be connected to well-connected peers *and more*. Specifically, the female MBA students who have the best placement outcomes are those who have a combination of big-city social capital (being connected to well-connected peers) *and* small-town social capital (a squad of two or three close female friends with whom they communicate frequently). Basically, successful women tend to look like Kim Ng, who has both big-city and small-town social capital.

What this all boils down to is that yes, everyone prefers similarity. However, the amount of time and effort that people have to put into networking differ depending on who they are, because the types of people and the types of relationships they need in their network differ. No matter how you cut it, women and non-Whites pay a networking tax that men and White individuals do not. Due to differences in access, they must put a lot more work into approach to obtain the same outcomes as men and White individuals. What this suggests is that those of us who are committed to more inclusive workplaces should put more effort into reaching out to women and non-Whites and to accepting outreach attempts from women and non-Whites.

ADDING MORE COMPLEXITY TO
THE TRUSTED TEN: MULTIPLEX TIES

At this point, let's insert another column to the right of your Trusted Ten spreadsheet and label this one "Type of Support." In this column, I want you to indicate what kinds of things you talk to your Trusted Tens about. Do you talk to them about how to get stuff done at work? Label that "Task." Do you talk to them about long-term professional goals? That gets labeled as "Career." And, finally, do you talk to them about your personal life, like family, religion, politics, hobbies, and so forth? Label that "Social." Once you've done this, I want you to see how many types of support your Trusted Ten give you and how that support is distributed. Does each and every one of your Trusted Ten give you all three kinds of support? Or, more likely, do some individuals give you task- or career-related support, but not social support, and vice versa?

Using my Trusted Ten as an example, my doctoral adviser, Brian, is both a trusted professional mentor and one of my best friends. I get it all from Brian: task, career, *and* social support. We have what network scholars call a "multiplex" tie, which means that we share multiple types of information with one another. Another person on my Trusted Ten provides me with mostly career-related support, which constitutes a "single-layer" tie. What the research says is that my connection with Brian is going to be more helpful to me than my connection with the people with whom I have single-layer ties. And, as you'll see in later chapters, Brian is someone who pops up as a sponsor frequently in my life.

Multiplexity can be thought of as a proxy for relationship closeness. Our conversations with people with whom we have single-layer ties tend to be fairly superficial. We stick to our one "safe" topic of conversation, and that's it. Obviously, this means that the quantity of information shared in a single-layer relationship is often lower, because, almost by definition, we'll probably have more to say about work and personal life than work alone. But what's important to know about multiplexity is that it doesn't just capture the quantity of information we share. It also captures the *quality*.

I have a colleague whom I'll call Nancy. Nancy and I are friendly at work, and our topics of conversation tend to be work related. Sometimes, Nancy and I will discuss exercises or cases that we use in our respective classes, and if there's an exercise she uses but I don't, or vice versa, we'll share our slides with one another. Contrast this with my relationship with Brent, a faculty member at a different university who is also on my Trusted Ten. Brent and I don't see each other very often, but when we do, we talk about it all: work, career, and personal stuff. There's nothing off the table in our conversations. That means, then, that when Brent finds out that I haven't done an exercise before, he goes beyond merely sending me his slides. He schedules time to talk over each step of the exercise with me, sharing little nuances of how to introduce the exercise, how to address common responses by students, or how to incorporate the exercise into an assignment. So what you can see here is that my single-layer tie with Nancy gets me relevant information, but not the same level of quality as the information that my multiplex-layer tie with Brent gets me when I ask the same kind of question.

Note that it's not that I don't trust Nancy or dislike her or anything like that. However, I think you'll find that the people with whom you feel the closest are those with whom you have multiplex ties.

Analyzing our Trusted Ten by categorizing relationships in terms of layers allows us to both identify if we are missing certain types of support from our network (much like the assessment step in the value-extraction approach to analyzing networks) and pinpoint which relationships have the potential to be turned into multiplex ties. Because multiplex ties, in fact, are better for our networks than are single-layer ties. Let's say, for instance, that you have many Trusted Tens with whom you entrust your deepest personal secrets, but lack Trusted Tens in whom you confide about task- or career-related obstacles. This means that your Trusted Ten are unlikely to be able to help you with professional challenges (because they don't know about them!), thereby limiting your ability to advance. Conversely, if your Trusted Ten are composed mainly of people with whom you discuss only task- or career-related issues, you may be professionally successful, but socially lonely.

The costs to the latter scenario were poignantly brought to life for me when, after completing this exercise in a session I was running, a Black participant named Jonathan revealed his dismay at the composition of his network: it was composed almost entirely of non-Black contacts with whom he had largely single-layer ties. He sat back in his seat with a shocked look on his face as he shared with the group that even though he was, by all metrics, an incredibly strong performer and highly valued in the company, he felt professionally lonely. It hadn't occurred to him that part of that loneliness may have come from his decisions about whom he spent time with and how. It wasn't that Jonathan didn't feel as though he had good friends at work or that he couldn't be himself at work. However, this exercise enabled him to finally understand the source of his unhappiness; in his steadfast focus on connections that would further his professional goals, he had ignored his need for identity-affirming relationships, which for most non-White individuals are with same-race peers.

Jonathan's experience reflects a trade-off that many of the women and non-White professionals I've worked with face daily because they know, implicitly, that the penalties they face when they are "authentic" are often larger than those faced by people in the majority group. Many women control how much, and which, emotions they express at work. They know that they can't be too emotional, because if they seem like they aren't in control of themselves, they'll be seen as less competent. But they also can't be too *un*emotional, because then it seems like they are robots or "ice queens" (consider: What's the male counterpart to "ice queen"?). And if women are going to be emotional, they had better not be angry, especially if they are Black. Research finds that expressions of anger are selectively used to discredit women and Black individuals in decision-making groups; in contrast, White men who express anger are no less influential than those who don't express anger.

For people from marginalized groups, then, there is a constant tension: Do I behave as I truly feel, at the risk of forfeiting being able to make important professional connections, or do I constantly monitor what I say and do, with the result of maintaining mostly single-layer ties? Most people choose the latter. Many Black Americans adopt Standard English at the office and switch to Black English, a fully separate language recognized by linguists, when at home, in a phenomenon called code-switching. I remember a time when I was with my adviser, Brian, a Black man, when he took a call from a family member. Before he answered the call, he warned me that I was about to hear him speak in a way that was going to be very different from how he normally spoke at the office. I found it telling (and sad) that he specifically told me "not to be shocked." Members of the LGBTQ+ community will "tone down" aspects of their sexual orientation in order to fit in with or avoid discrimination at work. The overarching sentiment among those who engage in such code-switching behavior is that they do it to put others at ease. In a study of Black executives, one participant put it this way: "Code switching is the art of shrinking [as] a survival tool. You must make yourself as invisible as long as possible."

Constantly monitoring our behavior takes a mental toll. The Black professionals in the study above describe coming home feeling emotionally and physically exhausted. But constant vigilance also costs us relational closeness. Recall that multiplex ties—the highest-quality connections—are those where we share multiple kinds of information. Code-switching and other forms of behavioral self-monitoring typically also involve monitoring the type of information we share with others. This means, then, that people who have learned how to survive at work by compartmentalizing who they are—by being one person at work and another person at home—probably have more single-layer relationships with their contacts than people who don't feel compelled to live dual lives. Single-layer relationships, however, are not the relationships that result in sponsorship. That all adds up to this: people from marginalized backgrounds might well have access to the right people in their networks, but they are less likely to be able to activate those relationships for sponsorship because their relationships aren't multiplex.

Access is not the same as activation.

TRANSLATING THE TRUSTED TEN INTO SMALL-TOWN VERSUS BIG-CITY SOCIAL CAPITAL

Who is available to us and whom we choose to approach (and who chooses to approach us) are the two factors that largely determine whom we know and how well we know them. If we spend just a little more effort in understanding who is available to us and whom we choose to approach (and not), we will have a much deeper understanding of our network and the level of social capital that we have.

As one final addition to your Trusted Ten spreadsheet, add a column labeled "Overlap." In this column, indicate whether the person you are thinking of is connected to anyone else on your list. If they are, write down the name of the mutual connection. We've already talked about how Brian, my adviser with whom I have a multiplex tie, is on my list. Are there others on my Trusted Ten with whom Brian is close? Indeed, there is: Miguel Unzueta, another one of Brian's students, who is like an academic older brother to me. But beyond that, I wouldn't say that Brian (or Miguel, for that matter) is close with the other people on my Trusted Ten. So on my list, Miguel would be listed as an overlap in Brian's row, and Brian would be listed as an overlap in Miguel's row.

What you want to pay attention to is how many people overlap with each other in your Trusted Ten. Brian and Miguel overlap with one another on my Trusted Ten, but they don't overlap with anyone else. I have a few other dyads and triads on my list who are connected to one another, but are otherwise not closely connected to the others. This is a good version of overlap; that there are some overlaps means that I am a part of several meaningful social cliques, but that those social cliques are otherwise not closely connected. I can therefore act as a broker between those groups.

If all the people in your Trusted Ten are close with one another, that's a problem; you are swimming in small-town social capital with little to no big-city social capital. Alternatively, if no one in your Trusted Ten knows one another, you have a lot of big-city social capital with little to no small-town social capital. And, as we discussed last chapter, what tends to work best for people is to have a good balance of both. We need sufficient small-town social capital to be sure that we can work effectively with other people, but also sufficient big-city social capital to be sure that we can get access to nonredundant information and people.

If the last paragraph describes your Trusted Ten (only small-town or big-city social capital, but not both), the next sections will provide some suggestions on how you can address these patterns in who you know.

WHY NETWORKING FOR SPONSORSHIP REQUIRES DIVERSIFYING OUR CONNECTIONS

When we start to consider who goes where and who approaches whom, we can start to see why we tend to have networks that are more homogenous and homophilous than we might like. We can also see how our networks might make us unwitting agents of social inequality. After all, if we sponsor only the people we know, then the powerful sponsor the powerful, creating a cycle in which those rich with social capital share their social capital with those who are similarly rich. If we are to break that cycle, we need to be more intentional about where we go, whom we approach, and *whom we sponsor*.

Given our networks' tendencies toward homophily and homogeneity, it's not surprising that a lot of networking advice tells us to focus on diversifying whom we know. Just as financial advisers recommend that we diversify our stock-market portfolios to mitigate risk, diversified networks can bring us benefits that a more homogenous network cannot. It's good advice. But the point of diversifying our networks is not just to protect ourselves from risk or to maximize the types of resources we can access. That is the networking as resource-extraction model. Rather, if our intention is to build collective value—to act as matchmakers and maximize the overall benefits to our communities—having a homogenous network won't help. When our Trusted Ten are too much like us (homophilous) or too much like one another (homogenous), our opportunity to add value to our social connections is reduced because value creation through sponsorship is about finding novel solutions (that is, protégés) to diverse problems. When all the people you know are like one another, it's probable that they face similar problems. Moreover, when all the people you know are like you, it's probable that they have access to the same solutions that you do. It is only when there is difference between you and the people you know (and the people they know) that the group is configured in such a way as to enable collective-value creation.

Consider: almost all my Trusted Ten are married with young children. This means, then, that many of us face the same problem of finding child care. It also means we all lack solutions to this problem, making it so that we are less capable of helping one another. But what if one or two of us were to have a more diversified network, one in which some of our contacts have children who are substantially older than ours and want work as babysitters? In this scenario, having even just one or two people with networks that are more diverse than the rest of the group's brings collective benefit because now the group has access to resources that it might not have otherwise.

This is why diversification of our networks is important if we are networking for sponsorship. When there isn't diversity, we have fewer opportunities to sponsor.

NETWORKING FOR SPONSORSHIP

So how do we more intentionally increase diversity in our networks? Here, we can go back to availability and approach. One straightforward way to diversify your network is to change who is available to you by changing where you spend your time. Instead of working at the coffee shop near your house, go to one farther away in another neighborhood. Instead of taking your kids to the nearest library, start frequenting ones in other neighborhoods.

However, I want to reiterate: just because we put ourselves in contexts with greater diversity does not mean that our networks will change, because unless we also *engage* with dissimilar people, just having more diversity available to us doesn't do anything.

Researchers have found that greater racial diversity in schools does not necessarily result in more cross-racial friendships. Rather, cross-racial friendships are more likely to come about when racial diversity exists *and* when there is a structural arrangement that forces cross-race interactions. Specifically, there are fewer cross-racial friendships in racially diverse schools in which electives are chosen by the students themselves than in racially diverse schools where the electives are assigned. Assigning students from different backgrounds and forcing them to engage with each other in shared activity is a structural solution to addressing our hesitation to approach people different from ourselves.

In life outside of school, however, we decide whom to make ourselves available to and whom to approach. And let's face it: a lot of us might have the desire, but we don't all have the means. Time is a scarce resource. Effort is a scarce resource. I have a close friend who has told me, "I'm forty-plus years old and have two kids. I don't have the time or energy to make new friends." As someone in a similar situation, I hear her! So I am going to suggest something that I hope is more manageable for the busy person: start with what you have.

First, are there single-layer ties on your Trusted Ten that could be converted to multiplex ties? Deepening an already existing relationship is much easier than starting one from scratch. But deepening a relationship means that you have to be willing to share just a bit more of yourself, to be willing to talk about subjects that you may not have been comfortable broaching before. I know that, for many of us, this seems like a daunting proposition. Just remember that deepening even just one friendship has implications that go beyond that specific relationship. Even if we are willing to share more with just one person about our problems, desires, and aptitudes, there are many people to whom they can sponsor us. In this way, the potential impacts of deepening one relationship can have exponential benefits for the collective.

Consider Kyle Webster, the illustrator whose network helped him to find a lawyer to guide him through the process of selling his digital brushes to Adobe. Like Webster, many of us are unaware of the resources that are already available to us in our networks. We need merely to ask our Trusted Ten to introduce us—sponsor us—to people who can fill those gaps. But the thing to remember is that now that Webster's public request has unearthed this connection, others in the network are similarly aware of this new resource.

When we have greater collective knowledge about one another, we all benefit through the improved problem-solving ability—increased sponsorship matchmaking capabilities—of the group.

Consider these other examples of sponsorship. Imagine that your friend asks you to help them move, but you really don't have the time (or desire). This is an opportunity for sponsorship! You could say, "Sorry, I can't, but I know you still need someone to help you with moving. My neighbor's son is a high school student on the football team and is looking to earn some extra money. Do you want me to put him in touch with you?" Win-win-win! Another example: You've been asked to join the Parent-Teacher Association (PTA) at your child's school. You work full-time and don't have the capacity to participate, but you also don't want to just say no. Then, perhaps you remember that your new neighbor, whose child also goes to the school, has mentioned to you that he's been having difficulty meeting other parents and getting integrated into the community. You suggest him as an alternative and introduce him to the PTA. This is also a win-win-win situation: the PTA gets a parent who wants to be there, your neighbor has an opportunity to get what he needs, and you are supporting the school without having to put additional strain on your work-life balance.

The problem, however, is that our ability to engage in the sponsorship described above depends on having information about what other people need or want. If you hadn't spent time chatting with your neighbors, maybe you would never have known that their son is looking to make some extra cash. If you hadn't asked how your new neighbor was doing, maybe he wouldn't have opened up to you about how he is having trouble meeting other parents.

Lack of information is what keeps many people from sponsoring; when we don't know what people need help with or what they want to do, it's hard to connect them to the right people or opportunities. So if we want to participate in the collective-value creation that sponsorship offers, we need to start getting out of our own way and be more willing to ask for help or what people need help with. These efforts will especially be fruitful for those who have a lot of big-city social capital and haven't been brokering connections across their Trusted Ten.

In addition to making it easier for us to act as sponsors (or to be sponsored), being more willing to engage makes everyone happier. Remember that increasing the diversity of our social diets—engaging with strangers and acquaintances, not just close friends and family—is a small gesture we can make that can have an outsize impact on collective happiness.

But what about those of us who have a lot of small-town social capital and want to have more big-city social capital? For those of you whose overlap column is bursting at the seams, there are two potential remedies. First, do what I suggested above—deepen single-layer ties—to see if the networks of your friends are as full of small-town social capital as your own. If not, then great: use them to sponsor you to new social circles. But if their networks overlap in the same way as yours, then you have a more difficult assignment: consider the people who are already available to you but aren't on your Trusted Ten. These are people you see on a regular basis but with whom you rarely ever speak. Why consider these folks? My guess is that there is probably more diversity available to you in your environment than you have taken advantage of. I, for example, sit on several not-for-profit boards, but I haven't made a concerted effort to connect with the other board members. The people on the boards on which I serve are a more diverse set than most other social contexts I typically find myself in. What's great is that we've all already shown ourselves to care about the same things, or else we wouldn't be on the board! Diversity in potential contacts already exists in my environment; I just need to be more willing to engage. I'm guessing that you can think of opportunities that exist in your life, too.

5 | THE PROBLEM WITH MERIT

Mark Anderson was so shocked by his boss's announcement that he had to pull his car over to the shoulder of the highway to continue the call.

"Why?" Mark finally managed to croak out. "Why wasn't I considered?"

On the other end, stunned silence from his manager. Cars and trucks roared past within just feet of Mark's car, his car swaying as they passed.

Then his manager said, "We didn't know you were interested in my job!"

Mark, having received only positive marks on his performance reviews up to this point, was flabbergasted and blindsided to find out he had been passed up for promotion to take his manager's position, his manager having just been promoted out of the role. Instead, his boss had just told him that the position was being given to someone more junior to Mark. The worst part: It wasn't that the other candidate had been judged to be better than Mark. It was that Mark's candidacy hadn't even been considered.

If he was being honest, Mark thought, he wasn't totally surprised. For years, he had noticed that he wasn't advancing at the same rate as his peers. He had remained a top performer, so what was going on? Was it him? Was it the company? It had been a mystery to him until that day on the highway when it all became clear. He told me, "Nobody was intentional about holding me back, but nobody was intentional about moving me forward either." Mark realized that his boss wasn't—and the ones before him weren't—*seeing* him.

Just as we can't sponsor people we don't know (which we discussed in the last chapter), we won't activate ourselves to sponsor people if we don't see them as being worthy of our sponsorship. In Mark's case, it wasn't that Mark's boss didn't know Mark or the quality of his work. Mark's boss had access to him, but knowing him wasn't enough to activate him as a sponsor. And the sad truth is that Mark's lack of recognition was a pattern. One has to wonder: How much of Mark's lack of progress was due to his being a Black man in a predominantly White company? (Oh, did I forget to mention that? Does this change how you see the situation? Why?)

It is no longer enough—has it ever been?—for anyone, no matter their race, gender, age, and so on, to just put their head down and do good work. But this is especially true for people who are numerical minorities of any type. Another interviewee, whom I'll call Joe, was inspired to join the US Air Force after the 9/11 attacks in New York City. His parents, Korean immigrants, were not in favor of this plan. Like most stereotypical immigrant parents, they wanted Joe to build a secure professional life in corporate America. But after a few years of working at a top-tier consulting firm, Joe was still enamored with the notion of serving. He hatched a plan to serve for a few years and later go back to the private sector. But when his commitment with the Air Force was set to expire, he was surprised at how much he enjoyed what he was doing. He liked being deployed for combat; he liked how fighting shoulder-to-shoulder with other service members enabled him to make lifelong friendships. But perhaps Joe's most important reason for staying in the Air Force was the personal fulfillment he derived from contributing to the national security of the United States, a passion he had developed while in college.

Given his decision to stay in the Air Force, Joe knew that he had certain milestones he would need to hit to advance up the chain. In the military, Joe told me, the path usually goes like this: Perform well and get promoted into higher- and higher-profile positions. At that point, a committee will select the most promising officers for special opportunities, among which the most desirable is to enroll in further developmental education, such as attending a one-year program at a war college. Being chosen for developmental education is as strong a signal as the military can send about an officer's promotion potential; almost everyone who goes on to become a colonel or general will have gone through at least one of these programs.

Joe set out to make himself as attractive as possible for these sought-after developmental education opportunities. He outperformed most of his peers on the metrics used for evaluation. He made a point of staying after hours, being the last person to leave the office. But, much like Mark, Joe was informed that he was not going to be chosen for additional developmental opportunities. His leaders agreed that he was great, but "we don't see you as someone who is going to be in our game plan to come back as a commander."

Joe was crushed. He asked himself, is it because I'm not fit for this? Is there something that I'm missing that others have? After some reflection, he realized that he, like many of the other Asian American and Pacific Islander officers he knew, was not being seen.

He was being overlooked. Not valued, despite his contributions. He knew that his bosses had noticed that he was putting in extra time at the office. But rather than inviting him to go out for beers with them after work, as they did with Joe's White peers, his bosses just gave him more work to do.

Mark's and Joe's situations are not unique. And we see this come up over and over again in the data. One study tracked the performance and promotion data of management employees at a large US retailer. The researchers found that the female employees at the retailer were 13 percent less likely to be promoted than their male peers. Was it because the female employees performed worse than male employees? Not so; if anything, the data indicated that women were *more* likely to be seen as high performers than were men. Specifically, women were 7.4 percent more likely to be rated as top performers and 21 percent less likely to be rated as low performers than were men. So why weren't they getting promoted?

As we saw with Mark's and Joe's experiences, performance is not the driver of who gets promoted; perceived potential is. And on this measure, it was found that women were more likely to be rated as high performers, but less likely to be rated as high in potential by their supervisors. If these high-performing women had gone to their supervisors and asked why they hadn't been promoted, I suspect that they would have received a similar response to what Joe had been told: we just don't see it. In fact, the data showed that women were 33 percent more likely than men to have the highest performance score *and* the lowest potential score, a combination that often results in the employee being branded a "workhorse," a good and dependable worker with little potential for growth into leadership positions.

Managers—men and women alike—are consistently inaccurately assessing the future potential of their female employees.

Can you imagine how frustrating and demoralizing it must feel to be a high performer and to know that others know you are a high performer, only to be told that people "just don't see it"? At some point, you are going to stop and say, "What more do you want from me? What, exactly, is it that you need to see that would convince you that I'm worthy?"

This is the question I want us to pose to ourselves: What, exactly, do we need to see to identify people as being worthy of our sponsorship? What are our standards? And, critically, are we consistently using the same standards in assessing the people we could sponsor?

THE IMPORTANCE OF KNOWING WHO KNOWS WHAT

Bias—inaccurate perceptions of other people—works against our ability to sponsor in ways that add collective value. This is because being effective matchmakers—problem solvers through sponsorship—requires us to have an accurate understanding of who has what problems and aspirations and who has what strengths and abilities. When we get this wrong, it's not just bad because people miss out on opportunities that they deserve. It's bad for the collective, because it means we are all being deprived of the benefit that results from pairing the right people with the right problems.

Consider what makes some teams more effective than others. Effective teams tend to have strong transactive memory systems (TMS), or a shared understanding of who knows what and who is good at what. Those of us who live with a partner will likely have an intuitive sense of how this works. Most household partnerships have a shared understanding of who is good at what or who likes to do what. Maybe one partner is more on top of arranging social events for the family, while the other has skills that make them more suited to managing the family's finances. In an ideal case, roles are distributed according to each person's strengths and interests. I, for instance, have consistently demonstrated a regrettably low level of competence when it comes to travel planning. I know this and Jeff knows this, and we have both agreed that I am hereby absolved of all duties related to planning family vacations. This is a good outcome for everyone involved.

In a similar way, the most effective teams are those where each teammate knows what other teammates are good at, so they can direct questions and tasks to the appropriate person. In teams with low TMS, people either don't know, disagree on, or have inaccurate perceptions of one another's strengths and knowledge base. This costs individuals, in the sense that they aren't appropriately recognized for their contributions, but it also costs the group, in the sense that the team doesn't perform as well as when team members are assigned to the roles that best suit their abilities. This, then, is the collective cost of bias: there is more collective value that could be had if we were more accurate about one another than we are. As sponsors interested in creating collective value, then, we should commit ourselves to ensuring that our evaluations are as accurate as possible.

Unfortunately, we are consistently inaccurate in how we evaluate others and consistent in how we are inaccurate. This is especially true for people with more power, and their inaccuracy has consequences for how well groups perform. There is a long line of work showing that women are more socially perceptive than men. In fact, their enhanced social perceptiveness is what makes teams with more women more collectively intelligent; the more people on a team who are sensitive to the social cues given off by other team members, the better the team can perform. However, social perceptiveness isn't some magical talent that women are just innately more likely to have. Other work has shown that people from lower social classes tend to score higher on emotional recognition tasks than higher-social-class individuals. These findings suggest that differences in social perceptiveness aren't due to gender per se but to power differences.

Indeed, it is high-social-class men—the higher-power gender of a high-power group—who seem especially oblivious to others.

The lack of social perceptiveness of high-power men also has real implications for the career trajectories of everyone else. One study finds that male research and development scientists, particularly high-power ones, are 10 percent more likely to work with other male scientists than they are to work with female scientists, even when controlling for other factors such as how productive the lower-power scientist is or where they are located. This matters because lower-power scientists who collaborate with high-power scientists are more likely to be promoted than those who don't. Perhaps that is why women in this context are less likely to be promoted than men. Importantly, however, there are some female scientists with whom high-power male scientists are willing to work. Who are these lucky women? By now, it should come as no surprise: the female scientists who work with high-power male scientists are those who have a sponsor—another male scientist who knows both parties and, presumably, vouches for the female scientist.

What we see here is the double-edged sword of sponsorship. In its bad incarnation, it can violate our notions of meritocracy. Although anyone can benefit from undeserved sponsorship, more often than not power and its impact on whom we know, whom we approach, and whom we notice all push toward a system in which people in higher-power social groups are more likely to be sponsored than those in lower-power social groups. When used in this way, sponsorship helps to maintain existing inequalities. Yet in its good incarnation, sponsorship *saves* us from violations of meritocracy; it enables us to rightfully recognize the contributions and talents of individuals who would otherwise go unnoticed. Sponsorship, then, can also be a way to mitigate existing inequalities. That is the kind of sponsorship we should aim for.

SPONSORS CAN BE A BULWARK AGAINST
UNMERITOCRATIC SYSTEMS

Last we saw them, both Mark Anderson and Joe were facing stiff headwinds in their careers. Mark had just been told that he had been passed over, yet again, for a promotion. Joe had just been told that although he was a high performer, his superiors did not see him as having the leadership potential to rise in the ranks of the military. Just like women scientists who face an uphill battle in being seen as worthy collaborators, these two non-White men struggled to have their value recognized by the mostly White men who were in positions to decide who was worthy of advancement.

But like the female scientists who collaborate with high-power male scientists, Mark and Joe had sponsors who changed the trajectory of their careers. Despite Mark's lack of advancement at work—or perhaps *because* of his lack of advancement at work—he worked to make his own opportunities. Outside of work, he had cultivated relationships with corporate executives at other companies by volunteering at a regional technology and innovation chapter. Once a month, he would, along with these other high-level executives from the area, gather in a room to listen to aspiring entrepreneurs pitch their business ideas. The group would then collectively give feedback to the founders. Through these events, Mark and the other executives would identify the most promising business ventures and provide even more hands-on guidance to the founders, sometimes becoming advisory board members for the new company. In this way, even though Mark wasn't valued at work, he grew a reputation outside of his company as someone who had a keen eye for identifying potential strengths and weaknesses in new start-ups. This paid off for him in a big way when he finally resigned in the aftermath of his nonpromotion.

After resigning, Mark decided to take a few months to center himself and take stock of where he wanted to go next. He was on the golf course when he received a phone call from a former

CEO, Alan, whom he had met through his volunteer work with the technology and innovation chapter. "What are you doing right now?" Alan asked. Baffled, Mark answered truthfully, "Golfing?" "Wrong answer," said Alan. "You're getting on a plane to San Francisco." Mark wasn't one to argue; he duly booked himself on the next flight to California. Once there, he met up with Alan, who took him to the headquarters of Kleiner Perkins, one of the largest venture-capital funds in Silicon Valley. Kleiner Perkins was looking for someone who could conduct due diligence on a company that they wanted to invest in, and Alan had sponsored Mark for the job, telling them that Mark was their guy. For the next several months, Mark embedded himself at the prospective investment company, scouring their financials and operations. When it came time to report back to Kleiner Perkins, Mark laid out all the reasons that he didn't think the company was a good investment. His assessment showed such a deep grasp of the company's inner workings and strategic imperatives, leadership at Kleiner Perkins chose to invest in the company anyway, installing Mark as interim CEO to fix the problems he had identified. Since then, Mark has been a very successful venture capitalist, starting several of his own venture-capital funds.

Joe too was able to turn things around with the help of a sponsor. In frustration, after being told that he wasn't leadership material, Joe asked to be assigned to a base in South Korea, which was as far away a place as he could go from the base where he hadn't been promoted. There, he was assigned to work under an Air Force colonel named Peter, who quickly noticed that Joe was a little bit different. Joe had gone to Yale as an undergraduate, which already made him a bit of an outlier in the group, but, more important, he was an avid consumer of the latest thought pieces on foreign affairs, politics, and diplomacy. Joe believed that the national security of the United States was based not just on its military might, but also on its ability to secure the cooperation of its friends and allies around the world. This put him at odds with most military officers, who tended to look down on the work being done by the State Department.

Unbeknownst to Joe, Peter similarly saw himself as a diplomat first and a military officer second. Noticing that Joe was a bit like him in his interests, Peter began mentoring Joe, asking him questions about what he wanted to do in his career. In these conversations, Peter shared his own career experiences, including things he had done that had been great opportunities and regrets about jobs that he had or hadn't taken, many of which were precisely the kinds of roles that Joe himself was interested in. Peter had worked as an exchange officer at the United Nations and at the State Department, which were both opportunities that Joe envisioned for himself as well. Over time, the two began to talk not just about what a career for Joe might look like in the military, but also about what a nonmilitary career for the two of them might look like. The widening of conversation topics—from task to career to personal life (a multiplex tie à la Chapter 4)—led the two to become good friends, and they remain in close touch to this day.

During this time, a team-leader position under Peter opened up, and Peter installed Joe first as a deputy on the team and later as the team lead, leapfrogging Joe over other officers with more seniority and credentials. This enabled Joe to work on combat operations and showcase his leadership abilities. When it came time for leaders at the base to decide whom to send off for developmental education, Peter went to the mat for Joe, arguing that Joe should get the opportunity over other candidates who were seen as more qualified (the biggest "knock" against Joe was that despite being an aviator, he was not a fighter pilot, one of the highest-status roles in the Air Force). This angered the other colonels in the room, who were similarly advocating for their protégés. Joe later heard through the grapevine about the heated discussion Peter's sponsorship had generated; Peter himself admitted to Joe that it had been a "knife fight." In the end, Peter had told the commander in charge of the decision that he vouched for Joe. "I know your top performers are deserving, but *I see this guy* and he's going to be in the Air Force for the long haul." The commander was persuaded, and Joe finally got what he needed to advance: enrollment in an in-residence Air Force education program, an opportunity reserved for the top 20 percent of the Air Force.

Joe told me that he can't overstate how important such educational opportunities are in setting the trajectory of an officer's career. "It's a snowball effect. Once you get one thing that highlights you, momentum builds and becomes unstoppable." After attending the program, opportunity after opportunity opened to him. He has been a squadron commander and was recently selected for senior developmental education, which goes to the top 15 percent of Air Force officers. In a karmic twist of fate, the program he will be attending is the same one that Peter attended, many years earlier, and is generally known to be one from which future generals are promoted.

Aside from feeling warm and fuzzy for these two underdogs who ultimately came out on top, I share with you their stories because I want us to think about just how much we lose as a society when we consistently misjudge or overlook talent in the way that Mark and Joe had been. Misjudged (female) scientists represent a loss to society as well.

There are likely countless people who have done everything by the book but are not seen. In the case of Mark and Joe, and probably for the rest of us too, it wasn't until someone was willing to fight for them—to sponsor them—that they received the opportunities that made it so that everyone could see them more clearly.

WHAT DOES IT TAKE TO BE EXCEPTIONAL?

I want us to come back to the questions opening the chapter. What do we need to see to judge people as being worthy of our sponsorship? We can start with an even simpler question: What do we need to see to judge people as being competent? One might imagine that competence looks the same, no matter who is the one doing the task. Alas, that's just not true.

Let's say that you are recruiting job candidates for an executive administrator role. What skills would you be looking for? Let's assume that you are interested in skills like decision-making, interpersonal relations, leadership, motivation, oral communication, problem solving, and willingness to seek and accept advice. These all seem like reasonable things to want in a person who would be managing a leader's affairs, right? Now, the question is, for any given candidate, how many examples of each skill would you need to observe before you would be satisfied that this person would be qualified enough for the position? How many examples of each skill would you need to observe before you would believe that this person would be exceptional at this job?

Note that the two questions are trying to get at very different ideas. The first—are they qualified enough?—is really a question about whether the person meets "the bar." Do they meet the minimum standards of the job? The second—would they be exceptional?—is really a question about whether the person is an ideal candidate. As it turns out, how we answer these questions differs depending on whom we are evaluating. Specifically, research participants put in the scenario above indicated that they would need to see significantly fewer examples of a skill before they would be convinced that a woman, Katherine, had the minimum qualifications than they would need to see from a man, Kenneth, even though Katherine and Kenneth had exactly the same qualifications. However, the opposite was true when participants were asked about exceptionalism; they needed to see significantly more examples of a skill before they would believe that Katherine was exceptional in that ability than they needed to see from Kenneth. They found similar results when comparing participants' responses to Mark

Washburn versus Marcus Washington (names that are stereotypically White and Black, respectively).

This is a phenomenon called "shifting standards," the idea that performance standards are subtly (or not so subtly) changed for women and individuals from marginalized communities such that they are compared against more lenient standards when people are thinking about the bare minimum but more stringent standards when people are thinking about top performers. The issue is that when it comes to sponsorship, most of us are thinking about exceptionalism, and what these findings suggest is that women and racial minorities need to be much more impressive—"need to work twice as hard to be considered half as good"—before we are willing to believe in them as protégés.

As potential sponsors, we have an opportunity to point out these inconsistencies when we see them. But our ability to do so hinges entirely on our ability to see inconsistencies in the first place, and it's not clear that we will. That is why some companies, such as Google, have tried changing their processes so as to diminish the likelihood that psychological bias will creep into how employees are evaluated. Leaders at Google noticed that project directors were consistently rating projects led by women as being easier than those led by men. Although it's possible that female leads were being systematically assigned to easier projects than male leads, another explanation is that they were in fact being assigned projects of equal difficulty, but evaluators changed their perceptions of the projects' difficulty after the fact based on the gender of the leader. Basically, high performance was not seen as a credible marker of actual ability for female leads, but was for male leads. To address this discrepancy, Google now has directors estimate how difficult a project is *before* they assign it to a project manager. This lessens the ability of evaluators to retrospectively skew their interpretations of performance in a biased way.

I, for one, applaud Google for their efforts. Sadly, psychological bias finds its way into almost any human-driven decision-making process (and even computer-aided ones, since our biases are often baked into the data used to train algorithms) because people will almost always find ways to rationalize the outcomes they want. Many companies now require skills testing during the hiring process. The idea here is that these tests aren't in and of themselves biased, so basing hiring decisions on them should, in theory, reduce the impact of any bias that hiring managers might have. However, evidence suggests that hiring managers work around such guardrails by selectively using the tests. Namely, they make women and non-White candidates take the tests, but not White men. This may be why companies that implement skills-based testing actually have a *lower* proportion of female and non-White managers in the years after implementing such policies.

Even when an unbiased process is in place, how that process is applied can vary widely in its consistency, thereby reintroducing bias back into the decision. Moreover, even if the information collected is unbiased, what people do with that information can also add bias back into the system.

SPONSORING BEST PRACTICES
IN ORGANIZATIONS

There are a couple of places where sponsors in organizations can step in to push back against biased systems and people. First, they can push leaders to commit resources to continual collection and analysis of evaluation data so that they can identify problematic processes. Google has an entire People Analytics division, staffed by social scientists with PhDs from some of the top universities in the world, dedicated to combing through Google's own human resources data to uncover potential bias and to devise potential solutions to address identified problems. They then run small experiments in-house to pilot potential interventions and determine which interventions actually work before scaling them up to the broader organization. Essentially, Google treats its own employee base as a social science lab. And while I grant that many organizations might not be willing to commit to an entire People Analytics wing, a smaller but still effective option is to give someone (ideally, a group of people) the resources to regularly collect data and report on their findings. Even this small step has been shown to, in and of itself, increase gender and racial diversity in organizations.

Knowing that someone is watching is sufficient to make people pay more attention to whether their behavior is biased, like the elite Yelpers who no longer rate restaurants lower if their server is a woman.

A second place where sponsors can work to counter bias is to push organizational leaders to commit to an evaluation scheme *before* any candidates are assessed. This is the evaluation equivalent of Rawls' Veil of Ignorance test. John Rawls was a philosopher who argued that when thinking about what constitutes a "fair" society, people need to set aside the perspective of who they are in the world as it exists now, to sit behind a veil of ignorance that shields them from knowing who they are in this yet-to-be-built fair society. The idea is that if we don't know who we will be, we'll be more attentive to how the operations of society affect everyone, no matter their level of ability or background. In a similar vein, sponsors who are dedicated to equity can advocate for processes that use predetermined evaluation schemes, in which evaluation criteria are laid out and the weight of each criteria is specified.

Let's go back to the shifting-standards example, in which we are hiring an executive administrator. Let's say that we (the hiring committee) have narrowed down the field of important skills to the ones identified above: decision-making, interpersonal relations, leadership, motivation, oral communication, problem solving, and willingness to seek and accept advice. The mere exercise of narrowing down the field is a step in the right direction! But now, the group needs to align on how much weight each of these dimensions should carry in the final determination of whom to hire. Is it more important that the administrator be a good communicator or that they are good at problem solving? What if someone is good at seeking and accepting advice, but they lack motivation? Basically, the task of the committee is to decide, in advance of seeing any of the candidates, what is most important for the success of the position.

By prespecifying what is important, and how important each dimension is, we reduce the likelihood that after the candidates have been interviewed, someone on the committee will put more weight on good decision-making skills than communication skills because the candidate they prefer has good decision-making skills.

There's one last place that sponsors can step in to address institutional bias, and that is enforcement. Recall that in the research above, part of the problem wasn't that the processes themselves were biased—everyone should go through skills testing—but that those processes were not being consistently applied across all candidates. I can't overstate how important enforcement is and how often it is overlooked in organizations. Having an evaluation scheme without enforcement of the application of said scheme is, potentially, worse than having no evaluation scheme at all. Why? Because when people are led to believe that a meritocratic system is now in place, without verifying that its outputs are, indeed, meritocratic, they can claim that the system is now fixed. If inequalities remain in who succeeds after its (inconsistent) implementation, then the fault must lie with those who have been judged unworthy, not the system itself.

A belief that the system is meritocratic allows people to sweep violations of meritocracy under the rug. As sponsors, our job is to keep those issues out in the open, for everyone to see.

SHIFTING STANDARDS ARE
A FEATURE, NOT A BUG

What I find laudable about Google's antibias approach is that they have tried to make changes to the system by which people are evaluated. Meaning, they didn't try to fix the problem by training managers to see women as more competent. They changed the procedures so that bias is less likely. On the other end of the spectrum, other organizational evaluation systems work in the opposite direction, by deliberately incorporating flexibility in how criteria are assessed. Ambiguity is a feature, not a bug.

At the risk of navel-gazing, I'm going to offer as tribute the performance-evaluation systems used at many universities to assess which professors go on to receive tenure. Tenure, in case you are not familiar, is a special state of employment that functionally equates to job security for the rest of one's career. Tenured professors cannot be fired except under very specific and extreme circumstances.

For nonacademics, the idea of tenure seems crazy. Why would you give someone guaranteed job security for life? The logic behind academic tenure is that job security frees faculty to challenge existing ways of thinking. This is how innovation occurs; by definition, innovation involves change from what is. But where there is change, there is invariably opposition. Tenure, then, is a bulwark against our natural tendencies to oppose change. Sometimes that opposition is warranted, but sometimes opposition is based on something that is less valid. Tenure is probably what made it possible for Marc Edwards, a professor of civil engineering at Virginia Polytechnic Institute and State University, to raise public awareness of the high levels of lead in the water supply in Flint, Michigan. When he first obtained unusually high readings of lead, he notified the appropriate authorities, who reassured him that his results were an anomaly. However, after repeated testing indicated otherwise and the government continued to stonewall him, Edwards made his findings public, ultimately forcing the government to take action on the water crisis. Had Edwards been a government employee, it's unclear if he would have publicized his findings, because doing so would probably have resulted in getting him fired. But having tenure, knowing that his livelihood was secure, likely freed Edwards to essentially whistle-blow on the government. For this reason, proponents of tenure argue that it benefits not just the individual faculty who have it, but also society at large.

Given the high stakes involved with tenure—after all, once granted, these people can't be fired—universities are understandably very stringent about who gets it. And it's not just high stakes for the university. Did I mention that academia operates on an up-or-out system? Meaning, at many top universities, faculty who are denied tenure are fired. Do not collect $200; do not pass go.

Okay, so we've established that tenure is super important for faculty and universities. So: What does it take to get tenure?

Here are the standards used by Carnegie Mellon University: "Indefinite tenure is granted to a candidate whose record shows that the leadership and reputation inherent in the attributes of a full professor are established or are clearly in the process of being established." Hmm . . . guess we should look at what it means to become a full professor then. Here, the policy states: "[A] successful candidate [for full professor] will usually be a recognized leader who has made outstanding contributions in teaching and other educational activities or in research, scholarly or artistic activities, and has achieved a national or international reputation."

Note how vague those requirements are. Nowhere in this description does it specify the metrics that candidates need to reach to be considered "outstanding." How many research publications are needed? How many times do papers need to be cited by other researchers to be seen as having an impact? Put simply, what are the standards for getting tenure? It is a question that I and others, mainly women and non-White faculty, have continually asked university leaders. And time and time again, they cannot (or will not) commit to any specifics. "We aren't a counting school" is usually the response. "We value quality over quantity."

Why? Why is there such resistance to providing a straight answer to the question, "What's the standard? What's 'enough'?" The answer is this: when we ask, "What's enough?" what we're really asking is, "Who is deserving? Who has merit?"

What even *is* merit? To answer this question, researchers interviewed MBA students and managers at a large technology firm about whom they thought deserved to get ahead in organizations, what merit is, and how merit should be evaluated. They found that people had strikingly different conceptualizations of merit. Some thought that merit should be based solely on performance—an output—but others argued that merit should also take into consideration inputs, like effort. A second area of disagreement was over to what extent objective versus subjective metrics ought to be used in determining merit. Finally, there was disagreement over how much merit should encompass only individuals' performance or should also include the impact they had on their teammates.

Basically, most people don't agree on what constitutes merit. Some see it in narrow terms (merit should be based only on individual performance as measured through quantifiable metrics), and others see it in broader terms (merit is a hazy, abstract concept that incorporates personal and interpersonal qualities that may not show up in objective metrics).

Importantly, people's own experiences with evaluation play a critical role in determining which version of merit they prefer. Those who haven't had many experiences with rejection or nonpromotion tend to have more inclusive and expansive conceptions of merit. Meanwhile, people who have been rejected multiple times or haven't gotten promoted tend to have more focused and narrow conceptions of merit. Perhaps not surprisingly, who has more positive or negative experiences with evaluation tends to depend on their gender and race. Remember how I said it is mostly female and non-White faculty who keep asking the university to provide clearer guidance about promotion standards? That's because it is usually female and non-White faculty who have trouble getting tenure. Women are less likely to receive tenure, even if they publish the same amount as their male peers.

I should be clear here that while I personally believe that there should be clear standards for promotion—and sponsorship!—I also recognize that how we think about merit cannot be disentangled from our personal experiences and desired outcomes. None of us is unbiased in how we decide who is deserving. So I'm going to be a bit provocative here and advocate that we do something a bit unorthodox: let's put less weight on performance to determine who is worthy of our sponsorship.

I know, I know. Some of you are throwing your hands up. The horror! Not prioritizing performance and ability? Who is this crazy woman?

Let me explain. Let's say that we, as individuals, want to approach sponsorship the same way that organizations should approach hiring and promotions. We then generate, for ourselves, an evaluation scheme for what would make us willing to sponsor someone. And for simplicity's sake, let's say that I have one and only one criterion: to even consider sponsoring someone, I would need them to demonstrate that they can accept and change their behavior in response to feedback. Simple enough, right? Here's the thing: I am probably biased in whom I see as needing feedback. I am probably biased in deciding which students I will "give a pass" to and for whom I will "hold the line." I am probably biased in how I give feedback, which impacts how students will respond.

Just this one example—responsiveness to feedback—has a bunch of potential bias baked into it. And other potential criteria are the same. One sponsor I interviewed told me that he looks for "workaholics." Let me ask you this: How can you tell someone is a workaholic? Willingness to travel for the job on a dime's notice?

Staying at the office late? Prioritizing work over family? What's the likelihood this sponsor will see an employee with young children as worthy of sponsorship, even if they are incredibly efficient in their work and are just as productive as someone else who might put in more time or have more flexibility in their schedule? Even work ethic—something I would guess that many of us would cite as a criterion for sponsorship—is a seemingly reasonable criterion rife with the potential for bias.

Most of us don't have access to objective measures of people's performance that organizations use in their evaluation systems,* which increases our susceptibility to bias. But also, despite the fact that many of us often feel like we are surrounded by idiots, my guess is that in reality, most of us are surrounded by people who are perfectly reasonable and competent. So, to really set oneself apart, one has to be exceptional. And we've already covered how problematic that is.

All this is to say, competence isn't as great a differentiator as we might think it is when it comes to deciding whom to sponsor. Which is why I'm advocating for us to prioritize something else.

WHAT SHOULD SPONSORSHIP BE BASED ON?

Throughout this chapter, we've covered a few research studies that implicate the accuracy of how we evaluate other people on the dimensions of competence and ability. Women and racial minorities are held to higher standards to be seen as exceptional. And even if women and racial minorities are high performers, their abilities

---

* And even then, I would argue that many of the objective criteria organizations use are approximations, not direct measures, of the qualities or outcomes that companies actually care about or want to maximize. If that captures your interest, consider reading *Mixed Signals*, by Uri Gneezy, which covers the intricacies of setting up good incentive systems.

are discounted. They end up being pegged as workhorses: dependable performers with low future potential. And because of the confirmation bias—a psychological tendency to pay more attention to information that confirms and to discount information that disconfirms our existing beliefs—once pegged as a workhorse, people will always be seen as just that.

Once someone has decided they hold a certain perception of us, it's really hard to change their minds. This tells us two things: having a sponsor to shape those initial impressions is critical, and sometimes people have to change where they go (whom they have access to) to get the sponsors they deserve. Consider Mark's and Joe's experiences. Mark met his sponsor outside of his day job through his volunteer work helping aspiring entrepreneurs. Joe asked to be transferred to an Air Force base in South Korea.

But another observation worth pointing out is that what attracted their sponsors' attention was not Mark's and Joe's performance per se. It was their shared values. Consider: Mark and Alan met via their work together supporting entrepreneurs. Everyone in the technology and innovation chapter had the same interests: helping aspiring business owners to build a successful company. Everyone there was choosing to be there, giving up time that they could have spent doing something else. We would assume, then, that everyone there was there because they were passionate about entrepreneurship. Knowing that Mark shared his passion, Alan could focus his attention on how Mark would support founders in building viable business models and point out areas of concern. He had the opportunity to witness Mark giving valuable feedback to founders. Similarly, Peter's interest in Joe was piqued when he noticed that Joe was passionate about foreign relations and, perhaps even more important, that Joe's perspective on foreign relations was similar to his. He saw in Joe a simpatico spirit, a man who, like him, believed that military might should be used as a last resort, not the first strike.

Knowing that someone shares our values, aspirations, and interests can change how we assess their competencies, especially when the protégé helps the sponsor pursue those shared passions. Rather than focus purely on present performance, knowing that someone shares our passions encourages us to envision what the trajectory of their future path might look like, often assuming that their passion will ultimately motivate them to greater and greater heights. Indeed, researchers have documented a phenomenon called the Passionate Pygmalion Effect, in which being perceived as having passion leads other people to treat us more favorably, such as by giving us more positive feedback, more training and promotion opportunities—sponsorship!—and more willingness to discount lackluster performance.

Knowing that someone shares our values and our aspirations makes it easier to see how their passions will translate into future performance. Into potential. Once we see their potential, we are more likely to believe in them. To trust them.

We sponsor the people we trust. We trust the people who share our values, our passions, and our dreams.

6 | WHAT IT MEANS TO SHARE

I occasionally peruse posts on Reddit, an online social news website and forum where users can post content to different subcommunities, called subreddits, each dedicated to a specific topic, like funny cat pictures, hiking, or politics. One of the subreddits I like is called CasualConversation, a community in which people are encouraged to pose thought-provoking questions or make a statement that invites engagement from other users. Some sample post titles are "I wish I had known a world without smartphones" and "What are some unwritten social rules everybody should know?" (According to the latter poster, one rule is to have one earbud out of the ear when hanging out with other people. Silly me, I thought the rule was to not have earbuds in at all. But I digress.)

Many of the posts in this community elicit information that people don't often think to share with others because they involve questions that people don't normally think to ask one another. As you might imagine, given my emphasis on sharing more information with one another in this book, I find these posts fascinating. One day, I came across a post that stood out to me, because it so clearly exemplified what we lose when we don't take the time to engage with one another.

The post was titled "Today I had one of the best conversations I've ever had." The original poster (OP) shared that a gentleman came into a music store, where they work, looking to exchange his guitar for a new one. When the poster was ringing up the gentleman's purchase, he noticed that the guy's ID was from California. So he asked him what part of California he was from. The gentleman told him but added that he used to live in Texas and began to describe some of the pros and cons of living in Texas versus California. Buried in this list of pros and cons was a point about his experiences fishing in both states. This led to a conversation about fishing that the poster says "resonated with me deep in my soul. . . . I told him how I had great memories of fishing with my dad as a little boy. . . . The memories of digging up worms and catching grasshoppers in a red Folgers can with my father, and fishing with him on the edges of a pond or on the boat came flooding back to me in an instant."

The Reddit poster said of this experience, "Here are two VERY different individuals from very different walks of life, one older African-American man (late 50s early 60s) who was from an extremely urban town on the West Coast, and a very young white man who grew up in a semi rural/suburban quiet part of the East Coast, and we bonded over arguably one of the most simple things that mankind has been participating in for millennia. I felt that our differences in this moment were totally irrelevant, and that this man had become my friend in just the 30 minutes I had interacted with him."

For this poster, the innocuous question of "Where in California are you from?" led to a conversation where he established true connection with someone, a small but meaningful moment for him.

The comments on the post are equally wholesome. The most upvoted comment states, "People like you are the reason why some keep going." The poster replies, "That is probably the best compliment I could ever hope to receive, thank you so much. . . . [I]t's amazing how a single question can lead to these experiences." Another commenter says, "Dude, those simple heartfelt interactions we have with ppl even random strangers are the best. You may have well made his day, sure seems like he did the same for you. We shouldn't be afraid to talk to each [other], we'd probably find we're all pretty much the same."

As we discussed in Chapter 4, there is surprising happiness to be found in talking with strangers. My guess is that a lot of the happiness that comes from talking with strangers stems from our willingness to ask questions that we might not usually think to ask, usually in response to someone sharing information that they might not usually think to share.

This premise—that good questions beget deeper personal information, which further begets good questions and deeper sharing—underlies one of the exercises I frequently use in the sponsorship programs that I lead. To give you a feel for what these sessions are like, I am going to share with you a few questions from the exercise. Take a few moments to think about these questions and answer them. And to make it even, I'll share my answers on the next page.

These are the questions:

1. If you were able to live to the age of ninety and retain either the mind or the body of a thirty-year-old for the last sixty years of your life, which would you choose and why?
2. Is there something that you have dreamed about doing for a long time? Why haven't you done it?
3. Imagine this evening, you are getting on a space shuttle to colonize a new planet across the galaxy. You will never be able to speak to anyone you know back on Earth ever again. What would you most regret not having told someone?

Here are my answers:

Healthy mind or healthy body?

With apologies to the ninety-year-olds out there who are perfectly physically and cognitively capable, I am answering this question assuming that it is imposing a strict trade-off between body and mind. Meaning, if I choose the option of having the body of a thirty-year-old for the rest of my life, I am forfeiting my cognitive capacities, and if I choose the option of having the mind of a thirty-year-old for the rest of my life, I am forfeiting my physical capabilities.

Assuming that's the case, I would choose to retain my mind over my body. Having a healthy body without the cognitive wherewithal to enjoy its capabilities, in my opinion, would be a waste. Also, I would worry about how my cognitive impairment would impact my family. When I think about the experiences of the people I know whose family members have passed with dementia or Alzheimer's versus those who have passed with clear and lucid minds, the latter seems preferable for everyone.

What is something you've long dreamed of doing? Why haven't you done it?

I have always wanted to learn how to surf. Given my affinity for the ocean, this seems like a huge oversight on my part.

I almost did go to surf camp many years ago, in the time between graduating with my PhD and starting my faculty job. But my then-partner couldn't afford to go, and I worried that if I went, it would hurt his feelings. It was bad enough that he didn't have the financial resources to make the trip, but what made it worse was that he was eight years into trying to complete a PhD, and here I was, gallivanting off to surf camp having secured an academic job at a prestigious institution after a comparably short five years in my program. Going (and celebrating) seemed too callous.

My present excuse for why I haven't done this yet is that I have young children, and it seems unfair to leave my family (really, my husband) to go to Costa Rica for a week to do nothing but surf and yoga. Doing things just for me continues to be something I struggle with.

What do you most regret not having told someone?

Ooof. This one is a hard one. I don't know that there's something that I regret not having told someone, but I will share two of my biggest regrets. Both involve my paternal grandparents and last words.

My first regret: I was keeping watch over my paternal grandfather at the hospital while my parents went home to rest. He called out and asked me where my brother was. I told him that my brother would be coming soon (he was scheduled to arrive the following day), and my grandfather grew visibly agitated. He raised his voice and said something in Chinese before lapsing into sleep. He never woke up.

My Chinese wasn't good enough for me to understand my grandfather's last words.

You might wonder, why do I care so much about understanding my grandfather's last words? For one, I suspect he wanted to bestow some last words of wisdom upon my brother, the last "true" Chow in his lineage (as I am a female descendant, my grandfather did not see me as a "true" Chow, because upon marriage, I would "belong" to a different family). What if my inability to understand him meant that I robbed my brother of some familial secret or creed? Despite being the least "Chinese" of my family (I barely speak the language. I married a non-Asian person. Heck, there's only one Asian person on my Trusted Ten!), I am steeped enough in Chinese cultural values to care deeply about fulfilling the wants and wishes of my elders. I'm not Chinese enough to have understood my grandfather's dying words, but I'm Chinese enough to care that I didn't.

My second regret: A few years before the incident above, my paternal grandmother told me over the phone that she was experiencing abdominal pain. Reader, I am ashamed to say that I brushed her off and told her that it couldn't be that bad. In today's parlance, I gaslit her. To her credit, she told me that she wasn't someone who typically complained (true), so for her to do so meant that the pain was pretty bad. I think I mumbled some sort of apology, and when the conversation ended, I gave her a perfunctory good-bye.

That was the last time we spoke. Shortly after our conversation, my parents took my grandmother to the hospital, and she passed away during a diagnostic scan. I wish—I wish!—to this day that I had taken her experience seriously and that I had given a more heartfelt good-bye, even if I hadn't known it would be our last. I wish I had told or showed her how much I appreciated her.

Because, truth be told, I had always held my grandmother a bit at a remove. She was constantly giving, not just to me but to everyone she encountered. But her generosity was so over the top, it had the ironic effect of pushing me away; I saw it as her trying to "buy" my love. To prove my independence, I denied her the thing she wanted most: my affection. Now, with the benefit of emotional maturity, I can see that all the presents, all the time she spent cooking my favorite foods, were her way of saying, I love you. She wanted us to love her back, of course, but she never demanded it of us. The demand was solely in my own head, and now it's too late for me to tell her how much she means to me.

[Who is cutting onions in here?]

———

What do my answers reveal about me?

My answer to the first question is probably not that surprising, given that I'm an academic. Academics prize the mind, so is it any wonder that I chose mind over body? But you also learned a bit about my thinking process, that part of my calculus involves considering my impact on others. This may start to give you an idea about my priorities—I tend to factor others' happiness into my decisions. This hunch could be confirmed by my answer to the second question, where this desire to make sure others around me are happy and comfortable can get in the way of my own happiness.

My answers to the last question give you a glimpse into the internal conflict I have about my Chinese identity and how that conflict has shaped me. They also tell you that I feel strongly about appreciation, both being appreciated and appropriately appreciating the other people in my life.

If I now challenged you to describe who I am, based on what you have read, I wonder what you would say. Has reading this chapter changed your sense of who I am? How? Why?

These questions are drawn from the exercise I use, called Fast Friends. Fast Friends was developed by social psychologist Arthur Aron to do exactly that: to quickly create intimacy between strangers. The exercise comprises three sets of questions, each requiring increasing levels of vulnerability and disclosure. Pairs have ten minutes to discuss each set of questions and cannot pick and choose which questions to answer.

The secret to Fast Friends is simple: these are questions that people would normally never ask one another, either because we don't think to ask them or because even if we did come up with questions like these, they seem inappropriately probing and deep. By coming in as an outsider and asking people to do things they would normally never do, I can serve as the "excuse" for violating these norms; people are willing to do the exercise because I, the crazy professor, am "forcing" them to do this awkward exercise.

But precisely because they aren't the normal kinds of questions we ask each other, Fast Friends induces vulnerability. When I debrief this exercise, people sometimes confess that they have just shared something with a stranger that they haven't even shared with their loved ones (these people then typically pledge to repeat the exercise with their partners when they get home).

Being vulnerable is the basis of trust. In fact, academics define trust as the willingness to be vulnerable to the actions of others. Trust and vulnerability go hand in hand; you cannot have one without the other.

When we are willing to make ourselves vulnerable, we imply that we trust others not to use our vulnerabilities against us. It is akin to approaching others with our hands up, palms open. This gesture is the universal sign for "I'm unarmed! Don't hurt me!" In using it, we give the other person the opportunity to harm us. We demonstrate that we are trusting that they will choose not to. And the reason the gesture works is that knowing that this vulnerability—this trust—is being offered leads others to trust us in turn. They respond by lowering their weapons, too.

In Chapter 2, we discussed how sponsorship won't occur unless the sponsor trusts the protégé, full stop. This isn't to say that protégés don't need to trust sponsors, but the risk to protégés isn't quite as high as it is for sponsors. When sponsors vouch for protégés, they risk their reputation and relationships. They make themselves vulnerable to the actions of the protégé.

When sponsors don't trust protégés, there is no sponsorship.

TALK ABOUT YOUR VALUES

Last chapter, I shared with you the story of Peter, an Air Force colonel, who chose to sponsor Joe, an overlooked Asian American Air Force member. Joe was by no means the most exceptional performer working under Peter. Peter himself acknowledged to the other colonels that their protégés might very well be more "deserving" of additional developmental education opportunities if deserving meant having fighter-pilot experience. But what made Peter willing to engage on Joe's behalf is that he had identified Joe as a kindred spirit. And how did Peter know this? Through the many hours he and Joe spent discussing Joe's career aspirations and their mutual interest in national security and diplomacy.

The story of Peter and Joe is a version of the prototypical sponsorship origin story. In many sponsorship origin stories, protégés and supervisors travel together for work, and what ends up happening is that all that time spent waiting together in airport terminals, cabs, and hotel lobbies makes it easier to leave work aside and talk about other things, like their families, hobbies, and life histories. They get to know about one another's values and aspirations. They build multiplex relationships.

They become fast friends.

This is precisely how the Fast Friends exercise works. Very few of the questions explicitly ask about accomplishments or professional achievements. The questions are about regrets, aspirations, and dreams. The questions are about motivations and values. In this way, Fast Friends takes advantage of the academic finding that trust isn't based on just one thing, but, rather, composed of multiple components. This is important, because when it comes to sponsorship and our willingness to trust potential protégés, too many of us are fixated on purely one dimension to determine trust: competence. And while it's true that competence is a core component of trust, it is by no means the only, or perhaps even the most important, one. Competence gets a protégé on a sponsor's radar; what pushes potential protégés over the top is that the sponsors also have conviction in the protégés' motivations. It matters less to sponsors that protégés know what they want to achieve than that protégés know *why* they want to achieve. A protégé who is driven by strong beliefs or values is one who will have the motivation to be successful. So long as a sponsor shares those beliefs and values, they will feel compelled to help the protégé achieve their goals through sponsorship.

Sharon, an interviewee for this book, had worked in health care for many years. One thing she observed was that hospitals consistently needed help with staffing, particularly nurses. She decided that she wanted to start a staffing company. However, family circumstances were such that she had to move to a new city, far removed from the professional network that she had cultivated over the decades. Starting a new business is daunting enough; to do so in a new city is even harder. Luckily, Sharon had a friend who connected her—sponsored her—to one of the top doctors in the region, who worked at a major hospital. After speaking with Sharon only once, the doctor told Sharon that he would put her company's name forward to the procurement office at the hospital, effectively becoming Sharon's first client.

Sharon was flabbergasted by his sponsorship. She had no track record, and he barely knew her. Why was this man willing to sponsor her? When asked, the doctor told her that he had seen her résumé, so he knew that she had the appropriate experience. Critically, however, was that during their single conversation, he could see how passionate she was about the importance of helping hospitals find good talent. Her conviction was the linchpin; she had the credentials, but beyond that, he believed that she would be willing to put in the work to make the company a success. He could tell from how she talked about the company's goals that she understood the challenges with and importance of finding good medical workers for the welfare of hospital patients. Being a doctor himself, he shared those concerns and wanted to find ways to address those same challenges too.

Sharon's sponsor's emphasis on motivation and values is echoed in the many interviews I conducted for this book. Performance and ability, when mentioned, are rarely the first things that people identified as the main driver for whom they choose to sponsor. Rather, what sponsors seem to care about is understanding the motivations underlying what protégés want and whether those motivations match their own. Sponsors want to know, are we motivated by the same values?

We tend to trust people who share our values. Consider: the people on our Trusted Ten aren't there because they are high performers; they are there because we think they are *good people*. Now consider that most of the people on our Trusted Ten are similar to us. That we see people who are like us as being good is not an accident; presumably, we don't see ourselves as morally suspect. Basically, those we see as being good people are the people whose value systems overlap with ours. We understand and want to help them because we understand and want to help *ourselves*.

In sum, how can we build trust with others? Talk about—or ask people about—their dreams, their aspirations, and their motivations. Knowing why people want what they want gives us insight into their values. To the extent we have similar values, and our dreams are informed by those shared values, we'll most likely want to help each another to achieve our dreams.

We will want to sponsor one another.

USING PSYCHOLOGICAL JUJITSU ON OURSELVES TO BUILD CLOSER RELATIONSHIPS

Sharing values and dreams with someone who isn't already a close friend is a big ask for a lot of people. Many of us are extremely private, and such questions might feel intrusive or inappropriate.

The first thing I want to say is that if you are a private person, that's fine. But research has found that there is personal joy in "being known" by others. The reward centers of the brain are activated when you talk about your own personality traits to others. While the notion that people enjoy talking about themselves may not be surprising to anyone who has had to sit through "conversations" with, say, narcissistic individuals, these findings suggest that those who avoid *any* form of self-disclosure might be doing themselves a disservice.

Withholding information about ourselves to others also takes away a key strategy for building closer relationships: the "fake it till you make it" mechanism. Another reason Fast Friends works to accelerate psychological closeness is that when someone bares their soul to you (even when they are forced to do so by some crazy professor!), you can't help but care about them. When people share personally revealing information with us and are vulnerable, we assume they like and trust us. We then like and trust them in return, which likewise increases our willingness to share personally revealing information with them.

The notion of "fake it till you make it" is also known as the self-fulfilling prophecy. The idea here is that when we have certain expectations, we will behave in ways that make those expectations come true. There's a classic study where students in the lab were told that they were either working with "maze-bright" rats or "maze-dull" rats. In reality, the rats had the same level of intelligence. However, rats who had been described as "maze bright" exhibited better performance in navigating mazes than those described as "maze dull," suggesting that the students were engaging with the rats in a way that elicited a performance consistent with their expectations. These studies were replicated with humans to similar effect: students who were described to teachers as having high intellectual potential performed better on subsequent standardized tests than students who hadn't been described one way or another. Why? Teachers asked "high-potential" students more challenging questions and gave them more opportunities to correct their answers when they provided an initially incorrect answer, which enabled them to learn more effectively. In contrast, when a "low-potential" student answered questions incorrectly, teachers would either provide them with the correct answer or ask a different student for their answer.

The self-fulfilling prophecy means that our beliefs and expectations for how our interactions will go can impact how we behave toward others, such that those expectations become reality. When we expect the best from others, we behave in ways that elicit the best from others. You can harness this power through a practice called "Giving an A," a strategy that Rosamund Zander and Benjamin Zander describe in their book *The Art of Possibility*. Benjamin Zander, a former conductor of the Boston Philharmonic, continually found that his musical conservatory students would be so hyperfocused on performing perfectly that they wouldn't take the artistic leaps that would push them into greatness. He and Rosamund then came up with the idea that if Benjamin began his classes with the statement that all the students were guaranteed an A in the course, they would be able to refocus their efforts from performance to the creation of art. As the two write, giving an A is "a shift in attitude that makes it possible for you to speak freely about your own thoughts and feelings while, at the same time, [allowing] you to support others to be all they dream of being. The practice of *giving an A* transports your relationships from the world of measurement into the universe of possibility."

Giving an A. Fake it till you make it. Self-fulfilling prophecy. However you want to think about it, the key is this: if our goal is to create the kinds of relationships where we will want to act as sponsors for others, one strategy we can use is to *go into more conversations with the expectation that we will, indeed, want to sponsor the other person*. When we go into conversations with the assumption that the other person is worthy and deserving, we just might find that they meet, if not exceed, our already lofty expectations.

ANOTHER WAY TO CLOSENESS:
ASKING QUESTIONS

Are you still skeptical of being vulnerable with other people? Or still working on coming out of your shell? An alternative approach, then, is the flip side of sharing: seeking.

On a flight many years ago, I found myself sitting next to another solo female traveler. I had brought a book, and after about a half hour of sitting in silence, the woman asked me about it. I don't recall the title, but it was related to work, so the conversation naturally turned to what I do for a living. I'm a professor, I told her. How about you? I'm a nurse, she responded.

At that point, we both had a choice. We had exchanged basic information. It would have been a natural place to end the conversation and move on with our lives. But I decided to be a bit provocative, so I asked her, "Do you like being a nurse?"

Here's where things got interesting. She could have said, "Yes, I love helping people" or some other pat response. But she made a different choice; she decided to be a bit more vulnerable. Maybe it was because I was a stranger on an airplane whom she would never see again. Whatever the reason, she decided to open up. She said, "No, not particularly." At this, my ears perked up. Most people don't admit to not liking their jobs. I asked her why.

She told me that she disliked how the health profession had become so bureaucratic. In the past, she used to work primarily with patients, and now she spent the majority of her time on managing paperwork. After expressing my sympathies, I opted to be provocative again. "If you weren't a nurse," I asked, "what would you do instead?" At this, she hesitated, deliberating before saying, "I… don't know." "Well," I asked her, "what do you enjoy doing the most when you aren't at work?"

This time, her answer was prompt: "I love helping people at my church." She proceeded to tell me how hard it had been for her when her father died, because she had to grieve his death, arrange for his funeral, and serve as the executor of his will all at the same time. Being in charge of all these things in the immediate aftermath of her father's passing did not give her the emotional space she needed to process his death. However, that difficult experience gave her expertise in managing someone's affairs after they pass. She now uses that expertise to help other families in her church when a loved one dies. She takes charge of making arrangements with funeral homes and organizing memorial services. She composes obituaries to notify the community. She provides phone and utility companies with copies of the death certificate so that services can be shut off. In short, she takes care of practicalities so grieving families can focus on emotional closure.

She said that helping people in her community in this way brought her the greatest satisfaction and fulfillment in her life. In this, I could see that her *why*—the value that most motivated her and from which she derived the most fulfillment—was helping other people in their times of need.

Here's the thing: there are many *whats* that can fulfill someone's *why*. This is a key insight that negotiation instructors try to hammer into students: there's a big difference between *what* people want (their positions) and *why* they want what they want (their interests). There can be many positions that will fulfill someone's interests. My flying partner's interest was to help others in their time of need. She had, for a time, fulfilled this interest by being a nurse. However, the *what* that she was doing—nursing—was no longer fulfilling her *why*. I then suggested that she consider moving on to a different *what*— starting her own company offering bereavement services.

She pondered this, and we began to have a conversation about what it might look like for her to start a business in this vein. I am, after all, a business school professor! I also happen to have some experience with angel investing (an early stage of investing that precedes venture capital). We mapped out people in her network that she should speak with, and by the time the flight ended, she was visibly excited about this possible new direction.

I should be clear: I know absolutely nothing else about this woman. I don't know her name, I can't even remember what city we were flying to, and I have no idea where she lives. I have absolutely no idea if she's a good nurse. I don't know if she graduated from a top school or if she's won awards. But none of that matters in comparison to what I *did* learn about her from our conversation: that she cares deeply about people and has found a meaningful way to contribute to her community. Seeing her passion and generosity made me trust her. I saw her motivation. If we had lived in the same city or if I knew more about the ins and outs of working in bereavement services, I would have connected her to people in my network. All because I now had a better sense of her values and her dreams. Her *why*.

Knowing her *why* made it so that I would have been happy to sponsor her to get to her *what*.

There are multiple paths to trust, and not all run through competence and ability. Yet most of us focus on competence because we've bought in to the networking-as-resource-extraction model of relationships. Because our goal is to figure out who has what we need, our conversations tend to revolve around *whats*. What are we good at? What have we done? What have we accomplished? It is much rarer to share information about our *whys*.

Every encounter we have, whether with an old friend or a soon-to-be new one, is an opportunity* to help other people articulate their values and dreams. When we ask questions and give others the space to expand upon their answers, we give them opportunities to self-disclose. Pay attention to what makes them light up. What do they seem excited about? Or, if they don't seem particularly excited about what they are telling you, point that out. After all, the things we lack enthusiasm for are often the things with which we are struggling. Pointing out their lack of enthusiasm, then, becomes an opening for them to share with you a bit more about what

---

* Opportunities are not to be confused with obligations. I'm not saying that we should approach every single encounter we have with this intention, only that we should be open-minded about making space for these conversations. Some people won't want to go there with you. Sometimes we don't have the time or cognitive capacity to do this for other people. That's all okay. I'm just putting on your radar that these conversations are possible and, indeed, desirable.

they might be struggling with. All of that, then, becomes inventory we can stock in our understanding of who is good at what or who needs what.

Critically, how we respond to other people's self-disclosures is as important to the building of trust as the fact that self-disclosure occurred in the first place. That I have chosen to share with you my regrets about my grandparents does not make me trust you more. If I shared these stories with you in person, the level of trust I would have in you would depend greatly on how you responded to my sharing. Were you attentive? Or did you seem uncomfortable with my sharing?

In a similar way, how I responded to the woman on the plane was of utmost importance in making it so that she was willing to share more and more as the conversation progressed. I was keenly interested in what she had to say, and I asked increasingly penetrating questions. Throughout, I was never judgmental one way or another about her responses (unless it was to affirm her experiences), nor did I try to make connections to my own life. I didn't try to convince her that being a nurse is, in fact, of incredible value to society (we called them heroes, after all, in the early days of the pandemic). I didn't try to console her when she spoke of her father's death.

All I did was listen and ask questions.

THE MAGIC OF LISTENING WITHOUT JUDGMENT

What does it mean to listen to someone? To truly, deeply listen?

When I pose this question to students, many start first with behavioral indicators of listening: eye contact, nodding, leaning forward. Once those physical cues are exhausted, they then begin to list off verbal indicators: asking clarifying questions, paraphrasing what has been said, saying uh-huh or yeah (what linguistic researchers call backchannels). Finally, once they've exhausted this set, students then turn to absence: not interrupting, not using the time to formulate your own response, not giving advice when it hasn't been asked for.

There's one they always miss: not judging.

Once we've converged on what good listening looks like, I then take them through an exercise that helps them to understand what good listening *feels* like. In this exercise, students are paired off. Each partner takes turns being the listener and the speaker across six rounds of questions. By design, every question is different for both listener and speaker to ensure that the person listening won't be distracted by thinking about how they themselves will answer the question when it's their turn to speak. After every other set—when each person in the pair has been in both the listener and the speaker role—the time increases. The first two rounds last two minutes each, the second two rounds last five minutes each, and the last two rounds last eight minutes each. So far, so good, right?

This is when I share with them some additional instructions. Critically, when in the listener role, the listener can *only* listen. They are not allowed to ask questions or paraphrase. Moreover, the speaker can *only* speak, and they must continue speaking until the time is up for the specific duration of the round. Nobody is allowed to speak between rounds. Essentially, the exercise is set up so that I've both helped and hindered their ability to demonstrate good listening; by not allowing them to speak, they can't do the things that are indicative of bad listening, like interrupting or giving advice. At the same time, by not allowing them to speak, they also can't do the things that are indicative of good listening, like asking clarifying questions or summarizing what the speaker has just shared.

There's usually a lot of grumbling at this point and a note of panic in the room, but I set up the timer, put the first question up on the screen, and off we go. The speakers start off strong, but after a minute, many run out of steam. They look at me beseechingly when I tell them that they should keep talking. Listeners fidget and give me similarly imploring looks as I patrol the room to ensure that people are following the rules. No one, as far as I can tell, is enjoying themselves. As I call "Time's up" after the first round, those in the speaker role exhale loudly, and some start commenting on how difficult it is to talk for two minutes straight. I tell them that it's not time to debrief the exercise yet, and we move on to the next two-minute round, when the pairs switch roles. When that round is finished and we move on to the five-minute set, the room is quieter, more focused. By the time we are in the third set—eight minutes—everyone has relaxed into the exercise. Speakers are less hesitant about what they have to say; they pause when they have finished a thought and then free-associate to the next idea. Listeners sit quietly and stare attentively at the speaker, few bothering to make eye contact with me as I pass by.

When the last set is done, I call a break. The class typically erupts in pandemonium, like the bubbling over of an uncorked champagne bottle. They excitedly tell one another things they wish they had said, had they been able to, or even just commiserate over how difficult the exercise was. Some are more pensive; others cry and hug.

When we return from break, I ask them what it was like to only be able to listen. Invariably, the first students to respond report feeling extremely uncomfortable with not being able to utilize their usual strategies to show that they are listening. They feel constrained by the inability to ask questions or to express their agreement or affirmation of what the speaker is saying. I'll then ask if there is anyone who had a different experience. At this point, someone usually offers that they found that not needing to respond freed them to pay better attention to what was being said. That not having to respond can make it easier to be a better listener. I let the class take a moment to let this idea sink in.

I then ask the class what it was like to be the speaker. As before, the first students to respond often report feeling extremely uncomfortable with having to generate content to fill two, five, or eight minutes straight. They share that they feel like they were just saying random stuff to fill the time. Then, as before, I'll ask if there is anyone who would like to share a different perspective. At this point, someone usually offers that once they realized that they wouldn't be getting a response from the listener, this freed them to say more about themselves than they had ever before. They were able to focus their attention on what they were saying, rather than on what the other person might be thinking. This is a perspective I elaborate upon. Most of us are constantly scanning our conversation partners for signs of agreement and affirmation. Do they understand what I am trying to say? Do they agree with me? Should I do more of that? Without those cues, many of us feel unmoored. We don't know where to go next.

Sometimes, that's exactly the point. *Good listeners do not tell us where to go next. They merely tell us to go forward.*

I want to be clear: I'm not saying that we should go through life listening to people with unemotional, blank faces. Most of the time, the most enjoyable conversations are a verbal dance where two people create an emotional reality together. The questions we ask, the smiles, the backchannel uh-huhs, all serve the purpose of indicating that we are on the same page, that we understand one another. This is why many students will say they believe it is impossible to have a meaningful conversation with another person if the person doesn't respond. But when I ask them if they feel closer to their exercise partner, they invariably say yes. The exercise precluded them from having a standard turn-taking conversation, but that didn't mean that they didn't build a deeper understanding of one another.

The best conversations foster a sense of connection. But the sense of connection we get from conversations isn't just because of effective turn-taking. Effective turn-taking is simply a marker of the real driver of connection: the knowledge that the other person thinks well of us and cares about us, no matter what we say.

The emphasis many of us put on turn-taking in conversations can have a hidden downside: hindering the ability of people to learn more *about themselves.* When someone is feeling uncertain, it can be helpful to pull back on some of the behaviors many of us have been trained to do to keep conversations going. When someone is uncertain or when they don't know the answer to a question, many of us immediately jump to problem solving or commiseration. Instead, when someone has a problem, consider just focusing on high-quality listening. Why is this a problem for them? How does it make them feel? We can certainly ask clarifying questions and smile to indicate that we are paying attention. But what we want to avoid is to give cues as to what we think is right or good. Our role is to act as a mirror to the speaker, reflecting the speaker to themselves and allowing them to see themselves the way they are, not the way we want them to be or the way they think we want them to be.

Good listening is, at its heart, about nonjudgmental and unconditional positive regard. No matter what the person is saying, the good listener gives them the time and freedom to explore the space. *Their* space. When we listen to others—really listen to them— we give them the opportunity to discover more about themselves than they might have imagined possible. What unspoken desires and dreams might they unearth? And through their journey of self-discovery, we discover them too.

MY HOPES FOR YOU, ME, AND THIS BOOK

So far, we've talked about the power of sharing information about our dreams, but you don't know mine yet. So here is one final question that I'll answer for you, drawn from the listening exercise I described above. Consider answering it for yourself, too!

What would it take to feel that your life had been a success? A failure?

As I've gotten older, I've started paying more attention to how people characterize one another at weddings and, sadly, at funerals. The ones who are remembered most fondly are the people who made people feel good about themselves. And I find myself wondering, how have I made people feel?

I don't (and won't) know what people will say about me at my funeral, but I do know what was said about me by the people who gave toasts at my wedding. One of my childhood friends described how, even when we were teenagers, I was good at debating. Another friend, from graduate school, touted my academic achievements and self-assurance when presenting and answering questions about my research.

I know that these comments were meant as complimentary. After all, when you're an academic, the height of achievement is to be acknowledged by your peers for your intellectual excellence and ability to argue a point. But I will tell you this: if all anyone has to say about me when I'm gone is that I was smart, that I was a significant contributor to my academic field, and that I was good at making a point, I will consider my life to have been a failure. *This is not how I want to be remembered.* I don't want my life to be measured by how many papers I have published or how many other researchers cite my papers.*

That realization has inspired me to change the trajectory of my career. Now that I have tenure—and don't have to worry about losing my job!—I'm focused on how I can help *others* to understand the impact they can have on other people's lives. My *why*—what drives me—is facilitating others' growth and thriving. And, perhaps not coincidentally, I happen to be in the perfect position to do just that. Being at a university where I can engage with hundreds of students

---

* I don't say this to demean those who use these metrics to measure the meaning of their lives. Just that they aren't the metrics I want to use.

(future leaders!) and professionals (current leaders!) puts me in a position where I can fulfill my purpose. I am immensely grateful for my livelihood, because when friends and colleagues tell me about instances when I've been the brightest and most vibrant version of myself, their examples almost always involve my leading a social or educational experience. I am a different self—my best self—when I am teaching or facilitating. In those moments, I can inform or reframe how people see the world, hopefully in a way that expands their understanding of how much they matter.

This book is the next step in my pursuit of fulfilling my *why*. My hope is that you will read this book and remember that some of the most revealing things we can share of ourselves are our *whys*. Remember that one of the most impactful things we can do for others is to help them to articulate their *whys*. With this information in hand—with the trust this information builds—sponsorship often becomes the obvious next step.

7 | THE DIFFERENT FORMS OF SPONSORSHIP

Halle Stockton, editor in chief and co–executive director at PublicSource, a local news outlet in Pittsburgh, has always been interested in journalism. When her high school student newspaper shut down, she convinced the faculty to let her publish stories in the faculty newsletter instead. When she enrolled at Pennsylvania State University, she spent more time at its student-led newspaper than she did in class. She rose through the ranks of the newsroom: reporter, editor, managing editor. She was a fixture there.

Stockton was sufficiently ambitious that she asked her college to nominate her to participate in a prestigious national journalism competition. They agreed to do so but told her to temper her expectations. Even the college dean, who knew her well, told her to just feel honored to participate. The competition tasked her and seven other finalists with roaming around San Francisco for ideas and then generating three articles within forty-eight hours. The assignment seemed daunting; this would be Stockton's first time in a big city, and she worried she lacked the kinds of social connections that the other contestants might have. Given the headwinds facing her, when Stockton won the competition, her win was even more validating and meaningful than it might have been for the average contestant.

Her university proudly announced the news to the community, which got the attention of her ethics professor. He already liked Stockton before her win; he was even more impressed by her journalistic chops after that—so much so that he decided to sponsor her by introducing her to a university trustee, who also happened to be a former managing editor for the *New York Times*. It took just one breakfast with Stockton for the trustee to gain an interest in her career. He offered to connect her with people and opportunities, which is how Stockton got her first journalism job after college.

Stockton is hardly the only journalist to have gotten her toehold in the field through personal connections. Thomas Friedman, a *New York Times* columnist, got his start in journalism when his girlfriend (now wife) used her connections to get an opinion piece of his published in the *Des Moines Register*. Friedman followed up with almost a dozen more opinion pieces and parlayed that experience into a job at United Press International, which sent him to Beirut as a foreign correspondent. There, he established himself as a leading journalistic authority on the Middle East and was hired by the *New York Times* two years later.

Sponsorship is an integral part of some of the most momentous events of our lives. Sponsors lift people up and make them visible to people who might otherwise never have noticed them. This can lead to love, like David Weinlick and Elizabeth Runze from Chapter 2, and career success, like Stockton and Friedman. Sponsors can solve problems, like Kyle Webster, the artist whose digital brushes are now used by millions worldwide. Sponsorship can also play a role in smaller moments too, as when an excited child comes home and shapes his parents' view of his teacher, when a newly arrived neighbor asks for recommendations for a new primary-care doctor, or when a manager gives a shout-out to an employee who went above and beyond to help the rest of the team.

Sponsorship is everywhere, because sponsorship is influence, and we influence one another each and every day, day in and day out.

THERE ISN'T JUST ONE WAY TO SPONSOR

Sponsorship is a specific kind of influence: impression management. Normally, when people think of impression management, they think of the things people do to manage how other people see and behave toward them. Sponsorship is a twist on this standard view of impression management; rather than managing how other people perceive us, when we sponsor, we manage how people perceive our protégés. And just as there isn't only one way to manage other people's impressions of us, there isn't only one way to manage people's impressions of one another.

Consider the many options we have available to us to get people to see us positively. When we share about an important achievement—self-promotion—we want to be seen as competent or talented. When we compliment other people—ingratiation—we want to be seen as warm. When people "pick their battles," that's also a form of impression management; by limiting how often we disagree with others—going along to get along—we want people to see us as likable. Strategically being the last to leave the office, as Joe, the Air Force officer we met in Chapter 5 did, is called exemplification, a form of impression management designed to get others to see us as dedicated.

There are various forms of impression management that can be used to defend ourselves from negative perceptions, too. When people resist seeking help from others at work, they don't want to be seen as incompetent. When we provide excuses for something bad that has happened, we are trying to protect our reputation by denying responsibility for the bad outcome. In deflecting blame, we seek to maintain others' perceptions of our ability or intentions (or both). Conversely, when we accept blame for a mistake and apologize, we imply that we share the group's values and acknowledge that we have violated them. We protect our relationships by expressing our commitment to shared values; we wouldn't apologize (authentically) if we didn't agree that our behavior was problematic.

Regardless of its specific form, impression management is meant to impact how we are seen by others, usually in terms of ability and reassuring people that we share their values. This should start reminding you of something: ability and shared values are also the hallmarks of trust. The fundamental purpose of impression management, then, is to increase others' willingness to trust us. Similarly, the fundamental purpose of sponsorship is to increase others' willingness to trust our protégés. As sponsors, we encourage others to see our protégés as competent, likable, and sharing our values— as trustworthy—and we persuade detractors that their negative perceptions of our protégés are unwarranted, ultimately giving our protégés the best opportunity to shine.

In essence, sponsorship encompasses a variety of strategies. What this means, then, is that we shouldn't think of sponsorship as all or nothing or see ourselves as being a sponsor or not. Sponsorship is an action—something we *do*—and not something we *are*. And if we see sponsorship as a type of behavior or a continuum of behaviors, it means that sponsorship is always an option. The question is *how* we choose to do it.

When thinking about different ways we can sponsor others, it helps to think about two factors: whether the audience already knows and has preexisting impressions of our protégé and whether we are seeking to maximize positive or negative impressions of our protégé. The combination of these two factors generates four categories of sponsorship types: **Prevent** (minimizing the creation of a negative impression), **Confirm** (maximizing existing positive impressions), **Create** (maximizing the creation of a positive impression), and **Protect** (minimizing existing negative impressions).

Prevent

Preventing refers to proactively ensuring that people don't develop negative impressions of our protégés. They don't know of our protégés one way or another, but we see a potential threat on the horizon and use our position to neutralize the threat before it becomes an issue for the protégé. Consider managers who ensure that their direct reports don't get put on dead-end projects at work or aren't assigned to work with coworkers who have a reputation for toxicity. Alternatively, consider an instance where you refer a friend to a hiring manager in your firm, but you strategically omit sharing the fact that your friend has just been laid off (which might lead the hiring manager to be less interested in them).

While Preventing can clearly be impactful, its impact is akin to those portrayed in the movie *The Minority Report*. In this movie, a police unit called Precrime relies on mutant humans called "precogs" to make predictions about who will commit a crime. The Precrime unit then swoops in to arrest the individual in question before the crime is committed. The end result is a nonevent; nothing bad happens. Preventing in sponsorship similarly results in a nonevent; the protégé isn't seen negatively. By ensuring that a protégé isn't assigned to work with a problematic manager, the sponsor prevents the creation of an association that might come to hurt how the protégé is seen by others. In other situations, some forms of Prevention are designed both to modify the protégé's behavior and to modify how the protégé is seen by others. We might discourage our children from playing with the neighborhood bully, thereby preventing our children from becoming bullies themselves (or being bullied) and from being seen as bullies through association.

Preventing could be particularly important for sponsors of protégés whose social identities come with burdensome stereotypes. Take non-promotable tasks, tasks that further an organization's goals but provide minimal to no career benefits for employees. An example of an NPT is when a senior employee is informally tasked with training and mentoring a new hire. It's a benefit to the company that newcomers are trained, but unless the senior employee gets credit for and is rewarded for training new employees, the time a senior employee spends on training is time that they could have spent on getting their own work done. For this reason, chronic engagement in NPTs ultimately harms people's career progress.

Unfortunately, a significant portion of NPTs, like organizing workplace social events or participation on low-level but essential committees, ends up being performed by women. Research indicates that this isn't because women prefer to do them or because women are better at them. Rather, neither men nor women want to do them. This means that frequently, nobody proactively steps up to do them, and many leaders end up distributing these types of tasks by asking for volunteers. When asked to volunteer, women tend to cave sooner than men; behold the woman who begrudgingly raises her hand to take on a task because she knows that it needs to be done, and if someone's got to do it, it might as well be her so that she knows that it's done right. Research also shows that people tend to ask women to do NPTs more than they ask men because they assume, correctly, that women are more likely to say yes. Given this, one thing a sponsor can do is to ensure that their protégés, especially women and racial minority protégés, are not assigned to these types of tasks. A sponsor might note that Jane has already been assigned to coordinate the July 4 social; surely, Tim can step up to organize the Thanksgiving party? Or, a sponsor might suggest, perhaps the team should use a system where these tasks are regularly rotated?

Some NPTs would be better dealt with not by equitably distributing them but by ensuring that the people who do them get appropriate credit and reward for them. Consider sponsorship's friend, mentorship. As we've discussed before, our social networks tend toward homophily (similarity to ourselves). This means that when people need help or advice, they tend to reach out to people who are like them. For a White man, it's usually not that hard to find—and ask!—another White man for help. But since there are fewer women and non-Whites in White male–dominated spaces, and even fewer senior leaders who are women and non-Whites, there's a discrepancy between supply (low) and demand (high) for women and non-White mentors. This increases the burden of mentorship for women and non-White leaders, as compared to men and White leaders. But while many workplaces value mentorship, most value it only to a point. So long as leaders engage in some minimal level of mentorship, they'll be seen as perfectly fine leaders; being an exceptional mentor doesn't usually get someone the promotion. This gives mentorship the semblance of an NPT, making it so that the women and non-White leaders who are doing more mentoring than men and White leaders are more likely to be overlooked when it comes to advancement.

The solution here isn't to find a way to equitably distribute mentorship relationships. Same-race mentor relationships give non-White employees a safe place in which to process potentially biased work-related incidents, and similarly for same-gender relationships. Organizations should therefore *want* same-race and same-gender mentors. But how can we ensure that women and non-White leaders aren't penalized for the extra mentorship that they do? Easy: reward them for it. That is, if mentorship is really that important, then make it a promotable task. Making exceptional mentorship the standard for promotion ensures that a person from a marginalized group who engages in a lot of mentoring won't be penalized for doing this important work and, instead, will be rewarded. So one thing a sponsor can do to Prevent a woman and a non-White protégé from being penalized for mentoring other women and non-Whites is to proactively push for changing evaluation criteria to include tasks and behaviors that are important to the organization but undervalued, such as mentorship.

Given its invisibility—the generation of a nonevent—and that it can also be seen as a form of mentorship, I'm not going to focus further on Prevention as a strategy, but it's one we should keep in our back pockets. In contrast, the other three forms of sponsorship—Confirming, Creating, and Protecting—have more clear-cut strategies associated with them because they have, unlike Preventing, observable consequences that are directly related to the sponsorship behavior.

Confirm, Create, and Protect

Confirming refers to actions that serve to reinforce other people's already existing positive impressions of the protégé. When we brag about our partners' work accomplishments to our friends, we are Confirming. When we advocate for our direct reports to get a raise, we are Confirming. When we inform our mutual friends that, unbeknownst to them, they share similar interests, we are Confirming.

Most of us Confirm without thinking much about it, but here's something you should know: when we Confirm, people not only like our protégé more, but also like us—the sponsor—more. We've just indicated to the audience that they have great taste *and* that we share their good taste. Confirming, then, is the pinnacle of win-win-win; when we can buttress others' positive perceptions of our protégés, the relationships between all of us—sponsor, protégé, audience—are strengthened.

Creating is similar to Confirming in that when we Create a positive impression, we are still saying nice things about our protégés. The only difference here is that the audience wasn't already aware of our protégé. Creating is a touch more intrusive, more obvious, than Confirming, because Creating, by definition, involves turning nothing into something, an action that by its nature will call attention to what is happening. When sponsors Create, they exert pressure on the audience to feel or behave a certain way toward a heretofore-unknown protégé, making it more overt than Confirming.

The pairing of Create and Confirm is a powerful combination. When sponsors Create and Confirm, they put in a bit of social capital to Create and then, assuming all goes well, coast the rest of the way by Confirming. If sponsors can successfully Create positive atmospherics around their protégés, their impression management at the Confirm phase is often much less obvious, which makes it more effective and less likely to elicit psychological resistance.

The Create and Confirm combination takes advantage of two related psychological phenomena: the confirmation bias and self-fulfilling prophecy (which we talked about last chapter). Confirmation bias refers to our tendency to pay attention to information that is consistent with a belief and to discount information that is inconsistent with the belief. As a negative example of this, consider the finding that teachers who watch videos of Black, Latino, and White students engaging in common classroom misbehavior are more likely to "see" and then discipline Black and Latino children rather than White children. Here, teachers hold negative stereotypes about Black and Latino students and are then more likely to pay attention to and interpret ambiguous behavior in the most negative light possible. Stereotypes also impact how people are evaluated at work. Law-firm partners reading a legal document identified more errors when they were told that the document was written by a Black third-year law student rather than by a White third-year law student, even though the documents were identical.

Confirmation bias can also work in a positive way. The same study that shows that law-firm partners identified more errors in a legal document written by a Black student than by a White student can also be described as one where fewer errors were caught when a legal document was thought to be written by a White student rather than by a Black student. Parents who believe their child can do no wrong similarly discount or excuse away evidence of their child's poor behavior. In effect, we tend to process information in a way that reinforces what we already believe. When those initial perceptions are negative, as when people hold negative stereotypes about certain social groups, confirmation bias can work to further increase these negative perceptions. But when those initial perceptions are positive, as when sponsors seed others with a positive impression of the protégé, sponsors increase the likelihood that the audience will, going forward, process information in a way that highlights the protégés' positive qualities and downplays their negative ones.

Once a positive impression has been Created, a protégé might be more successful not just because they are seen as being more competent, but also because they are treated in a way that makes them more likely to succeed. The studies described in Chapter 6 in which teachers were told that some students were "high potential" probably led teachers to interpret ambiguous behavior from "high-potential" children more positively than those who hadn't been labeled as such. If a "high-potential" child hesitated to answer a question, the teacher might interpret the hesitation as thoughtful cautiousness rather than as them not knowing the answer or understanding the material. Consistent with this possibility, the researchers saw that the students were treated differently by their teachers. "High-potential" children were given harder questions to solve, more opportunities to rectify errors, and more attention by the teacher than students who hadn't been described as high potential.

You may have seen this in your organization. These "water walkers" (people who are so favored, they walk on water) or "golden children" are put in plum assignments, serve on highly visible committees, or are charged with leading small initiatives. With these opportunities and helpful connections, water walkers then have the requisite track record and sponsors to be considered for more and more leadership positions in the future. This is what Joe, the Air Force officer, called "the snowball effect"; snowballs often fall apart in our hands when we start pushing snow together. But once we have the foundational snowball mass formed, adding to the snowball becomes easy. Once one opportunity is given, it triggers the provision of additional opportunities. Success breeds success. This is the power of Create and Confirm.

Yet . . . there will be times when, despite a sponsor's best efforts, a protégé will come under criticism from others. Or someone might observe a situation in which a subordinate is being treated unfairly. These are situations in which sponsors might choose to Protect their protégés by minimizing the level of negativity that an audience feels toward a protégé and the degree to which the protégé is penalized. To do so, sponsors can express disagreement with or confusion over the audience's negative impressions of the protégé. The sponsor Protecting a protégé wants the audience to take a different view of or behave differently toward the protégé.

It's hard to disagree with other people without their noticing. Protecting, then, is often one of the most explicit, and therefore risky, versions of sponsorship we can engage in.

Why is explicitness important? In Chapter 2, we briefly discussed that relying on power when sponsoring is often less effective than relying on status. There are two reasons for this effect: The first is that power's tendency to enhance people's self-centered tendencies and status's tendency to enhance people's other-oriented tendencies lead most people to trust those with power less than they trust those with status. The second is that status obfuscates the degree to which people identify sponsorship as a form of influence, while power amplifies this perception. This second point is key; the less obvious it is that we are trying to influence other people, the more effective our influence is, which is why, now that you understand the different kinds of sponsorship there are, we need to discuss why it is important that we make our sponsorship as invisible as possible.

THE IMPORTANCE OF STEALTHY SPONSORSHIP

When I first enrolled in college, I originally planned on majoring in political science. But when I took a course on game theory, I found myself less interested in the math and more in the psychology behind what drove people's decisions. I decided that I wanted to be a clinical psychologist. Getting into clinical psychology graduate programs is incredibly competitive, and one way to be a more attractive candidate is to conduct research as an undergraduate and obtain other relevant training. So I promptly volunteered as a research assistant for a psychology faculty member and worked as a counselor for an anonymous suicide hotline. After a year or so of this, I realized that I did not, in fact, want to be a clinical therapist but that I did enjoy doing research. So I decided to pursue a PhD.

My father was supportive, except he implored me not to go to graduate school in social psychology; as an accounting professor in a business school, he knew that there was a field called organizational behavior that would be significantly more lucrative. He suggested that I consider taking a class so I could learn more about it. I remember scoffing at him. What did my dad know?* In my mind, I thought that organizational behavior meant working as an in-house therapist for employees, which had nothing to do with the study of

---

* I'm embarrassed to admit that I had no idea what my dad did until I got to graduate school. Upon arriving, I mentioned my father's name offhandedly to a faculty member, who then asked me if I was talking about THE Chee Chow. Upon looking up my father's CV, I was both horrified and proud to discover that he is actually an extremely influential accounting professor with hundreds of papers and thousands of citations. Whoops.

social psychology. Did he not understand that I didn't want to be a therapist in any capacity? I rejected his advice.

Fast-forward to my senior year of college. A friend of mine told me that she had taken a course called Introduction to Organizational Behavior the prior year and that she thought I should take it. Based on her endorsement, I decided to give the Intro to OB course a whirl. Once in the class, I was mesmerized. The work in organizational behavior was precisely the kind of research I wanted to do; it was tethered to the methodological and conceptual precision of social psychology but focused on real-world applications that could have obvious practical impact. The class set me down the path of getting a PhD in organizational behavior.

In both instances, my father and my friend made similar suggestions: that I take a course in organizational behavior. Yet I took my friend's advice but not my father's. Why was I so quick to dismiss my father's advice? He had more than thirty years more experience than I did as an academic; surely, he would have some relevant information that I should use. Well, for one, I am as guilty as the next almost-adult of thinking that I know better than my parents. But also, like most adolescents, I didn't want to be told what to do or what to think. I wanted to feel as though I was making my own choices. Given the power differential that is often inherent in many parent-child relationships, my father advising me to take a particular path felt like a constraint on my independence. But when that same suggestion came from a peer, I didn't see her suggestion as an imposition, because it couldn't have been. She didn't have power over me. But what she did have, in my eyes, was status.

The status my friend had made her sponsorship of organizational behavior more effective than my father's because I didn't experience her suggestion as anything other than her sharing relevant information. I didn't feel pressured in any sort of way, nor did I think she was trying to change my behavior. Her influence was invisible to me.

The more invisible influence is, the more effective it is, because people like to feel that they are in control of their own choices. Most of us, even those of us who come from the most collectivistic societies, want to feel that we choose our own destinies. The best sponsors, then, recognize that need for independence and will find ways to sponsor that mask sponsorship for what it is: influence.

ONE WAY TO MASK INFLUENCE:
FOCUS ON PROCESS, NOT OUTCOMES

If you're looking for a job, one of the first questions you might ask yourself is if you know someone who can introduce you to someone who is hiring. Russ Ewing was no exception to this; during Ewing's first year in the Tepper MBA program, he went through his mental Rolodex in search of someone who might help him land a summer internship in asset management. Having analyzed his network, Ewing realized that he knew exactly one person in the asset-management world: Fred, the little brother of his roommate from college.

That Ewing, a Black man, knew only one person in the industry that he wanted to work in is consistent with research showing that although White and Black job seekers are equally likely to use their networks in getting a job, White job seekers are more likely to know people in the companies where they want a job than are Black job seekers, which might help to explain why it takes Black job seekers longer to find employment. This research also finds that of the people who know someone in a company where they want a job, White job seekers' contacts are more likely to directly connect the job seeker to someone in the company than are Black job seekers' contacts. And, in fact, that almost happened to Ewing; his roommate's little brother, Fred, generally did not refer people from his network to be hired. Part of the reason for his reluctance may have been that Fred himself was one of only two Black employees in the firm. However, Ewing impressed Fred enough that Fred brought his name up to Allen, the other Black employee who was a senior executive deeply respected by the company's CEO.

When Fred mentioned Ewing to Allen, Allen immediately took notice. If Ewing had met Fred's very high standards, then he must be very good indeed. And after talking with Ewing himself, Allen agreed with Fred's assessment. He took the matter to the CEO of the company, who, unbeknownst to Ewing, deputized Allen to look discreetly for non-White candidates to hire. The firm's clients had noticed the lack of diversity in the firm and had been taking the CEO to task on this point. The CEO instructed Allen to inform him if and when Allen came across any qualified non-White candidates. In effect, the CEO had a problem that he trusted Allen to help him solve. And Allen, having a network with more non-White people than the CEO, indeed knew people who could solve the CEO's problem. It was a perfect sponsorship opportunity, but the next question was this: After identifying good people, how should the company proceed in hiring them?

The CEO and Allen hadn't quite thought that far. The original plan was to fast-track those appointments and bypass the roadblocks that non-White candidates might normally encounter in the hiring process. But what would a fast track look like? How could they ensure that their efforts would not be so overt as to attract undue attention that might lead to backlash throughout the firm? Fred and Allen came up with an ingenious solution: they proposed a firm-wide program for hiring first-year MBA students as summer interns, which the CEO readily approved. It just so happened that the inaugural intern class was disproportionately composed of non-Whites, among which Ewing was one. Fred and Allen, with support from the CEO, had found a way to sponsor Ewing and other non-Whites by creating a process that gave interns the opportunity to show the firm's employees how great they, the interns, would be as colleagues. By changing the process, they changed outcomes.

A similar idea undergirds a pilot intervention undertaken at the University of Chicago's Department of Medicine. The faculty noticed that women were less likely to receive research, teaching, and clinical awards than were men, much lower than their representation among the faculty. Was this truly a pipeline problem, where maybe there are just fewer deserving women? Or was this an issue of women lacking the necessary sponsorship to be recognized? The department decided to form a subcommittee of three to four volunteers, who were tasked with identifying eligible women award nominees, notifying worthy nominees of the group's intent to nominate them for an award, and ensuring that all the materials necessary for the nomination were submitted. The subcommittee nominated one woman for each available award. Subsequently, the percentage of women in the department who won awards increased significantly, suggesting that the lower rates of winning prior to the intervention were not because there weren't as many worthy women, but because not enough women were being sponsored (nominated). Their intervention, which tackled the nomination process, was designed to address the systematic lack of sponsorship for women, to great effect.

These changes to process are reminiscent of the suggestions I provided about how sponsors can help women and non-White protégés avoid being overburdened with or penalized for engaging in NPTs. There, the idea is that sponsors can advocate for a different process by which opportunities (or dead-end work, as it were) are distributed. Alternatively, sponsors can push to change evaluation processes and criteria so that NPTs become promotable tasks. Whatever the case, sponsors are clearly exerting influence because they are explicitly seeking to change the existing process. However, because their focus is on changing a process rather than on generating a specific outcome for a specific person, they are practicing stealthy sponsorship. They can talk about the organizational benefits to making these changes or the potential costs to the organization if these changes are not made. In doing so, they highlight that they are good organizational members who care about the group. This bolsters their status in the firm *and* gets them what they want, which so happens to be something that makes the organization a better place for everyone.

HOW TO GAIN STATUS SO YOU CAN BE A STEALTHY SPONSOR

You'll have noticed a recurring theme of this book is how important it is for sponsors to have status. Sponsors with status are more effective because of status's association with trust. Status also often helps to mask sponsorship's true self as a form of influence. So this might be a good place to tackle a question that may have been on your mind for quite some time: How much status do I have?

First, the good news: most of us are reasonably accurate in our assessments of our own status. Social psychologists have found that asking someone for their perception of how much social status they have is remarkably consistent with their peers' assessments of how much they are liked. If anything, people who are inaccurate about their status underestimate their status, rather than overestimate. People brought into the lab to have a discussion with a stranger leave the interaction thinking that their conversation partner likes them less than the partner actually does. Basically, people like us more than we think they do! The reason most of us are accurate (or underestimate) how much status we have is that the social penalties to overestimating our status are so high. We become the targets of gossip. We are called "too big for our britches," or people feel like they should "take us down a notch."

This is all to say, don't worry too much about how much status you have. You probably have a good sense of it, and if you are wrong, it's probably that you think you have less than you do.

But let's say that you don't know how much status you have, and you want to ensure that you have as much status as possible. What should you do? One way is to again use the age-old trick of "fake it till you make it"; to gain status, act like you have status. Note that acting like you have status is not the same as acting like you have power. While we might expect people with power to act like the world revolves around them, people with status are expected to act as though the world revolves around other people. People who are high in status are supposed to be reasonable and pleasant to be around, much more so than people who are high in power.

Simply put, if you want to be high in status, don't be a jerk.

The answer to the question of how to gain status is, of course, more nuanced than that, but not much more. The reality is that research shows that the people who gain the most status are those who show themselves to be willing to help others in the group. This is because status is the currency by which we reward good behavior in groups; we grant status to people who demonstrate through actions and deeds that they care about the group, potentially even more than they care about themselves. This is why we hold martyrs in such reverence; they care so much about the group and its values that they are willing to make the ultimate sacrifice.

I'm not advocating for you to become a martyr. But I do suggest conveying to other people that they have status in your eyes. Giving others status means treating them as though you respect and admire them. It means paying attention to who they are and what they want. And coincidentally, when we do that, it also means that we can be better sponsors for them. And then guess what? They'll sponsor you!

Being a sponsor—granting others status—gets us sponsors. And the more people sponsor us, the more status we will be known to have, which will, in turn, make our sponsorship all the stealthier.

8 | TO CREATE AND CONFIRM IS TO SHOW AND TELL

When Clarence Dozier started at his first job in a law firm in the early 2000s, he was one of three Black associates who had been hired that year, out of more than a dozen new hires.

A few months after his start date, Dozier walked into a client meeting and was surprised to see another Black lawyer in the room. It was sufficiently rare that Dozier took the unusual step of introducing himself to the other lawyer. "Here's my card," the other lawyer told him. "Let's have lunch sometime."

Dozier, curious, showed the card to a colleague, wanting to know more about the identity of the mysterious Black lawyer (word of mouth being the primary option for surreptitious information gathering in those pre-LinkedIn days). The colleague, eyes wide, spoke in hushed tones. "That's the general counsel of our largest client!" Dozier was shocked and immediately intimidated. He decided that, rather than risk sharing inappropriate information or otherwise embarrassing himself in front of the Black GC, whose name was Daniel, he would not be reaching out to him, let alone going to lunch.

Several months after this encounter, Dozier ran into Daniel at another event. This time, Daniel cornered Dozier, telling him that he had been waiting for his call. And this time, Daniel was even more imperative: Dozier was to call his assistant and schedule monthly meetings with him. From that point onward, Dozier met every month with Daniel, many times at the Duquesne Club, an exclusive invite-only business club where high-ranking corporate executives would go to see and be seen. During their lunches, Daniel asked Dozier about the cases that he was working on and to discuss, in general, what his experience was at LawFirm. Daniel was doing double duty; he was mentoring Dozier but also, by showing up with him at the Duquesne Club, Creating atmospherics around Dozier so that other people thought that he was a big wig too.

After a year of doing this, Daniel announced to Dozier that their monthly meetings would be changing in tenor. "From now on," he told Dozier, "I am going to be giving you cases, and our lunches are going to be about your caseload." Dozier was surprised at this development; strictly speaking, Dozier worked for LawFirm, not Daniel's firm. While it's possible for clients to request certain lawyers to lead their cases, Daniel's firm was technically the client of one of LawFirm's partners, who was always listed as the lead lawyer on their cases and received credit for the billing that came from working on those cases. However, as the saying goes, don't look a gift horse in the mouth,* and shortly after this conversation, a strange thing began to happen: every couple of months, when lists of who had brought in new business went out to the entire firm,

---

* If you are curious what this saying is alluding to, it is that a horse's age can be discerned by looking at how worn down its teeth are. A person who looks in the gift horse's mouth is someone who, in front of the gift giver, is evaluating the quality of the gift, something that most people would find rude.

Dozier would be listed as the lead lawyer on cases coming from Daniel's firm.

To understand why this is important, we should go over how promotions work in the legal world. LawFirm is an independent law firm, a conglomerate of lawyers who are basically loaned out to complement a company's internal legal team in cases where extra expertise or work is needed. In independent law firms, promotions are largely based on billable hours, or the amount of money that lawyers bring in via working on different cases. The more billable hours a lawyer works, the more "value" the lawyer provides to the firm and, thus, the more likely they are to be promoted. Given this setup, lead lawyers have a lot of power because they decide who gets to work on their cases, controlling access to a highly desirable resource: billable hours. Being listed as the lead lawyer on the new cases coming out of Daniel's firm, one of LawFirm's largest and most important clients, made Dozier one of those power holders, and his visibility within the firm skyrocketed. Other lawyers flocked to him, wanting to be put on his cases so that they could get more billable hours. Dozier was on the fast track to becoming a partner in LawFirm, a highly coveted position.

Later, Dozier decided to take an internal position at another company, essentially taking on a similar role to the one his sponsor had in his firm. When he broke the news to Daniel, Daniel was disappointed. Daniel revealed that he had orchestrated Dozier's accelerated career trajectory, having negotiated with Dozier's boss to agree to the unusual arrangement of putting Dozier, and not Dozier's boss, as the lead lawyer on the cases. Daniel had hoped that Dozier would become a partner at LawFirm; he wanted there to be more Black leadership present in the top positions at an extremely large and reputable independent law firm. Despite his disappointment at these quashed dreams, Daniel continued to mentor Dozier until his retirement. To this day, Dozier remains grateful to Daniel for his sponsorship. He told me, "There was no way I was going to bring in business from the firm's largest client without a sponsor like that."

Although few of us will ever have a sponsor who is in a position to pull strings on our behalf in this way, Dozier's sponsor provides us with a master class in Create and Confirm, the two most effective tools of a stealthy sponsor. Since Dozier was a newcomer—to the industry, to the firm, to the city, to him—Daniel started small. He first deliberately lent some of his social capital to Dozier by going to the Duquesne Club with him, knowing that when other important people saw the two of them together, they would infer that Dozier must be an important person worth knowing. Meanwhile, he mentored Dozier, using this time to figure out what Dozier was capable of and his worthiness for further, more costly, sponsorship. After the initial year of meetings, Daniel was convinced. He then upped the ante by convincing Dozier's boss to give up some of his visibility in LawFirm by putting Dozier's name down as the lead lawyer on the cases coming out of Daniel's firm instead of his own. In this way, he Confirmed Dozier's rising-star status; if people had noticed Dozier from the Duquesne Club, they certainly paid even more attention to him now that he controlled who would work on some of the most profitable cases at LawFirm.

Dozier's experience shows us that the most effective sponsorship starts early and is done with intention. In this case, Daniel was willing to expend a lot of social capital on Dozier because he had a particular mission: he saw Dozier as one of a few Black lawyers who had the ability to rise to partner level at a national law firm. Most of us, on the other hand, probably don't have that kind of ambition for our protégés, because we don't have that kind of power and we don't plan that far ahead. That doesn't mean that the overarching lesson isn't worth learning: the most effective sponsorship starts early, *before* impressions of a protégé have been set. We may not have the careers of our protégés fully mapped out, but if we approach sponsorship with a clear idea of what our standards are for sponsorship (Chapter 5) and know in advance what small forms of Create and Confirm we are willing to perform for anyone who rises to our standards (this chapter), we will be well on our way to being highly effective sponsors.

So what, specifically, can we do to Create and Confirm? The same way that children bring a valued belonging to show-and-tell at school, we can also engage in show-and-tell of our protégés. And, just as kids first show and then tell, sponsors can first show off their protégés to Create a strong initial positive impression and then build on that by telling information that Confirms an audience's positive feelings toward the protégé.

CREATE BY SHOWING

You might be familiar with the phrase "Show, *don't* tell." It's a piece of advice that is often given to writers to enliven their writing. The idea behind showing, and not telling, is that often, when people "tell," they are so focused on conveying factual content that they omit the small details that give characters a sense of life and realism. Telling doesn't make people care about characters in the same way that Showing does because Showing lets the audience draw their own conclusions about our protégés. It gives them the freedom to see the protégé the way they want. That we've set up the situation in such a way that we've all but ensured that they'll see our protégé at their best is not something that most of them will have considered.

Take the story of Sona Movsesian, late-night show host Conan O'Brien's personal assistant and cohost of the podcast *Conan O'Brien Needs a Friend*. Sona began her career in the page program at NBC, one of many interns who aspired to break into the entertainment industry. She found out that Conan was moving his production to Los Angeles, and she immediately decided that she wanted to be a part of his team. She stalked the internal job board at NBC for weeks, waiting for the production-assistant positions to be posted. As soon as they were up, she immediately applied.

These are highly sought-after positions, so the odds were not in Sona's favor. What she didn't know, however, is that a publicist from *The Late Show* (which Conan was leaving) texted Conan himself, saying, "Sona's a rockstar." With that small act of sponsorship, Sona's application got pulled from the production-assistant candidate pile and put into Conan's personal-assistant candidate pile (which was not advertised due to the obscene numbers of applications they would likely receive). Sona then interviewed with Conan and they hit it off, mainly because she broke character as an intimidated interviewee when Conan told her that it was just a casual conversation and that she should make herself comfortable. Without missing a beat, she said, "Great, I'll just lay here on your couch." Conan laughed and hired her.

At first Sona was very formal with Conan, treating him with the professional distance that seemed appropriate for her role. But they quickly developed a rapport that consisted of Conan provoking her in hopes of getting her to laugh. What really cemented their friendship was an ongoing joke in which Conan lambastes the various ways Sona shirks her job responsibilities by napping and binge-watching TV shows on the clock, and Sona cops to it immediately and without shame. Her nonchalance about her (lack of) work ethic led Conan to give her the moniker of "the World's Worst Assistant."

Prior to reading this book, I doubt that you would have given much thought to what Conan was doing. But at this point, it should be plain to see that Conan functionally foisted Sona and several other crew members onto our collective consciousness with his sponsorship. Yet none of us likely thinks about his behavior as sponsorship per se. Why? Because Conan Showed; he didn't Tell. He didn't invite Sona onto his show and tell us, the audience, that she is funny. Instead, he deliberately chose to include Sona in bits that would showcase their offbeat dynamic. In this way, Conan utilized one of the easiest ways to Create: inviting a protégé to spaces or events to which they would otherwise not have access.

CREATE THROUGH INCLUSION

Exclusivity almost always serves as a signal, whether we want it to or not. This is because when places or events are exclusive, entrance is limited. This applies to all sorts of exclusive spaces and events. When we throw a party, it's exclusive, because most parties are not open admission. What this means, then, is that attending a party can be used as a signal. It signals that the people there have the means (the host likes them) and the motivation (they like the host) to be there. The signal that comes from being invited to and attending a private event can be used to jump-start a connection between people who meet there for the first time. Attendance suggests that they are likely to share some things in common, because at the very least, the host likes them both!

This signal is why Daniel's decision to publicly take Dozier to lunch at an exclusive business club was such a savvy sponsor move. Because the club is not open to everyone, only Very Important People must go there. And if Dozier was there with someone that people already knew to be Very Important, then Dozier must also be Very Important. This is also why Heidi Roizen's dinner parties, in which she invites the who's who of Silicon Valley to her house for informal dinners, are so impactful; the people who attend the parties know that Roizen has carefully curated the invite list. They trust that she has selected the party attendees for a reason. They can then engage with one another with the assurance that everyone there is interesting and worth knowing.

One time, a chief financial officer of a Fortune 100 company came to speak to a group of Latino and Black professionals in a program I direct. He shared with us his upbringing and background, and one thing that stood out to me was that although his parents, immigrants from Puerto Rico, did not have a lot of money (his father was a mechanic, and he did not mention if his mother worked), they made sure to send him to a prestigious private boarding school in New England. When he graduated from college, he was hired into an analyst role at Citigroup by the father of his boarding-school roommate, who was in charge of investments at Citi. His parents implicitly understood the value of being included in an exclusive space. Being included in exclusive spaces gives protégés a chance to show off their abilities, creating their own relationships so that they can find even more sponsors.

Inclusion is a signal. It's a signal that all of us should be thinking about more intentionally whenever we find ourselves in a situation in which we control access over who is and isn't invited to an event. Consider who you invite to your next dinner party or who you ask to join you for lunch. Can you make room for one more person, someone who makes sense for other people in the group to meet? Why not ask the coworker you don't usually invite to join the group when you go out for coffee?

For my part, after working on this book for quite some time, I've tried to put some of the lessons of this book into practice. Taking a page straight out of Heidi Roizen's playbook, I've significantly expanded our guest list for informal dinner parties. I'm normally someone who prefers to host small gatherings (introvert here!) of friends from the same group (the notion of having different social circles collide without me there to facilitate makes me anxious). But I want to walk the talk, so to speak, so my guest list has expanded and diversified for these kinds of events. And what I've found is that as the dinner parties have grown, they have become even better experiences for the attendees than when they were smaller. Multiple guests have told me they feel honored that they made the list—and are pleased about the connections they have made with people they would most likely not have met otherwise. And what's more, Jeff and I now have a reputation as people who know people.

It helps that all my friends are people who have passed my own quality standards. I trust them all to comport themselves in a way such that my providing the context for them to meet will be largely sufficient; they'll impress each other on their own terms. In this way, great protégés make sponsorship easy; when a protégé is great, all a sponsor needs to do is set the stage and let the protégé do their thing. One of my favorite examples of this comes from my friend Tynina Lucas, who very early in her career benefited when her firm's chief procurement officer sponsored her by inviting her to attend an executive board meeting. Entering the room, Tynina noticed that the room was set up in the traditional boardroom-meeting format, with a large table in the center surrounded by chairs, with additional chairs placed around the perimeter. If it had been me, I would have almost certainly made a beeline for one of those peripheral chairs, because most people intuitively understand that the seats at the table are reserved for "important" people and that "less important" people sit by the walls.

Not Tynina. She took a seat at the table, and who should sit down next to her but the CEO of the company himself! She actively participated in the meeting, and the CEO was so impressed with her contributions that by the end, the two of them were laughing and joking like old buddies. That evening, over dinner at the Waldorf (!), everyone jockeyed to sit at Tynina's table. When they returned from the trip, the chief procurement officer told Tynina that she had been a hit and that the executive team wanted "to see more of her." Tynina went on to get promotion after promotion in the firm, in no small part because her sponsor put her in a situation where other people could see for themselves how great she is.

Janet Lee, the general counsel for Ansys, similarly Shows off protégés by putting them in the limelight and then just gets out of the way. She will sometimes strategically feign a lack of availability and send her protégés to important meetings as her representative.*

---

* Note: this only works if you don't get caught.

Lee does this to afford her protégés more exposure. "It makes them look more [leader-like] and capable of carrying loads. It looks like they are totally trusted by me and reflects well on them."

There are signals in who goes where. We can use those signals to our advantage, to direct attention to our protégés and give them the opportunity to impress others.

HOW TELLING WORKS

Once a sponsor has successfully Created through Showing, they can move on to Confirming through Telling. Conan used Showing to successfully establish Sona's persona as the World's Worst Assistant (but also world's funniest assistant?) by featuring her in bits for *The Tonight Show*. He also continued to showcase her abilities by having her cohost his podcast, *Conan O'Brien Needs a Friend*. But now that Sona has a following of her own, large enough that her book, also titled *The World's Worst Assistant*, became a best seller, Conan immediately insisted on writing the foreword for the book. He made the jump to Telling. Show, *then* Tell.

Telling is a key part of sponsorship because the content of what is being told typically involves information about someone's accomplishments or abilities. When people share this kind of information about themselves, it's a form of impression management called self-promotion. Here's the thing about self-promotion: it's a double-edged sword. On the one hand, it's important for people to know who is good at what or who has done what. On the other hand, people don't particularly like self-promoters because they seem self-focused; after all, why would someone be tooting their own horn unless they thought very highly of themselves? This dual effect is sometimes dubbed the Self-Promoter's Paradox: people think self-promoters are competent, but they also tend not to like self-promoters. In other words, self-promoters often face a trade-off:

ensure that other people know about their abilities and accomplishments or be liked.*

Sadly, the self-promotion penalty is larger for women than it is for men. Why? Society expects women to be more other focused and selfless than men. Being full of oneself can then lead people to rate self-promoting women as being even less likable than self-promoting men. Racial minorities are similarly penalized for self-promotion. One study finds that self-promotion by Black employees is associated with lower job-performance ratings and perceptions of "fit" with the company.

Yet if collective value comes from having an accurate inventory of who knows what, who is good at what, and who needs what, then this is precisely the kind of information that needs to be shared for us to benefit from it. How else are we to know whose problems these incredibly capable and skilled people should be matched to? Enter the sponsor. When we promote others—not ourselves—we help everyone. We add information to the network about people's abilities without requiring people to share that information themselves, shielding them from the likability penalty that usually comes from self-promotion. But wait, there's more! Not only is the person being promoted seen more positively, but there's no cost to the person doing the promoting! If anything, people who amplify the achievements of others can experience a sponsorship boost themselves

---

* Don't let anyone tell you otherwise. People who self-promote to friends and family (not in the context of an interview) often believe that when they share their good news, other people will feel as happy and proud of them as they do themselves. Reader, they are wrong. As with unsolicited advice, most people don't like unsolicited self-promotion. When someone engages in unsolicited self-promotion, we feel annoyed, like the self-promoter less, and think of them as a braggart. But if someone asks you what you've been working on or if you have any exciting news to share, self-promote away! They asked, which means that it isn't unsolicited!

because when we share about someone else's accomplishments, we are showing ourselves to be other focused. After all, why would you say nice things about the other person unless you were thinking about them (and not, presumably, yourself)? And recall that the way groups reward other-focused members is by giving them status.

Sponsoring others through Telling elevates you, lifts up your protégé, *and* increases the group's transactive memory system of who is good at what and who can be trusted, which is necessary for groups to coordinate effectively. Win-win-win!

CREATE THROUGH TELLING

Although Showing is preferable to Telling in the Creating stage, there will be times when it isn't possible for sponsors to first Show off their protégés to the audience. Take applicants for college admissions. There are simply too many applicants for college admissions officers to see for themselves how talented each one of the applicants might be. They must therefore rely heavily on one of the most ubiquitous forms of sponsorship via Telling: letters of recommendation. Letters of recommendation are the shotgun version of sponsorship; the sponsor shoots out a message about the protégé in the hopes that if the letter just so happens to end up in the right hands, the protégé will get their shot (har har).

There is also the more sniper-precise version of Creating through Telling, which is when a sponsor personally vouches for a protégé for a particular opportunity. An example of this comes from Tiffany, a senior director at a major health-care company, who credits her love of economics and her entry to her career to her MBA professor, Dr. Peterson.

When Tiffany took Dr. Peterson's course, it was Dr. Peterson's first year teaching. However, what Dr. Peterson lacked in pedagogical experience, she made up for by having prior working experience in health care. She could relate theoretical economic concepts and analysis techniques to concrete corporate problems, such as health-care planning. The immediate applicability of the course content made her class memorable; it was, bar none, Tiffany's favorite class during her MBA program.

Like most students, once the class was over, Tiffany thanked Dr. Peterson, not expecting to see her again. But she took the lessons from the course with her. At her first job postgraduation, Tiffany used an analytic technique she had learned from the class, which impressed her superiors. Tiffany then did something a bit unusual: she reached out to Dr. Peterson to share the impact of her teaching. (Side note, if there is a professor who has had a positive impact on you, please tell them about it! It will make their day/week/month/year/life.)

To Tiffany's surprise, Dr. Peterson not only responded, but also suggested that Tiffany come to work for her. In the years since Tiffany had graduated, Dr. Peterson had left academia to rejoin the corporate world and was now a very well-respected figure in the private health-plan space. Tiffany balked; she lacked direct experience or relevant qualifications. But Dr. Peterson persisted, telling Tiffany that she believed in her ability to get up to speed quickly. "You don't need experience," she told Tiffany. "You just have to be smart. And you're smart."

Tiffany said she'd think about it. Meanwhile, unbeknownst to her, Dr. Peterson set the balls in motion. She told her boss, the firm's chief medical officer, that she wanted to hire Tiffany. The CMO, like Tiffany, was incredulous. She raised the same concerns about Tiffany's lack of experience, but, again, Dr. Peterson emphatically stated her confidence in Tiffany's abilities. The CMO, who had great respect for Dr. Peterson, decided to give Tiffany a chance. Dr. Peterson's Telling was how Tiffany got the job.

When sponsors Create by Telling, they broadcast information about a protégé's accomplishments, abilities, or ideas to people who would otherwise be unfamiliar with the protégé. In fact, the less a sponsor's network overlaps with the protégé's, the more effective they are at helping to create the protégé's reputation. In some cases, there might be no overlap at all, as in the case of Sal Khan, the founder of Khan Academy, an online education platform. During an interview on *How I Made This*, a podcast where company founders discuss their company's origin stories, Khan described how his mental and physical health was deteriorating in the face of mounting financial stress, having quit his high-paying investment banker job to dedicate his time to creating a platform that would democratize world-class education. But the bills were piling up, and he was running out of savings. He was on the verge of calling it quits when an early supporter of Khan Academy excitedly called to tell him, "Bill Gates just plugged you at the Aspen Institute!"

The Aspen Institute is a prestigious gathering of the world's foremost thinkers, and an interviewer had asked Gates to speculate on the most exciting development in the education sector. Gates touted the content provided by Khan Academy, which was so high quality that he used it to help teach his daughters. What I think is notable about Gates's Telling is not just that he name-dropped Khan Academy and talked about how impressed he was with the quality of its content. Gates also shared Khan's entrepreneurial origin story of giving up his lucrative investment-banking career in hopes of building a platform that would provide a free, world-class education to anyone in the world. In sharing this, Gates made it possible for attendees to see that Khan Academy was a manifestation of Khan's values and dreams. And, as we discussed in Chapter 6, knowing Khan's values and aspirations engendered trust and goodwill among potential investors. Indeed, after Gates's Telling, Khan's financial woes were over; within days, he received calls from interested funders to back Khan Academy.

When sponsors Create via Telling, they are actually doing two things at once: they introduce the protégé to the audience, who would otherwise be unaware of them, and they seed the connection with the fertilizer of their personal backing and good words. You might know this phenomenon as "strategic introductions," as when someone makes sure to introduce you to the "right people." When I first thought about writing this book, I thought about who in my network I could ask about book writing. Katy Milkman immediately came to mind; she had just published a great book on self-improvement called *How to Change*, and the two of us were on friendly terms. So I reached out to Katy and told her that I was thinking about writing a book and asked if she would please share with me a list of the literary agents she had considered working with. Now, if Katy was a less generous person, she might have simply shared the email addresses of the literary agents she knew and told me to name-drop her in my emails to them. I would have been fine with that; it was as much as I would have presumed our relationship to have warranted!

But Katy, bless her soul, is a good sponsor and went above and beyond. She asked me to provide her with a paragraph or two about my book idea and then emailed each literary agent herself, CC-ing me on those emails. In her emails, she mentioned how much she respected me and provided a sentence or two of her own about why she thought the agent might be interested in my work. I'm incredibly grateful to her for her sponsorship, because it is through her that I was able to find an agent so quickly (a feat that takes most authors much longer).

Katy's sponsorship is also a good example to illustrate how there are variations in how people sponsor that can impact its effectiveness. If Katy didn't want to sponsor me, she could have just given me the email addresses of a few agents. Alternatively, if she had wanted to sponsor me but not in a way that would put too much of her own reputation on the line, Katy could have written to the agents saying, "Hey, my friend Rosalind Chow is thinking about writing a book. Would it be okay if I passed your name on to her?" That would have satisfied the purpose of putting me on their radar—if they said yes, it would mean that I should at least expect them to read my email—but that level of sponsorship isn't particularly compelling. A more assertive version would involve putting us both on an email, with a similar message of "Hi, Agent Smith, my friend Rosalind Chow (CC-ed) is interested in writing a book. Hope you two can find a time to connect!" That's a step up in terms of how overtly Katy would be sponsoring me, since by including me on the email, the agent would know that it would be plain to see if they didn't respond. Thankfully for me, Katy gave me the white-glove version of sponsorship; she not only directly connected me to the agents but also provided additional information to the agents about me—she Told them about me—giving them a reason to care. Gates did something similar in his sponsorship of Khan; by sharing his positive assessment of the quality of the Khan Academy content *and* giving people Sal Khan's backstory, he made Khan a more compelling protégé.

THE RISK OF CREATING VIA TELLING

Creating through Telling calls upon the sponsor's social-capital resources in a way that Creating through Showing does not. When sponsors Tell to Create, they associate themselves with the protégé and implicitly ask the audience to trust their judgment. This is when the status of the sponsor matters; trusted and high-status sponsors are more likely to be successful in their sponsorship than low-status sponsors. If the CMO had had less respect for Dr. Peterson, she likely would have denied her request to hire Tiffany. But because Dr. Peterson had a strong relationship with the CMO and status within the firm, the CMO believed her "guarantee of quality" about Tiffany's future performance.

Note, however, that what this also means is that Dr. Peterson needed Tiffany to live up to her advertisement of her abilities. When we tell someone, "Trust me," what we are saying is that we know that they are taking a risk by going through with whatever it is that we are trying to get them to do. Their trust in us is the collateral we have put on the table to compensate them for taking this risk. In the event that things don't work out as advertised, we must accept the consequence that the trust that they showed us is now lost. If hiring Tiffany had ended up being a mistake, the CMO probably wouldn't have given Dr. Peterson carte blanche on hiring a replacement.

The other risk to sponsoring via Telling is if the sponsorship attempt fails. Each time a sponsor sponsors a protégé, especially when their sponsorship is extremely overt, they receive information about what their social capital is truly worth. When their sponsorship isn't effective, sponsors are confronted with the possibility that they have less social capital than they had thought (or at least hoped). Let's return to Derek Jeter. Jeter started his baseball career on the inauspicious Kalamazoo Central High School baseball team, which he describes "respectfully" as "not good at all." Even so, people saw right away that he was different. Baseball scouts started showing up at his practices, with one scout in particular standing out in the mind of his coach, Don Zomer. Zomer remembers the day clearly: "I see this guy in the stands and I wonder what he's there for, and after about a half hour, he introduced himself as Hal New-houser and I just about fell down."

Newhouser, a former baseball star himself, was there as a scout for the Houston Astros. He was known to be careful and under-stated, a scout whose assessments were never prone to hyperbole, as most other scouts' tended to be. In his report, he wrote that Jeter was a special player and a special kid. This caught the attention of Newhouser's supervisor, who had never known Newhouser to have been that positive about any player before. But the Astros were wary of signing Jeter, who had been promised a scholarship to attend the University of Michigan. They worried that he would use the schol-arship to hold out for a signing bonus of $1 million or more, an unheard-of amount at the time for any draftee, let alone an untested teenager who was just graduating high school. Newhouser went to bat (pun intended) for Jeter, adamant that Jeter should be the Astros' number-one draft pick. He told them, "No one is worth $1 million, but if one kid is worth that, it's this kid." The Astros ended up passing on Jeter, who wound up going to the Yankees. And the rest, as they say, is history.

Most people think of Newhouser in the context of Jeter's career; he is a modern-day Cassandra, the Greek priestess cursed by Apollo to never have her predictions believed. I see Newhouser as a cautionary tale of sponsorship that illustrates how sponsorship involves risks to sponsors. Newhouser was not a "nobody." He was famous in his own right, a former baseball player who had won two Most Valuable Player awards and was an inductee into the Hall of Fame. Yet even as someone with a lot of social capital—four decades of experience in the game and a reputation for careful assessment— he could not convince the Astros to take Jeter. When the Astros passed on Jeter, Newhouser was so disappointed that he quit the game entirely. His perspective was that if he couldn't convince the Astros to take Jeter, any future sponsoring he might do would likely be similarly dismissed. For a talent scout, that was unacceptable. He had put his entire reputation on the line, and the Astros' decision had shown what his judgment was worth in the eyes of the people making the decisions: not much. Given that, he chose to retire instead.

CONFIRM THROUGH TELLING

When people think of sponsorship (at least the ones who know what it is), many think of advocacy. "Sponsors talk about you in the rooms you aren't in" is one way I've heard it put. Confirming through Telling is how people get promotions; having a sponsor in the room to enumerate a protégé's contributions is a powerful way to ensure that the protégé gets credit for and rewarded for their work.

For those of us who feel less comfortable engaging in overt sponsorship, there are "smaller" ways to sponsor others, smaller in the sense that the outcomes associated with the specific sponsorship behavior may not seem that important in the moment but build up to have large impacts. Janet Lee of Ansys believes that influence is better exerted through "micro-actions and words." In her mind, the proverbial "pounding the table" that many people associate with sponsorship is not as helpful as getting ahead of the issue and making it so that such blatant sponsorship isn't necessary. Lee therefore specializes in what she calls "drive-by" sponsorship, where she strategically creates "atmospherics" around her direct reports by crediting them when giving presentations to clients or telling her colleagues about how impressed she is about their contributions to a project. Her drive-by sponsorship takes the form of actions that tend to fly under the influence-detection radar, which, as we discussed last chapter, is usually more effective.

These small acts of credit giving can have big effects, especially for protégés who are unlikely to have their abilities seen *unless* this information comes from a sponsor. Lee noticed that a Latina with "rock-star talent" was constantly having other people take credit for her work. Lee intervened with her signature drive-by sponsorship; rather than helping people who came to her with questions herself, she would tell them to seek help from the woman, saying, "You should go to [her]! She's the expert in this!" Here, Lee combined Show and Tell, but flipped the ordering; she Told so that the protégé would be given a chance to Show.

Having people take credit for your work or not getting credit for your work is something that, unfortunately, is more likely to happen to women and non-Whites. This has downstream consequences for people's careers. Researchers studied randomly composed teams competing in a military competition to investigate whose verbal contributions would be recognized and rewarded by their teammates. They found that men, but not women, who spoke up to offer suggestions to the team were more likely to be voted by teammates for leadership positions. You might think that this is a problem only in the military, where women are relatively few in number. Not so; when the researchers conducted a study in which participants listened to a male or female voice making the exact same suggestion, participants rated the female speaker as being lower in status than the male speaker and as having exhibited less leadership.

A related phenomenon is when women's ideas are erroneously attributed to men. Women staffers in the Obama White House noticed that when they spoke in meetings, men would co-opt and take credit for their ideas and insights. To address this problem, the women banded together to ensure that the men couldn't steal credit. When one woman made a key point, the other women would repeat it and credit the original speaker, forcing the men to recognize the woman's contribution. Evidently, President Obama noticed their efforts and began to spontaneously call on women aides more frequently.

What I appreciate about the female staffers' solution was that they informally systematized Telling so that credit would be given where it was due. I have seen other leaders implement a variation on this theme. One leader shared with me that they begin their weekly team meetings by going around the group and having each person express appreciation for someone who helped them in the week prior. Some leaders up the ante by pairing these reports of help giving and expressions of gratitude with requests for additional assistance for the coming week, as when a team member first thanks others for their help in their progress in the past week and then describes what they plan to tackle in the coming week. As they outline their plan for the coming week, they can share areas where they could use some help. In that moment, other team members can chime in to commit to providing that help. This method effectively makes it so that good group contributors get a double boost in the eyes of the team; helpers are recognized both when they publicly commit to providing the help and when they have followed through. The system also has a side benefit of creating a culture where people do not see asking for help as something problematic; it's just what they do.

Of course, not all of us are in a position where we can implement the above process. Even so, there are additional ways to ensure that we are more likely to notice, and so, Tell people about others' work. One leader shared with me her institution of Thankful Thursdays, in which she would write an email to someone every Thursday to share with them an example of something they did that made a positive impact, either on her or on others. While privately thanking individuals for making a positive impact isn't the same as sponsoring them, committing to Thankful Thursdays made this leader more sensitive to the positive things her colleagues did around her. Intentionally paying attention to the ways that other people are a positive influence in our lives puts us in a position to sponsor them. Moreover, as with other forms of sponsorship, these kinds of practices benefit the collective because it shows people in the group that positive, contributory behavior is something that is valued and rewarded. It also makes people feel appreciated, which makes them more likely to continue helping others.

SHOULD WE TELL PROTÉGÉS?

One question that I sometimes get is whether sponsors should tell protégés that they are sponsoring them. On the one hand, some sponsors believe that there should be transparency between sponsors and protégés. They think that if a protégé knows that someone is spending social capital on them, they will feel pressured to rise to the occasion. On the other hand, sponsors believe the exact opposite, that sponsors should never tell protégés that they are pulling strings for them behind the scenes because the protégé might choke under pressure.

I can see the rationale behind both of those answers. On the one hand, a sponsor who constantly keeps track of what they are doing for the protégé might come off like a parent who keeps a running tally of how much they spend on their children. Keeping track turns a relationship from one of closeness to one that's transactional. The tallying sponsor signals to the protégé that they expect there to be some sort of return on investment, that there are obligations associated with their sponsorship. On the other hand, a sponsor whose protégé is completely oblivious to the sponsor's support won't experience gratitude for the support they have received, an emotion that often leads protégés to engage in sponsorship to others in turn. Moreover, gratitude is a feeling that brings people closer together; after all, what is appreciation other than acknowledging that our actions and lives are connected?

On balance, I think sponsors should, as many parents do with their children, consider the temperament of their protégés. If their protégés are communally oriented, knowing that they are representing the sponsor can be an incredible motivator. Protégés who are more independent and self-focused, on the other hand, might be better off not knowing about the sponsorship until much later.* Regardless of where you fall on this question, one piece of advice I would give is to always have a good idea of what your protégés' aspirations are, lest you run the risk of sponsoring protégés for opportunities that they don't want and that do not showcase them at their best, putting sponsors in the dreaded position of needing to Protect their protégés.

---

* However, one risk of not telling self-oriented protégés about sponsorship is that they become convinced that they did everything on their own, which might well make it so that they expect others to do it "without help" as well, thereby ending the sponsorship cycle.

9 | PROTECTING WITHOUT (RESORTING TO) POWER

I am standing outside the door of a dorm room. Loud music is thumping inside, and I can also hear screaming. Not a "we're having fun" kind of screaming, but a "someone's mad and things are going down" kind of screaming. As the residential assistant on duty, I've received complaints about the noise and, now evidently, a potential altercation.

I square my shoulders and knock loudly on the door. No answer. I throw my weight behind my fist, banging on the door until it is opened by a large, burly man. He stares at me, wide-eyed, and behind him I can see several other faces in various poses of surprise, confusion, and alarm. Some of the faces are attached to other large men, and that is when I realize that I've come to break up what might very well be a party of football athletes gone wrong.

I, all four feet, eleven inches of me, am either extremely brave or extremely stupid.

Thankfully, I don't have to find out which one because that's when the simulation ends. It's the last day of resident-assistant training, and I'm pretty sure I've just failed one of the test scenarios. Now, no one tells me that I've failed, but I am gently reminded that calling security is always an option. "It's okay to call for backup," the trainers tell me.

It's okay to call for backup.

Greg Spencer, whom you met in the Introduction as my initial skeptic and later converted supporter, is the current CEO of Randall Industries, one of the largest minority-owned chemical manufacturing firms in the United States. Spencer began his career in the Air Force during the Vietnam War and, upon his return, worked as a warehouse employee for US Steel. He quickly ascended into management positions, first overseeing steel-plant labor operations before moving into human resources, in which he rose to the level of general manager of human resources before being hired away to EQT, a national natural-gas producer. At EQT, Spencer became a member of the C-suite before striking out on his own as an entrepreneur by purchasing Randall Industries.

While he was at US Steel, Spencer witnessed an example of Protecting that he will never forget. Sometime in the 1980s, in his role as general manager of human resources, Spencer approved what he thought would be a routine transfer of a high-performing Black salesman, Andrew, from Iowa to the Atlanta sales region. Andrew had just gotten married, and his wife wanted to be closer to her family in Atlanta. To Spencer's surprise, the sales manager of the Atlanta region opposed the transfer, saying that Andrew "would not do well" in the sales territory. Spencer found this opposition odd; after all, Andrew posted strong sales and had high customer ratings. After some discussion with the Atlanta sales manager, Spencer determined that the opposition was racially motivated and decided to approve the transfer over the objections of the sales manager. This led the Atlanta sales manager to complain about the transfer to the executive vice president of sales, who then complained about the transfer to the vice president of human resources (Spencer's boss). Thankfully, the VP of HR trusted Spencer, saying, "This is Greg's job, and I support his decision." With his boss's support, Spencer went through with Andrew's transfer.

Despite getting what he wanted, Spencer was wary. He knew that the conflict had unleashed strong feelings and that the new president of US Steel was going to find out about the conflict. He wasn't sure how the president would respond, but just in case, Spencer decided to get ahead of the issue, informing the president directly. And to Spencer's great surprise and admiration, the president not only made a company-wide statement about how US Steel would not tolerate racist behavior in the firm or racist clients, but also made a special point of taking the company's private jet to Atlanta to personally introduce Andrew to existing clients as their new US Steel sales rep. Andrew, for his part, was never made aware of how much conflict his transfer had caused and went on to become a top salesperson in the region before leaving US Steel for a senior executive position at General Mills.

What I find interesting is that when Spencer shared this story with me, he said that it wasn't a story about a time he had sponsored, but about a time when he had witnessed sponsorship. From his perspective, his role in the situation was negligible, presumably because he wasn't the one whose power was pivotal to the story. But from my perspective, that's simply not true. Spencer, the salesman's first sponsor, had been forced to call for backup, first from the VP of human resources, and then from the president of US Steel. Now, it's true that maybe the VP of human resources would have approved the transfer over the objections of his White colleagues regardless of who had initially approved the transfer. But I doubt that was the case; nobody likes conflict, and most will do their best to avoid it altogether, even if they privately disagree with what's happening.

No, something else must have been at play here, and my guess is that the VP of HR's willingness to step into a conflict between a Black employee and White employees likely stemmed from his respect for Spencer. In fact, Spencer himself held a lot of status in the firm, in no small part due to his having been hand chosen to serve on a "special projects" advisory committee that reported directly to the prior president of US Steel. In short, it mattered that Spencer was Andrew's sponsor; had it been someone else with less status or who lacked relationships with other leaders, I doubt that the outcome would have been the same. That the president then went out of his way to sponsor Andrew himself in the new territory was just the cherry on top.

Let us not underestimate the influence we can wield via our status and relationships. Even when we lack power, it's still possible to lean on our status to call for backup.

THE COST OF PROTECTING

Raise your hand if you've ever witnessed someone being treated unfairly. Now raise your hand if you've ever stood by and said nothing.

I'll admit it: my hand is raised.

That is why I so admire sponsors who Protect, especially those who are fully aware that they are likely to be penalized for Protecting. A woman named Donna told me about her experience working as the chief human resource officer (CHRO) at a national financial services firm. The CEO was, to put it mildly, abusive; he regularly yelled, banged on, or punched furniture openly in meetings, and he threw papers at people, even other C-suite members. His erratic behavior was an open secret; everyone knew about it, even board directors. Perhaps this is why the board essentially coerced the CEO into promoting Donna, known for her no-nonsense sensibilities and ability to get things done, into the CHRO role. But, as we've discussed before, sponsors who use their power to force their protégés upon a resistant audience might technically get what they want, but otherwise poison the well for the protégé. People do not like feeling as if they haven't had a choice, and the CEO straight up told Donna prior to her taking the role that he did not support her promotion.

The responsibilities associated with Donna's role meant that she was the one who received reports about the CEO's problematic behavior, and it was also her responsibility to address the issue. Can you imagine having to tell your extremely volatile boss that his behavior is inappropriate? A lesser person might have strategically overlooked that part of the job description, but Donna felt strongly that she had a responsibility to speak up on the behalf of her colleagues. So she scheduled a meeting with the CEO and explained to him that there had been complaints about his behavior and that it needed to change.

Predictably, the CEO was infuriated with Donna's Protection of her colleagues. Because Donna mentioned that several of the complaints had come from other senior executives, the CEO took it upon himself to individually interrogate all the senior team members about whether they had been the ones to report him to Donna. And, perhaps predictably, the other senior leaders disavowed their complaints, each denying having said anything. With this information in hand, the CEO met with Donna, told her that her accusations were baseless, and said that she had lost his trust (not that she had it to begin with). He unceremoniously fired her on the spot.

Donna spoke up on behalf of the other employees because it was important to her to live by her values. Protecting others cost her her job.*

Of the numerous sponsors I've spoken to in the process of writing this book, the vast majority of stories about Protecting in particular, not sponsorship in general, involve women and non-White individuals, either as sponsors or as protégés. Indeed, Donna, from the story above, is a Black woman who was working in a White- and male-dominated space. Another example comes from Cassie, a professor, who told me about how hard she had to fight for equitable treatment for one of her protégés. Cassie directed a women's leadership program at her university, which became so successful that additional instructors were needed to meet demand. One who had regularly filled in for her was Clara, a practitioner who, while not having a PhD, was a skilled facilitator who provided rich learning experiences and managed clients well. Clara's teaching was well received, and over time she was teaching as much as a part-time teaching-track instructor, a position that, unlike her current per-contract arrangement, would afford her benefits, job stability, and access to more teaching opportunities. Given her stellar teaching ratings and the demand for her services, Cassie expected Clara's "promotion" to be an easy case.

To her surprise, the college administration objected, arguing that hiring non-PhD holders as instructors would lower the quality of teaching at the school. Cassie countered, pointing out that Clara's record indicated no such thing. Moreover, the college had recently promoted a male teaching faculty member who, like Clara, did not

---

* The part of Donna's story that angers me to this day is that, in my mind, the board deliberately put her in a precarious role—a phenomenon called the glass cliff—to do a job that they didn't want to do themselves, which would have been to fire the CEO or, at the very least, put him on notice. Donna was, in effect, sacrificed so that the board could avoid dealing with the CEO mess themselves.

have a PhD, to the highest teaching-track rank. Why, Cassie asked, the double standard? Relenting, the administration agreed to let Cassie bring up the matter for the approval committee to discuss and vote.

The committee meeting turned out to be an ambush. An anonymous letter had been distributed, accusing Cassie of intentionally violating hiring processes and pushing Clara forward despite objections from faculty members in her own group (which was news to Cassie). In a move reminiscent of Donna's abusive CEO, an investigation was then conducted by the school's dean, in which he interviewed every tenured faculty member in Cassie's group about the allegations. The interviews did not reveal any evidence of wrongdoing, and Clara was eventually promoted to a part-time position. Cassie, however, was deeply hurt by the experience, noting that there had been nowhere near the same level of opposition to the hiring of male teaching faculty both before and after this incident, suggesting that others were not being subjected to the same level of scrutiny and opposition that she, her leadership, and Clara had been.

This is but one example of several that Cassie shared with me about her experience Protecting women and diversity, equity, and inclusion programs at her school. Protecting was something she felt empowered to do because she felt that despite vocal DEI resisters, she was generally well regarded and respected in the school. Her Protecting, however, exacted a price. For her efforts, she was rewarded with damaged relationships and broken trust. Her conclusion that she had pushed too hard on issues related to DEI within the institution with too little support had real consequences: after years of frustration, she left to join a different institution, one with a stronger commitment to the issues that Cassie holds dear.

Sponsorship, and Protecting in particular, can have extremely high personal costs. But when I asked Cassie if, knowing what she knows now, she would do it again, she said yes without hesitation.

Donna, the Black female CHRO who was fired for Protecting her colleagues from the abusive CEO, told me the same.

These two separately expressed that despite the opposition they had faced, not doing something wasn't really an option they had considered. Donna told me that she "wouldn't be able to live with herself" if she hadn't acted in accordance with her principles. Others saw their trials as a necessity in helping the institutions in which they work to change. Cassie ended her interview with the following: "The cost was worth it." She is inspired by Vice President Kamala Harris's sentiment that it hurts to break barriers, but that the breaking—and the pain—are necessary for change that needs to happen.

This is what has struck me the most in collecting the stories for this book: the sheer number of sponsors, many of whom are women and racial minorities, who have chosen to risk their reputations and livelihoods to Protect deserving protégés and to challenge seemingly inequitable decisions in the hopes that institutions will change.

USING STATUS TO PROTECT YOURSELF
WHEN PROTECTING OTHERS

Surely, you are wondering, you can't be suggesting that we all be martyrs? What a privileged view!

Indeed, I am not.

Protecting doesn't *require* martyrdom, but it almost always involves conflict. However, there are ways to Protect that can temper its costs. To give you a sense of what that looks like, consider the case of Tom, a former CEO of a large materials manufacturer. When Tom was first starting out in his career, he mostly provided mentorship, as many of us do. But he noticed something curious: most of his mentees were female and racial minorities. It wasn't intentional on his part; as far as he was concerned, he mentored top performers, full stop. But part of what he was also looking for were "people who [will] challenge you" because "leaders need to know their areas of weakness." In Tom's experience, women and racial minorities were more likely to have the qualities that he sought.

His mostly White male peers, however, would invariably question Tom's female and minority mentees' interpersonal qualities, despite acknowledging their strong performance. They were "too outspoken" or "too difficult to work with." From Tom's perspective, those were just excuses. So when Tom rose to higher levels in the firm, he began to more openly Protect women and racial minority workers. There was the Black woman who seemed to constantly be "scapegoated." Another protégé, a White woman, was someone he wanted as a successor, but top leadership objected, saying that she "didn't connect" with them. In both cases, Tom pointed to his own experiences working with the women, directly contradicting the negative claims being made about their working styles and potential. And in both cases, he helped his protégés to prevail, rising to become leaders in the firm.

Tom's sponsorship went beyond one or two protégés. Once in a position of power, he expanded his Protection by changing organizational processes to address inequities. While giving introductory remarks to the company in his first days of leadership, he was struck by the observation that everyone in the room was a White man. He told me that he stopped in the middle of his talk, telling the group, "I see a lot of baby boomers like me in this audience. That's got to change." He immediately hired a new human resource manager to change the company's hiring processes. Despite the changes being unpopular, he notes with satisfaction that within five years, the firm was more diverse.

Tom is also proud that one of his first actions as the president of the company was conducting a pay-equity audit. As most new leaders do, he began his term by conducting a "listening tour," which led him to meet with the Black and Women's employee resource groups (ERGs). People in both groups asked him if they were being fairly paid. He had no idea, so he told them that he'd find out. The audit revealed that they were not, and Tom immediately adjusted compensation across the firm. This did not endear him to the board of directors, who were irked that he hadn't asked for permission to make the changes first. When challenged, Tom asked them in return, "Did I do something that you wouldn't have?" He had not. He just did it faster than they wanted.

In the case of revising hiring processes and adjusting inequitable compensation, Tom leaned on the power he held as the CEO and president. He went head-to-head with detractors, akin to a linear approach to battle in which both armies line up and then engage in a direct clash where the winner is determined by how many people on each side are left standing after the initial charge. Tom had an explicit goal to change the culture at the company to be more inclusive. This upset some of the firm's senior members, some of whom, he notes, "didn't make the trip." In the end, Tom's vision prevailed; the company is ranked highly on *Forbes's* list of the world's top companies for women.

But complete reliance on power is not a sustainable approach. Tom also had a strategy of first talking to influential individuals in the firm to "make sure they had the facts, not opinions," when he was about to announce an unpopular decision. In this, he followed one of organizational change management's central tenets: build a guiding coalition (or, in my parlance, call for backup). He first leveraged his relationships to convince other highly respected individuals to come to his side. He could then point to the support of those high-status members of the company when he made the official announcement, effectively adding their social capital to his own to make the decision more compelling to employees who might otherwise be opposed or undecided. He called for backup.

Having status can protect the Protector. Why? Because people generally respond better to disagreement when it comes from someone they trust and respect than from someone they don't. Jackie, a former corporate vice president, described for me an instance in which a former male boss, Henry, was complaining to her about one of Jackie's direct reports, Jane. The basis of Henry's complaint was that Jane consistently declined to travel for work due to her commitments to her two young children. However, Henry had young children at home too, but he didn't see them as an excuse to duck out of traveling for work the same way that Jane did. Jackie thought his interpretation of the situation lacked understanding and empathy. She explained that although, on the surface, their two situations looked similar, they were not, in fact, the same. Henry had a stay-at-home wife who could take care of the children while he was away. In contrast, Jane was going through a divorce and did not have family in the area, making her a single mom. The cost for Jane to travel for work, then, was much greater than it was for Henry. Although irritated in the moment by Jackie's Protection of Jane, Henry stopped complaining about this issue.

Later, Henry criticized Jane for not being as outspoken in meetings as he wanted. Jackie again defended Jane, explaining to Henry that in the meetings he had observed, Jane had been invited to provide information only about a very narrow, specific topic to high-level executives. Given this, it wasn't Jane's place to challenge the leaders. Again, Henry wasn't pleased in the moment with Jackie's defense of her staff member, but he later revised his thinking about Jane and supported Jackie's decision to give her a sizable raise commensurate with her performance and contributions.

What's notable is that when I asked Jackie if her defense of Jane caused a schism between her and Henry, she said no. "I had broader political capital," she told me. "The CEO, my boss's boss, openly respected me, and I made my boss look good all the time. So I knew I could afford to spend some of my political capital in my staff's defense with my boss." Here, then, is a situation where a sponsor's Protection of a protégé is helped by their having status in the eyes of the audience. If Henry had held Jackie in lower regard and if she had been less respected in the company, her sponsorship might very well have backfired, leading Henry to have even more entrenched negative views of Jane and, potentially, negative feelings toward Jackie herself. Indeed, Jackie's outspokenness had already led her to be "put in the proverbial doghouse" at a prior time by Henry, but she had managed to rebuild his trust in her over time. By the time these incidents occurred, her willingness to directly challenge Henry was actually one of the reasons he trusted her so much. He told her, "One of the reasons [you are] valued in the company [is that you] say what people need to hear, even if they might not want to hear it."

Jackie was willing to challenge Henry because she knew that he trusted her and valued her opinion; the status she had with him was strong enough to buffer their relationship from the frustration Henry may have felt in response to her Protection of Jane. Her experience illustrates how the risk of Protecting can be mitigated by a sponsor's status and trust with the audience.

PROTECTING WHEN YOU DON'T HAVE STATUS: SPONSORSHIP JUJITSU

There will be times when sponsors don't know how much status they have or think that they lack status. This does not absolve them from Protecting because, to go back to the fighting metaphor, even the smallest opponent can be highly effective when they use the right techniques.

Enter: sponsorship jujitsu.

First, full disclosure: I don't practice jujitsu, although I've been intrigued with the possibility for many years. Jujitsu appeals to me because of my small stature (I don't clear five feet, remember?), and jujitsu is one of the rare fighting styles in which a smaller fighter can subdue a larger opponent. The core philosophy behind jujitsu is to use an opponent's strength against themselves, rather than taking it on directly. The style relies on yielding rather than direct confrontation.

One of the best examples of sponsorship jujitsu I have heard of involves a faculty member who single-handedly changed the decision trajectory of a tenure case. As I mentioned in Chapter 5, tenure decisions are incredibly consequential for professors because being denied tenure is the equivalent of being fired. It is such an important decision that universities have extremely long and intricate processes for deciding whether a professor gets tenure. First, the tenure candidate writes a document, usually three to five pages, summarizing their research and explaining why their research is rigorous and impactful. To back up these claims, the candidate also provides a few of their research papers. These materials are then sent out to highly respected professors in the candidate's area of research at other institutions for comment. These external experts read over each tenure candidate's materials and write a letter evaluating the quality of the research and its impact on the field and weighing in on whether the person should get tenure.

Once all of the external letters are collected, a small committee of faculty at the home institution (where the professor is going up for tenure) then goes over the material and makes a recommendation to the senior faculty at the college. The college-level committee then votes on whether the college should recommend the candidate for tenure, which goes to the college dean, who almost always goes along with the faculty's assessment. Each college's dean then submits their recommendation to a university-level review committee, which is composed of a mix of other respected faculty on campus and the deans of the other colleges. The university committee is typically there as a safeguard; they make sure that the college has followed proper protocol in evaluating its faculty. For the most part, the university committee approves the deans' recommendations. The university committee's recommendations, in turn, go to the university provost, then the university president, and then, finally, the Board of Trustees.

Like I said, it's a process.

In this case, the college dean had decided against supporting the candidate's case for tenure to the university committee. Under normal circumstances, the university committee wouldn't think twice about the decision, but here something didn't quite add up. The report generated by the small internal college committee was scathing; the candidate didn't publish in the right journals, they used questionable research methods, and their research lacked impact. But the letters of evaluation from the external experts were glowing, almost all recommending that the candidate receive tenure. What was going on?

At the beginning of the discussion about this case, most members of the university committee, while not exactly pleased with the discrepancy between the internal report provided by the college and the external evaluations, were willing to let it go. In universities, there's nothing to be gained by digging too much into another college's business; the motto is "Live and let live." So what if the decision seemed a bit dodgy? But there was one lone dissenter, a female faculty member (always a woman!) whom we'll call Grace who refused to let the rest of the committee move forward. Grace insisted that further explanation be given as to how the college had found the candidate's research so wanting when, in fact, the external letter writers claimed otherwise. After all, wasn't the committee's very purpose to ensure that tenure decisions were conducted appropriately?

Grace began by asking questions. Who was on the committee that wrote the internal report, and what were their qualifications? With each question she asked, the dean's answers raised more. The internal committee that wrote the scathing report did so without having access to the letters provided by external experts. Moreover, the internal committee had conducted a vote on the case without access to the external letters. Both the report and the vote, then, constituted assessments based on incomplete information. However, the report and vote were key pieces of information on which most of the faculty on the college-level committee depended when making up their minds about whether to support a case.

The issue of incomplete information was one problem that Grace's questioning uncovered. Her questioning also revealed that the voting members of the internal committee had been composed of faculty who were hostile to the candidate's field and research methods. What this meant was that the conversation in the committee had been less about the candidate's work per se than about the validity of the candidate's scholarly discipline.

In this way, Grace's questioning revealed that the procedures used by the college—how they composed the internal committees and the use of reports and votes that were based on incomplete information—were inconsistent with what the rest of the university considered to be good practice. Moreover, in the same way that college deans tend not to meddle in one another's affairs, faculty are expected to exhibit intellectual humility and to defer to the experts in other fields. In this case, that deference had not been honored; faculty at the college had voted to deny the candidate tenure despite exemplary letters in favor of the candidate, showing a distaste and lack of respect for the candidate's field. This kind of scholarly disdain is not considered appropriate in an institution that prides itself on intellectual curiosity.

With this information revealed, the other committee members took notice. They then began asking questions of their own, prompting the dean to provide ever more inadequate answers. Why were the journals the candidate published in considered inappropriate? Why was the research method of the candidate considered inferior? The dean's answers revealed that, yes, most other colleges would consider the journals in which the candidate published to be top-tier journals. Yes, most other colleges would consider the research methods that the candidate used to be valid and appropriate. By the end, the college's decision had been thoroughly discredited, and the university committee voted to support the candidate's case for tenure, which was ultimately granted.

There are a couple of points I want to make about this. First, as a general note not necessarily related to sponsorship, dissenters can be valuable assets for groups. All it takes is one dissenter in a group to greatly improve the group's decision-making quality. Even if other members don't agree with the dissenter's assessment, merely the existence of a dissenter makes it more likely for other group members to raise their own concerns. The consideration of additional viewpoints, in turn, increases the quality of the group's decision.

Second, sponsors who are trying to Protect a protégé don't have to do it in a way that marks them as being oppositional. Grace was able to exert influence merely by asking questions.

Now, I acknowledge that there are situations where people use questions in bad faith, as when conspiracy theorists pose outlandish questions to inject doubt about otherwise seemingly objective facts. "What if the Holocaust was all a ruse?" and "How can we be sure that we landed on the moon?" are examples of this kind of questioning. It has, to some observers, become such a ubiquitous rhetorical tactic that it now has its own term in *The Urban Dictionary*: "JAQing off" or "the act of asking leading questions to influence your audience, then hiding behind the defense that you're Just Asking Questions."

So how can you ensure that your question asking doesn't make you look like a JAQ-off? First, only ask a question if you have genuine curiosity about the answer. If your opinion won't change based on the answer, then don't ask it. But more important, make sure that your questions highlight your commitment to group values. Grace was a faculty member speaking to a group of peers and higher-ups. As a result, she didn't have the highest social standing in the room, and if she had been more overtly oppositional, her approach could have focused the group on her rather than the merits of the case. She would have "protested too much," leading people to question her motives in putting up a fight.

What made Grace's line of questioning so impactful is that she prefaced them by pointing to shared values and goals. She justified her opposition to moving on to the next case by reminding the group of their official charge: to ensure that the faculty member being evaluated was being treated fairly and consistently, in accordance with the processes laid out by the university. She wasn't being difficult just to be difficult; she wanted the group to do its job. She reminded the group of the consequential nature of their decision and their (presumed) desire to make a just decision.

Pointing to shared values and goals reminds people that you care about the group. And recall that when you show yourself to care about the group, people grant you status. Indeed, research finds that appealing to common values is a way for people to disagree without incurring social penalties for dissenting. Appealing to the group's higher values has the added benefit of alerting potential allies that backup is needed.

BACKING UP SHARED VALUES

Calling for backup helps only if the call is answered. As in war, numbers matter. Allies matter. So if you aren't the first to stand up and Protect someone when you see them being treated inequitably, you can still be the second. The third. The fourth. Be a horde. Don't sit back down just because someone stood up before you did. Back. Them. Up.

Why? When only one person dissents on the behalf of a protégé, they are a lone voice. But when more people stand up with them to Protect, it starts feeling like the group is taking a stand. It's clarifying its values, and those values indicate that what is happening is not, in fact, consistent with the group's values. This can be incredibly impactful, especially for those whose inclusion—their standing in the group—is being questioned. When women or racial minorities observe—not personally experience!—biased behavior, their feelings of safety in the group are higher only when the biased behavior is directly confronted by an initial ally *who is then supported by a second ally*. In fact, having only one ally speak up doesn't restore a sense of safety among marginalized group members much more than if no one had stepped forward to confront the biased behavior at all.

Sponsors who Protect can be the stone that produces ripples that touch every corner of a lake, but only to the degree that others add their weight to the issue.

As a postscript, Grace's dissension had a larger impact than helping the candidate get tenure. Her questions revealed significant discrepancies between the college's evaluation processes and those used by the other colleges at the university, and the university subsequently formed a committee to audit the college's evaluation processes, in hopes that the college would make fairer decisions going forward. In this way, the Protection of an individual protégé can open the door to more systemic changes that make the institutional landscape fairer for everyone. Protecting isn't always just about protégés. It's also about Protecting values.

ASSUME POSITIVE INTENT

Because Protecting can be seen as a form of conflict, it might be helpful to bring to bear what research on conflict resolution has to say about the matter. Here, I'll offer that the best way to approach conflict—of any type—is to assume positive intent, particularly as it relates to information. Many disagreements stem from the fact that we don't share brains and can't just do a Vulcan mind meld. What I know isn't necessarily what you know, and vice versa, but our tendency to assume that we are all working from the same set of materials gets us into trouble. So one angle a Protecting sponsor can take is to ask if everyone is working from the same set of information. Do we know something the other person doesn't? Does the other person know something we don't? This was the tack Grace took when she asked questions about the college's process; she didn't assume she knew how they ran their evaluation system and sought clarification. It wasn't that her questions were problematic; the college dean's answers were.

In some cases, it will be revealed that there is some level of information asymmetry or additional information is needed. At this point, you can ask whether that information is available or obtainable. If so, offer to be the one to do the research, and *make sure you report back*! In this way, you can show that you care about the group and are genuine in your desire to contribute. When the women's and Black ERGs asked Tom if they were being paid fairly, he acknowledged that he didn't know the answer. He didn't dismiss their question out of turn; he said he would look into it, and he did. After commissioning an equity audit, he closed the loop by providing the results to the leaders of the two groups and by adjusting compensation throughout the company. When we show ourselves to have integrity, people trust us.

Sponsors can also preemptively seek and provide additional information when Protecting protégés. I was once on the board of a nonprofit with a mission to serve any and all individuals who are struggling with life's transitions, widely defined. It helps individuals "aging out" of the foster care system, elderly individuals who don't have the means to enter assisted-living housing but who need additional care, individuals with special needs who require guardianships or would benefit from specialized job training, and teenagers who are struggling with mental health issues. It's a nonprofit that I support wholeheartedly; it exists to fill the gaps in social services that are not already filled by other nonprofits.

One of the fastest-growing services the nonprofit offers is legal services to immigrants and refugees. Originally, these services were largely utilized by Jewish refugees fleeing oppression from former USSR countries, but they have been increasingly used by refugees from Central America and war-torn Afghanistan and Ukraine. Yet the board had only one member with personal immigration experience. Moreover, like most US nonprofit boards, the board was mostly White, while the populations the nonprofit served were increasingly non-White. Recognizing the discrepancy, the board had been involved in a years-long process of diversifying, seeking new members with backgrounds that would give them a deeper understanding of the populations served. I myself was a product of that effort, and it was my understanding that part of why I had been asked to join the board was so that I could use my network—my big-city social capital—to identify additional board members who would similarly add more diversity to the board.

With that in mind, I proposed a former staff member of CMU, Carmen. Although Carmen had no prior nonprofit board experience, she had other relevant skills and experiences that made me think she would be a great fit for the nonprofit. First, Carmen had been instrumental in securing a lucrative partnership between CMU and a large foundation for CMU's Africa campus in Rwanda, evidence that she had connections and fund-raising skills that all nonprofits need. But Carmen was also an immigrant from a Central American country who had firsthand experience navigating the labyrinthine American immigration system. She also had personal contacts with Latino immigrants in the region who would benefit from the services of the nonprofit. As far as I was concerned, Carmen was a perfect board candidate.

Given what I saw as incontrovertible evidence that she was exactly who the board needed, I thought nothing of it when I couldn't make it to the meeting where the candidates were discussed. Clearly, I was overconfident; I found out later that Carmen's nomination had been set aside because committee members thought she lacked demonstrated interest in the nonprofit's primary areas of focus.

My initial response at this news was irritation. I thought the decision was shortsighted. Carmen had a lot of relevant expertise and skills that would benefit the board. But also, if one of the board's priorities was to diversify its membership, she should have been a shoo-in. I had a brief vision of storming into the next committee meeting, of accusing the other board members of harboring only superficial commitments to the goal of diversifying the board. It would have been my personal "pounding the table" moment. In an alternate vision, I imagined telling the committee chair that if my nominations weren't going to be taken seriously, I wouldn't be providing more of them (as Newhouser, the scout whose recommendation to the Astros to hire Derek Jeter from the last chapter, did).

Thankfully, I didn't do any of those things. Instead, I decided to ensure that the committee had all the information they needed to make an informed decision.

I went back to Carmen, asking for clarification on her work for CMU's Africa campus in Rwanda. She told me that her success in wooing the foundation partner for the Rwanda campus was because of her excitement about the Rwanda campus's potential to elevate the trajectories of displaced African students. Carmen was passionate about using education as a vehicle toward economic mobility, and she successfully sold her vision for how the funds would be used; the foundation partner agreed to the partnership with CMU on the condition that a portion of the funding would be set aside for scholarships exclusively for African refugees to attend programs on CMU's Rwanda and Pittsburgh campuses. Building on her expertise in working with international populations, she now works to bring services to underserved populations in the United States, mainly parents and families of immigrant service workers.

With this information, I could now articulate Carmen's *why*: to ensure that underserved people have access to the services and opportunities they need to thrive. With this information, I could sponsor her more effectively. I could tell a story about how Carmen's personal *why* was entirely in line with the mission—the *why*—of the nonprofit.

At the next board meeting, I apologized to the nomination committee for my previous absence. I expressed concern that perhaps the committee didn't have adequate information to make an informed decision about Carmen's suitability. I then shared the additional information I had learned about Carmen, which, once out in the open, completely changed her reception by the nominating committee. Carmen was overwhelmingly supported to join the board, and since her inclusion on the board, she has actively used her connections to uncover potential corporate funding opportunities for the nonprofit, particularly for legal services for refugees.

My sponsorship of Carmen got the nonprofit a fantastic board member who used her unique expertise and connections to get funding for the nonprofit. Carmen is now gaining valuable experience on a nonprofit board, which will help her be considered for additional opportunities. I get the satisfaction of knowing that I made this pairing possible and am now seen as being well connected.

Win-win-win.

Note that continuing to push for Carmen was a gamble on my part. My efforts could have been shut down by the committee. They could have told me that Carmen would need to be reconsidered in the next cycle or that she didn't have the qualities they were looking for. Basically, they could have implied that I lacked the standing to keep her candidacy open or that I didn't have a good grasp of the group's values and that my contributions were unwelcome. By Protecting Carmen, I made myself vulnerable to the possibility that my status was lower than I thought or wanted. I am glad that this wasn't the response and that they were open to being persuaded. I credit at least part of that openness to my approaching their resistance by assuming positive intent.

PROTECT BY GIVING OTHERS STATUS

Sometimes all the relevant information is at hand, and the conflict is, instead, about people's *interpretation* of that information. When that's the case, the way these disagreements often get settled is based on who has the most power. However, as we've discussed previously, resorting to power should be exactly that: the last resort.

Let's imagine a pair of parents who disagree with a teacher's conclusion that their child Johnny is not, in fact, gifted. This is an example that counts as Protecting because the parents' intent is to change the teacher's beliefs about or behavior toward Johnny. One way for Johnny's parents to Protect him would be to threaten to escalate things to the principal. The principal has power over the teacher that the parents do not and could, if swayed by the parents' complaints, compel the teacher to classify Johnny as gifted. Now let's imagine that this strategy works; the principal forces the teacher to pull Johnny into the advanced group. But consider how the teacher is going to think about Johnny going forward. The parents may very well have gotten what they wanted—Johnny is now classified as gifted—but they haven't necessarily changed the teacher's mind about Johnny's "real" classification. And what do we imagine the parents' relationship with the teacher will be like for the rest of the year? What their reputation might be among the other teachers who are yet to teach Johnny? What this illustrates is that while relying on power as a sponsor can be effective, in that it might change how people behave toward a protégé, it's not a great way to build positive relationships with other people. Nor is it necessarily a great way to help our protégés build a positive reputation of their own.

Sponsorship that relies on the exertion of power doesn't exert its effects through trust. To maintain trust between sponsors and audiences, it's better to rely on status—respect and admiration. However, when we rely on status, we shouldn't point to why others should respect us; if we have to tell other people to respect us, more often than not, it means that they don't. Instead, we can encourage others to give us status by first giving *them* status. We can point to the group's values and goals and acknowledge or remind the other person how they have lived up to those shared values and goals.

Consider an alternative scenario to the above. Imagine that Johnny's parents begin their meeting by reiterating their respect and appreciation for the teacher's efforts in teaching Johnny. In essence, they point to their and the teacher's shared goal of ensuring that Johnny has the best educational experience they can arrange. Then, the parents frame their questions as coming from a desire to better understand the evidence being used in evaluating Johnny's giftedness. Here, they are assuming positive intent and acknowledging that perhaps they aren't all working with the same information. By asking how the evaluation process works, the parents might surface information that reveals that the teacher used a more advanced test than was appropriate (something that in fact occurred to the classmate of one of my children), and upon taking the more appropriate test, Johnny does, in fact, test into the gifted category. Alternatively, Johnny's parents could open similarly to the above, but here they provide the teacher with additional evidence of their own about Johnny's math abilities, showing them Johnny's progress on math workbooks at home. But rather than use this evidence to contest the validity of the teacher's assessment, they could ask how they can help make it so that the abilities that Johnny evinces at home translate into his performance at school.

How conversations "open" matter. The point is to cast ourselves as partners, not opponents, in a shared quest to do what's best for the group. We don't insist that we know all the answers; we make room for the possibility we could be wrong. By being open to being wrong, we grant that the other person might be right. We give them status. This makes it more likely that the other person, in turn, is more willing to consider that they might be wrong. Role-modeling the open-mindedness that we want others to have makes it more likely that they will, indeed, be open-minded, much like the self-fulfilling prophecy. In this way, we can encourage other people to be more receptive to evidence that will ultimately change their *minds* about our protégé, not just their behavior, which will allow our relationships to remain strong.

———

Protection doesn't always take the power-forward, strident, overt, table-pounding version that is so often associated with sponsorship. By now, you know that in a matchup between power and status, status wins. Just because we lack formal power in a situation does not mean we cannot or should not Protect our protégés. There are ways to Protect that reduce the potential cost to the sponsor: We can appeal to shared values. We can ask questions. We can gather more information. And we can call for backup.

When all else fails, remember this: Protecting is a critical function of sponsorship because, sometimes, what is at stake is larger than a single protégé's plight. Sometimes, the collective needs principled sponsors who are willing to shine a light on inequities even if doing so comes at great personal cost. So let us champion the Protectors among us and ensure that they are rewarded for the collective value they bring. Our world is better for their sacrifice.

10 | TIME TO STRETCH

In the fall of 2023, Kim Ng had just presided over the Marlins' most successful season in twenty years, largely credited to her careful curation of the team's roster. The Marlins' owner, Bruce Sherman, said so himself: "Not easy being in her role at all. Can you imagine that? First female GM in all of baseball history. Unbelievable. And all the moves, all the trade moves, have been excellent." It wasn't just that Ng was picking good players; she was also successfully making headway in changing the culture of the team. "We went from rigid-control B.S. to a place of 'we need ideas!' It's a breath of fresh air," shared a staff member, suggesting that Ng's penchant for constantly seeking innovation, whether homegrown or not, remains firmly in place. Marlins president of business operations Caroline O'Connor echoed this sentiment, saying, "[Ng] gets people to voice their opinions and creates a collaborative environment for the team. . . . She's a very thoughtful leader." Skip Schumaker, a Marlins manager, similarly praised her leadership approach. "The respect I have for how she leads is at the very top. . . . Players love her; she knows how to have difficult conversations. . . . [S]he lets us do our jobs. She gives ideas and recommends, obviously, but doesn't second-guess. You know what that does for a manager and staff? It's incredible."

It was a surprise, then, when in late October 2023, Sherman informed Ng that he would be hiring a president of baseball operations, effectively demoting her to second in command. In response, Ng opted not to renew her contract with the Marlins, ending her term as Major League Baseball's first (and so far only) female general manager. Observers were incensed. One commentator was blunt: "If a male general manager achieved what Ng did after all of the turmoil she endured during her tenure with the Marlins, they would have been signed to a multiyear extension and provided with the budget to compete for the World Series." He went on to say, "The truth is, hiring a president of baseball operations after Ng's performance this past season . . . is a sign of disrespect. Let's call it what it is."

When this news flashed on my phone notifications, my heart sank. I was outraged for Ng. It felt like just another example of a woman who had risen to the occasion and, instead of being rewarded for her accomplishments, was told, "Thank you for your service. Now sit back down." This phenomenon isn't merely anecdotal; one study looking at CEO gender and likelihood of dismissal finds that male CEOs are more likely to be retained if their firm does well. Well, duh. But that's not true for female CEOs; female CEOs are just as likely to be fired regardless of whether the firm does well or not under their leadership. Meaning, you can be a female CEO who leads your firm to high performance and still be shown the door.

Ng's effective ouster was also frustrating because it threw into sharp relief the difference in how she was being treated compared to someone she had sponsored: Skip Schumaker, who, prior to being hired by the Marlins, had been a bench coach for the St. Louis Cardinals. Until he joined the Marlins, Schumaker had no prior manager experience, which made Ng's hiring of him a bit of a gamble. Ng reportedly did so over the objections of other decision-makers, the majority of whom voted to hire someone else. Schumaker is aware that Ng sponsored him, saying, "[Ng] could have picked anybody, and she decided to pick me. And I promise you, not everybody in the room wanted me. I know. I'm not dumb." Her sponsorship paid off, but not for Ng herself; in an ironic twist, Schumaker went on to be named 2023 manager of the year a few months after Ng left the Marlins in protest of her demotion.

Aside from her sponsorship of Schumaker, Ng spent most of her time mentoring others. "I try to be proactive in helping others, particularly women in the workplace," she has said. "Whether it's giving advice, mentorships, providing camaraderie or letting others know they aren't the only ones out there dealing with difficult situations in terms of being a woman or someone of color." But in her position as GM of the Marlins, Ng was responsible for hiring and firing the coaching staff, where women have been making inroads. Why didn't she sponsor more women coaches to the Marlins?

Research suggests that Ng would have had multiple valid, evidence-based reasons to avoid sponsoring other women. For one, many women believe others see them as having less legitimacy as a leader, which is likely only exacerbated in situations where they could be seen as a "diversity hire." Others worry that because there are so few of them, their every move comes under greater scrutiny. Indeed, women CEOs appear to have significantly different leadership experiences than do men CEOs, in that women CEOs have been shown to be more likely to be challenged by activist shareholders, and more likely to be challenged by multiple activist shareholders at the same time, than are men CEOs.

Believing themselves to face this extra scrutiny, women might be particularly sensitive to how they are seen by others and especially to the possibility that they will be seen as being biased in favor of other women. Here, too, research has shown that their concerns are warranted; women leaders are given lower leadership ratings when they advocate for diversity-related practices. Men leaders, on the other hand, are neither penalized nor rewarded for vocally supporting diversity-related practices.

With so many headwinds facing women leaders, is it any wonder they might be hesitant to sponsor or to have higher standards for people who look like them?

But here's the thing: it's sponsorship from other women that enable women to attain leadership positions and succeed in those positions. One of the biggest predictors of a firm appointing a woman CEO is the gender composition of the board of directors; the more women on the board of directors, the higher the likelihood of a firm having a woman CEO. In other words, to become leaders, women need other women in decision-making positions to sponsor them. Sponsorship also impacts women leaders' ability to perform once they attain leadership positions. Women CEOs have the greatest positive impact on firms when the board is composed of at least 20 percent women board members who are themselves well connected. Meaning, to do their best work, all CEOs need a supportive board of directors. Women CEOs, however, tend to receive that level of support only when their board has a sizable proportion of women board of directors who have the social capital to Confirm and Protect the women CEOs from their more numerous internal and external detractors.*

In effect, to make leadership more diverse, people from marginalized groups tend to need other people from the same group to

---

* Male CEOs also benefit from having gender-diverse boards. However, the social capital of the female board members matters less for male CEO success.

sponsor them. But how does a person from a marginalized group get into a position to sponsor? If the way to getting more women into CEO positions requires that we have more women on boards, then how do we get more women on boards? Perhaps unsurprisingly, having a woman chairing the nominating committee is one key factor in driving diversity in gender composition of a board. But for a woman to be the chair of the nominating committee requires that at least one woman is on the board in the first place, which means that at least one majority-group member—a man—must first step up and sponsor someone who doesn't look like him. And the need for majority-group sponsors doesn't just end with boards; women CEOs are also more successful when their men predecessors pave the way for them by consistently putting them in clear succession-planning positions and publicly giving their blessing when they step down.

There's no way around it: succeeding at the highest levels requires that people from marginalized groups be sponsored not just by people from their own group but by people from the majority group as well.

Some people will bristle at this advice; they resist the idea that people from marginalized groups need to be "saved" by majority-group members. Here, I want to be clear that I'm not advocating for anyone to save anyone else. Saving implies that the other person couldn't have done it on their own, and I would never suggest this. Sponsors don't save people. They share their power—control over information and access to people—so that it doesn't have to be so challenging for exceptional people to get where they want to go and meet the people who should know them.

If sponsorship is a form of power sharing, then we need those who have power to share it. It's that simple.

More of us need to sponsor people who don't look like us, but doing that will require change. Change in where we go. Change in whom we choose to approach. Change in how we engage with people. These are all changes we can choose to make, and if enough of us do, our collective efforts will change the social environment not just for ourselves, but for others too.

YOUR (STRETCH) SPONSORSHIP TEN

Who you choose to sponsor is what will determine the progress we make toward making the world more inclusive and equitable. In the spirit of using sponsorship to increase diversity and inclusion in our social spaces, I'll end by offering one last exercise: Your (Stretch) Sponsorship Ten.

The (Stretch) Sponsorship Ten is a variation on the Trusted Ten that was introduced in Chapter 4. It's called "stretch," because I am going to challenge us to think of people for whom sponsorship would not be an obvious next step in our relationship.

Just as you did for the Trusted Ten exercise, I'd like you to open a spreadsheet or take out a blank sheet of paper.* Create a table with ten (or so) rows and columns. Label the first column "Name" and populate it with the names of people you admire and respect, but *don't know particularly well.* These are the people who you could see yourself one day including on your Trusted Ten. In fact, the way I generated my Sponsorship Ten was to think about the people I enjoy spending time with and whose presence energizes me. So another way to think about this list is as "the people who bring me joy who are not already on my Trusted Ten."

Avoid choosing people you feel you *should* know or be close with because of your job. In fact, consider taking work-related people off the table completely. If you want to keep people you know from work on the list, that's fine, but don't put down the names of people you know you would be sponsoring regardless. I wouldn't put down the names of doctoral students working with me, for example, since

---

* For convenience, there's also a blank version of the exercise in the Appendix.

I already consider sponsorship of them to be part of my professional responsibilities.

Having done that, set that list aside and look back at your Trusted Ten. Identify the three or four characteristics on which your Trusted Ten show the greatest level of homophily (similarity to you) or homogeneity (similarity to one another). The characteristics on which my Trusted Ten have the greatest homogeneity are educational attainment (lots of PhDs), age (most everyone is thirty-five or older), parental status (almost all of my Trusted Ten have kids), and industry (more than three-quarters work in higher education). Once you've identified the characteristics on which your Trusted Ten network could use additional diversity, label the next three or four columns of your Sponsorship Ten with those characteristics. Because of what I study, I also included "Gender Identity" and "Race/ Ethnicity" as columns on my Sponsorship Ten list. Similarly, you are free to include or add other characteristics as you see fit.

Now, populate the rows under those columns with the appropriate information for each of the individuals on your Sponsorship Ten. Having done that, I want you to take stock of how your Sponsorship Ten looks compared to your Trusted Ten, especially on those characteristics of your Trusted Ten you've identified as needing greater diversity. You might notice that your Sponsorship Ten is not helping you to diversify your Trusted Ten (because, after all, the hope is that these people will end up there!). If that's the case, now is the time to interrogate how you generated your Sponsorship Ten. Can you be more expansive in who you can think of? Why have you chosen these people *and not others?*

When I did this exercise, I realized that I still had way too many PhDs on my list. At least a quarter of the people on my list were junior faculty at other institutions whom I'd sponsor anyway. I decided not to count them toward my Stretch Sponsorship Ten; I forced myself to think even more broadly about the people I've met over the years whose presence affected me positively.

Okay, so at this point, you should have a list of individuals who (hopefully, but not necessarily) add diversity to your network on the dimensions on which your Trusted Ten are homogenous or homophilous. For my part, I ended up with a list of twelve people, of whom exactly half were men and half were women. My list was also more than half White, but I had a good mix of Asian, Black, and Latino individuals for the other half (so while better than my Trusted Ten, still not great). I had also identified three individuals who were younger than those on my Trusted Ten and two individuals who were older. When it came to educational attainment, three of the people on my list either had or were working toward their PhDs. However, everyone else on the list had degrees that would diversify my Trusted Ten. I had three MBAs (who are almost completely missing from my Trusted Ten), one MD (also missing), and one JD. On the child-rearing front, I must admit that my Sponsorship Ten did not show signs of greater diversity: only two of my Sponsorship Ten do not have children. In addition, only a quarter of my Sponsorship Ten do not work in higher education. Taken together, if I am successful at converting the individuals on my Sponsorship Ten into additions to my Trusted Ten, my network will be more diverse, but not significantly so. Still, more diverse is better than less!

You might be wondering why I've instructed you to populate your Sponsorship Ten by first identifying people you enjoy spending time with and *then* checking to see if their inclusion on your Trusted Ten would diversify it. Why not start with the dimensions on which your Trusted Ten are homogenous and identify people for your Sponsorship Ten who will address that issue? I could have, for example, made a point of saying, "I need more Asians in my Sponsorship Ten!" and then scanned through my mental Rolodex of "Asians I know who live in Pittsburgh."

To identify a need and then find someone who would fulfill that need is to take the value-extraction approach to networks. That's not how I want us to approach our social relationships. Doing it this way flips the ordering: find a person who we think is great, and *then* see if they fulfill a need. If your Sponsorship Ten ends up looking too much like your Trusted Ten, you should continue to identify people who are different from those you already know but who are also people you already respect and admire. And if, after doing that, you still can't generate a more diverse set for your Sponsorship Ten, that's a cue to reconsider where you spend your time, with whom you speak, and what you speak with them about.

Remember: one of the main points of this book is that we shouldn't approach our relationships with purely instrumental motives. Nobody wants to be your token [insert characteristic here] friend. That's not a good way to build the kind of relationships that lead to sponsorship. To the contrary, the point of the Sponsorship Ten is to push us to take a relatively small step—identifying the people we already respect, the people who have status in our eyes—and to push ourselves to think more intentionally about how we can deepen those relationships. Once these relationships are strengthened— once we know more about their values and dreams—we can more effectively sponsor them for appropriate opportunities or connect them to appropriate individuals.

The Sponsorship Ten is about connecting people we already know to be great to others in our networks so that everyone in the collective can benefit from their greatness.

USING THE SPONSORSHIP TEN TO CLARIFY YOUR VALUES

Whatever the case may be in terms of homogeneity of your Sponsorship Ten, label the rest of the columns on your Sponsorship Ten with the following: "Qualities I Admire," "Strengths/Areas of Expertise," "Dreams/Aspirations," and "Opportunities to Create and Confirm." Then, populate the rest of the spreadsheet.

You can think of the "Qualities I Admire" column as asking, "What do I respect about this person?" or "Why do I like this person?" What about this individual made you put them on this list? Your answers on this column will likely reveal information about *you*. I filled this column with personality attributes that I thought characterized my listed individuals. Several adjectives seemed to come up more often than others. Specifically, the term "positive" showed up a whopping seven times in my descriptions of my Sponsorship Ten. What this suggests is that the people I admire and enjoy spending time with are people who have positive attitudes. This is in stark contrast to my earlier years, in which I found cynicism and having a quick wit much more attractive. The other most frequently mentioned term was "socially oriented" (also seven times), which, upon seeing it, I recognized as meaning that I knew the person to be active in efforts to address social inequality (broadly construed).

I also found it interesting what terms *didn't* show up; as an academic, you might expect that I would care a lot about someone being well educated or, at the very least, interesting or smart. And indeed, "interesting" shows up on the list three times. But that's a lot less than I would have anticipated. "Smart" shows up on my list exactly once. This isn't to say, by the way, that the people on my Sponsorship Ten lack these qualities. Indeed, I would say that most of them are, in fact, interesting and smart people. It's just not what I find most attractive about them.

If I had to characterize the people on my Sponsorship Ten, I would describe them as people who are socially and politically aware, kind, and thoughtful. They, despite clearly being cognizant of the many injustices and calamities the world might be facing, are able to maintain a sense of calm and positivity about their ability to contribute to making things better. At least that's the face they present to me! I too care deeply about taking into consideration how my actions might impact other people. I also care deeply about social issues and want to contribute to making the world better; why else write this book? That the people on my Sponsorship Ten similarly share these values is no accident.

Your data (because that's what this is!) can provide similar insights about yourself. Maybe your Sponsorship Ten is composed of people who have high intellect, ambition, and devotion to religion or family. Whatever it is, one of the benefits of this exercise is that it enables us to identify our values by looking at more tangible and concrete evidence of our preferences, in contrast to standard values exercises in which we are forced to identify our two to four top personal values without context. That being said, it's still a good idea to cross-check what your Sponsorship Ten says about your values against your gut instinct about your values. If the terms that you use to describe your Sponsorship Ten are inconsistent with what you understand your deepest values to be, you may need to take some time to reconcile the two.

The next column, "Strengths/Areas of Expertise," is where you have identified what your Sponsorship Ten are good at or areas that you would feel comfortable vouching for them in terms of topical expertise. My Sponsorship Ten are a varied bunch, with areas of expertise ranging from applied mathematics to playing brass instruments to criminal justice. Note that, again, we filled out this column *after* we identified who should be on the list, rather than identifying first the types of expertise and abilities that we'd like to have access to via our networks and then finding individuals who possess those skills. The point here is to take stock, not to evaluate "worth."

While the "Strengths/Expertise" column was probably straightforward enough, I'm guessing that the next column, "Dreams/Aspirations," was probably much more difficult to complete. That's okay—this is why these people haven't made it to your Trusted Ten list (yet!). Greg Spencer (my initial skeptic turned friend, mentor, and sponsor) is on my Sponsorship Ten list. Greg is extremely well respected in the region and a leader in many different communities.

I know that he has a general passion for racial equity, and once he saw me teach, he could see that I shared that passion. Our shared passions are probably why he was willing to sit as one of the first interviewees for this book, and I know that he speaks of me fondly to others. I also know that he is fulfilled by teaching others. Yet I have never been able to sponsor him in turn, and I'd like that to change. If anything, doing the Sponsorship Ten reminds me of how grateful I am to know some of the people on this list, a useful outcome in and of itself.

The last column, "Opportunities to Create and Confirm," is where we get to try out our sponsorship wings. Hopefully, you will have enough information about a few of your Sponsorship Ten to be able to generate at least one or two obvious opportunities to engage in sponsorship. My friend Marie has a background in environmental science and horticulture, and she's passionate about urban planning and climate change. So passionate, in fact, that she led a nonprofit with the mission of providing free native saplings for people in the region to plant to help support native wildlife. As it turns out, I also happen to know another person who is also passionate about sustainability and works in the Sustainability and Resilience Division of Pittsburgh's Department of City Planning. The two of them almost certainly have overlapping interests and shared aspirations. Better yet, the city employee is likely aware of grant opportunities for which Marie could apply, and the program directors managing the grants would probably be excited to receive applications from a person with Marie's background and experience. Win-win-win!

A note of caution here. I would err on the side of leaving the cell blank if you're not certain of the answer in this column because inappropriate matching is costly for sponsors. Being wrong about dreams and aspirations will make it so that we will unnecessarily—and potentially damagingly—expend social capital sponsoring protégés to people or for opportunities for which they are a bad fit.

So if you are not confident of an answer for this column, this is a cue to take the time to get to know the person better, until you feel you understand their goals.

USING OUR SPONSORSHIP TEN TO
POINT US IN THE RIGHT DIRECTION

The Sponsorship Ten exercise puts into clear view many of the topics and phenomena we have discussed throughout this book. Naming specific stretch protégés encourages us to search more expansively across our social circles to identify people we have **access** to and whom we are curious to learn more about. How difficult this task is can reveal information about our own habits. Difficulty generating more than two or three stretch protégés could indicate a lack of variety in the places we spend our time; if we spend too much time in a given space or in a given social circle, it's likely we already know everyone there, making it more difficult for us to think of stretch protégés. This is a problem of **availability** and suggests that we should further diversify where we spend our time. Alternatively, if we in fact experience a great deal of physical and social-circle variety, but still have trouble identifying stretch protégés, or if the protégés we identify are homogenous on some dimension, it could be that we are not fully engaging with the variety of individuals available to us. This, then, is a problem of **approach**, suggesting that we might consider putting a bit more effort into engaging with the taciturn parent who always stands off to the side at our children's birthday parties or inviting a coworker to join the rest of the group to lunch.

In effect, an analysis of our Sponsorship Ten points us in the direction of how best to diversify our networks so as to be more inclusive. If our networks are too homogenous, is the solution to change where we spend our time, assuming that's possible? Or is it to change how we spend our time with the people we already know?

Beyond that, identifying what we admire about our Sponsorship Ten provides us with information about our standards for **activation**. But while most people's decisions about activation are based on a potential protégé's performance or capability, here we focus specifically on values and, to some extent, traits. I focus on values for multiple reasons. First, as we've discussed, having shared values is a critical component of trust. Second, focusing on values—as opposed to abilities—opens us to a wider range of individuals we might consider for sponsorship because to the extent that the performance we notice is often influenced by characteristics like someone's family income, race/ethnicity, gender identity, height, weight, and so on, people's values are not as strongly, if at all, dictated by those same characteristics. Third, seeing trends in the types of people we admire can tell us about ourselves. What do we value? How we answer that question has implications for our reputations; if it is true that we are the company that we keep, and that the people we admire tend to be people who share our values, then the very values we admire in our Sponsorship Ten are likely to be the same values for which we are or are yet to be known.

In contrast, difficulty identifying what we admire about people on our Sponsorship Ten suggests that we lack clarity on our values. Even if that's not the case, the fact is that if we don't know what we respect about others, we are unlikely to sponsor them. An alternative outcome is that we can easily identify people for our Sponsorship Ten, but what we admire is different for all of them. One possible explanation for this is that you are exceptionally easygoing and can see the good in pretty much anyone. For some, this is a laudable indication of open-mindedness and tolerance. However, the potential downside is that if you can't identify what your standards are for sponsorship, then neither will anyone else. Being seen as someone who doesn't have standards is not helpful if what we want is to be effective sponsors.

I anticipate that there are few who are truly standardless when it comes to their Sponsorship Ten. Rather, we might see that there are, in fact, trends in whom we admire, but that the characteristics we list depend on the context from which we know someone. We might list "ambitious" as an admired trait for individuals we know from work and "open-minded" for non-work-related acquaintances. One potential explanation for this difference could be that we receive much more information about our work colleagues' ambitions than our social acquaintances and the inverse for open-mindedness; maybe the conversations we have at work are much more focused than those we have outside of work. If that's the case, that's easy enough to rectify; we simply need to ask more questions and be more open with people at work. However, there's another possible explanation. Perhaps we use ambition as a standard when evaluating—which is not what we are supposed to be doing here—people we know from work, and we use open-mindedness as a standard when evaluating non-work-related acquaintances. This would be an example of having inconsistent standards.

I can already anticipate the outrage people are going to feel for my suggesting that they have inconsistent standards. I'm not trying to shame you! If anything, I see this as illustrating just how thoroughly the ideology of value extraction has permeated our culture. And lest you want to argue that it makes sense that we use different standards to evaluate—there's that word again!—potential protégés depending on the situation, recall that the generation of the Sponsorship Ten is, by design, agnostic with regard to opportunity; inclusion on the list isn't based on a specific opportunity we are sponsoring people for. It merely asks us to identify the individuals we admire but don't know well. Given that, why *not* admire ambition among those outside of work? Why *not* care about open-mindedness in work colleagues?

Finally, you may have noticed that I focused our attention solely on opportunities to Create and Confirm and not at all on

Prevention or Protection. This is because I want to steer us toward stealthy sponsorship, to think about how we can begin our sponsorship when it is still possible to sponsor in ways that are less obvious and less likely to evoke the negative reactions that many would-be sponsors fear. Stealthy sponsorship levels the playing field so that we can all be sponsors, no matter how much formal power we may have.

————

So many of us think about sponsorship from the perspective of being a protégé while neglecting the very real agency we have to act as sponsors. We want others to open doors for us and forget that we can open doors for others. I hope this book helps to challenge this asymmetry of focus and to disabuse us of the myth that sponsorship is the province of the few and the powerful. We can all open doors for others, or, if we cannot open the door directly ourselves, we can encourage others to open them.

Sponsorship is a social phenomenon in which all of us participate, whether as sponsor, as protégé, or as the audience of others' sponsorship. If that's true—and I hope I have convinced you that it is—then more of us, not just those with power but *definitely* those with power, need to be mindful of how it works and to wield it responsibly and equitably. When the right people are chosen for the right opportunities, everyone benefits: sponsor, protégé, audience, and the broader collective. The alternative—leaving sponsorship to those with power—can (and already does) contribute to a world where the powerful tend to sponsor only those who have some level of power or status already.

The more we sponsor others, the more we will be elevated in turn. Sponsoring others—giving up power—results in other people giving us status. In effect, the path to greater status is through *giving others status*. And one way to indicate that you are giving someone status is to listen to them, deeply and with genuine interest. To listen is to defer. Deference is what we give to those we respect and value.

When we ask about others' dreams and values, we say to them, "I am here. I am listening. I care about you." When we find opportunities for them to make progress toward their dreams, we implicitly tell them, "I saw and heard you. I was thinking of you." When we sponsor our protégés, we tell the audience that our protégés are worthy of respect and admiration. Good sponsors give their protégés status.

When we ask about others' challenges and problems, we say to them, "I am here. I am listening. I care about you." When we connect them with people who can help them with their challenges, we implicitly tell them, "I saw and heard you. I was thinking of you." When we find the right protégé for the right audience, we show the audience that we have thought carefully about what they need. Good sponsors give their audiences status.

To gain status, give others status.

To find sponsors, be a sponsor.

The more doors you can open for others, the more doors will be opened for you.

APPENDIX

TRUSTED TEN WORKSHEET

Whom do you trust (not family members)?
Whom would you go to if you needed help with a sensitive problem?

Name of Contact	Gender	Race/ Ethnicity	Age	Sexual Orientation	Occupation
1					
2					
3					
4					
5					
6					
7					
8					
9					
10					

* **work** = we only talk about specific work tasks, expertise-based issues
career = we only talk about career aspirations, strategies or
opportunities for promotion
social = we only talk about family/personal things

Education (HS, BA, MA, PhD, etc.)	Marital Status	Religious Affiliation	Disability (y/n)	**Multiplexity** What do you talk about with this contact (work, career, social, all of the above)*?	**Overlap** Does this person know another person who is also on this list? If yes, who?

Exercise based on Uzzi (2005) adapted by R Chow (2024)

STRETCH SPONSORSHIP TEN WORKSHEET

Who are people you admire and respect,
but who are not on your Trusted Ten?

Name of Contact	Gender	Race/ Ethnicity	Age	Sexual Orientation	Occupation	Education (HS, BA, MA, PhD, etc.)
1						
2						
3						
4						
5						
6						
7						
8						
9						
10						

Qualities I Admire	Strengths/Areas of Expertise	Aspirations/Dreams What is this person's *why*?	Opportunities to Create & Confirm Who in your network should know about this person?

Exercise based on Uzzi (2005) adapted by R Chow (2024)

ACKNOWLEDGMENTS

I am immensely grateful for the door-openers in my life who have Showed me off, Told others about me, and Protected me when I wasn't there to speak for myself.

This book would not exist if it hadn't been for Leanne Meyer putting my name forward to lead the Executive Leadership Academy and for Evan Frazier's willingness to take a chance on an untested (and non-Black!) faculty member. Cohort One, thank you for letting me into your lives at a critical moment. I will never forget you. Susan Caplan, you make this work seem effortless. I see you.

Amy Gallo's uplift and encouragement was the galvanizing force I needed to start working on this book in earnest. Katy Milkman introduced me to the incandescent Celeste Fine, who immediately understood what I wanted to say and, more importantly, imagined for me greater aspirations than I dreamed for myself.

Colleen Lawrie championed the book to the team at PublicAffairs and pushed to give me the space I needed to make this book the best it could be. I am forever grateful for your unwillingness to compromise on what you knew I could deliver.

Keith Meatto patiently transitioned me from writing like an academic to writing like a normal person. Teaching someone with existing bad habits is harder than teaching someone with no habits at all; thank you for listening and refocusing my efforts.

The amazing team at Hachette Book Group, Jenny Lee and Brieana Garcia, and the DEY Media team, Rimjhim Dey, Andrew

Desio, and Jessica Zagacki, combined their marketing and publicity efforts to sponsor me in the extreme!

Team Onagadori's members generously shared their wisdom and connections; I hope to be able to contribute in turn.

To the interviewees who agreed to share their stories with me: thank you. I hope I have done your stories justice.

I would not be a professor if it were not for the mentorship and sponsorship of numerous amazing academics: Linda Babcock, Mark Fichman, Lori Holt, Brian Lowery, Elizabeth Mullen, Nathan Pettit, Katherine Phillips, Ray Reagans, Denise Rousseau, Lara Tiedens, Laurie Weingart, Batia Weisenfeld, and Anita Williams Woolley. Thank you so much for your guidance, friendship, and protection.

A special shout-out to the best academic family I could have asked for (in order of siblinghood): Eric Knowles, Miguel Unzueta, Caitlin Hogan, Aneeta Rattan, Shantal Marshall, Taylor Phillips, Sora Jun.

Thank you to the students who have taught me: Nazli Bhatia, Jin Wook Chang, and Elizabeth Campbell. I have learned so much from each of you. And when I didn't think I could do it anymore, Taqua Elleithy and Jose Cervantes showed me that I can, in fact, keep going.

Through life's vicissitudes, these friends have been constants: Sara Blumenstein, I-Chant Chiang, Brian Kovak, Kristen Kovak, Sarah Kuehn, Jeff Markel, and Carol Robinson. You have my undying gratitude for sticking with me through thick and thin.

No acknowledgments would be complete without recognition of our first sponsors: our parents. But I would go back further to recognize the sacrifices of my maternal and paternal grandparents, who were willing to let my parents go to the United States for college and to pursue the opportunities available only in a different country. Now that I am a mother, I cannot fathom the strength it must have taken them to let their children go so far away, not knowing when they would see them next.

Immigrant parents are the ultimate sponsors; they step into the unknown so that they, but more often, their children, can go and be seen in the spaces where the opportunities are. Thank you, Mom and Dad, for giving me the best opportunities in life. Thank you, too, to Vincent, for keeping things real.

And last (but only to take advantage of the peak end effect), Jeff, you are the gravitational force who holds our family together. You make me my best self. ILYMED.

BIBLIOGRAPHY

INTRODUCTION

Brands, Raina A., and Martin Kilduff. "Just Like a Woman? Effects of Gender-Biased Perceptions of Friendship Network Brokerage on Attributions and Performance." *Organization Science* 25, no. 5 (2014): 1530–1548.

Gregory, Sean. "How Kim Ng, MLB's First Female GM, Finally Got the Top Job." *Time*, March 3, 2021. https://time.com/5943601/kim-ng-fi.

Kepner, Tyler. "With Jeter and the Marlins, an Awkward Marriage Ends in Divorce." *New York Times*, February 28, 2022.

"Marlins GM Kim Ng Said Some Interviews Likely Weren't on the 'Up-and-Up' Before Historic New Role." NBC News, November 16, 2020. www.nbcnews.com/news/us-news/marlins-gm-kim-ng-said-some-interviews-likely-weren-t-n1247917.

Mengel, Friederike. "Gender Differences in Networking." *Economic Journal* 130, no. 630 (2020): 1842–1873.

Palmer, Joseph. "The First Female GM in Baseball Is Leading the Marlins' Play-off Charge." *Guardian*, July 27, 2023. www.theguardian.com/sport/2023/jul/27/trailblazer-kim-ng-is-leading-the-marlins-mlb-playoff-charge.

Sheinin, Dave. "Ng Breaks Gender Barrier, Makes Baseball History." *Washington Post*, November 14, 2020. www-proquest-com.cmu.idm.oclc.org/newspapers/ng-breaks-gender-barrier-makes-baseball-history/docview/2460203800/se-2.

CHAPTER 1: HOW TO NETWORK LIKE A SPONSOR

Anderson, Cameron, and Gavin J. Kilduff. "The Pursuit of Status in Social Groups." *Current Directions in Psychological Science* 18, no. 5 (2009): 295–298.

Blader, Steven L., and Ya-Ru Chen. "Differentiating the Effects of Status and Power: A Justice Perspective." *Journal of Personality and Social Psychology* 102, no. 5 (2012): 994–1014.

Brands, Raina A., and Martin Kilduff. "Just Like a Woman? Effects of Gender-Biased Perceptions of Friendship Network Brokerage on Attributions and Performance." *Organization Science* 25, no. 5 (2014): 1530–1548.

Burt, Ronald S. "Structural Holes and Good Ideas." *American Journal of Sociology* 110, no. 2 (2004): 349–399.

———. "Structural Holes Versus Network Closure as Social Capital." *Social Capital* (2017): 31–56.

Cross, Rob, and Robert J. Thomas. "Managing Yourself: A Smarter Way to Network." *Harvard Business Review* (September 7, 2017). https://hbr.org/2011/07/managing-yourself-a-smarter-way-to-network.

Dannals, Jennifer E., Julian J. Zlatev, Nir Halevy, and Margaret A. Neale. "The Dynamics of Gender and Alternatives in Negotiation." *Journal of Applied Psychology* (January 2021). https://doi.org/10.1037/apl0000867.

Ellwardt, Lea, Giuseppe Joe Labianca, and Rafael Wittek. "Who Are the Objects of Positive and Negative Gossip at Work? A Social Network Perspective on Workplace Gossip." *Social Networks* 34, no. 2 (2012): 193–205.

Fragale, Alison R., Jennifer R. Overbeck, and Margaret A. Neale. "Resources Versus Respect: Social Judgments Based on Targets' Power and Status Positions." *Journal of Experimental Social Psychology* 47, no. 4 (2011): 767–775.

Granovetter, Mark S. "The Strength of Weak Ties." *American Journal of Sociology* 78, no. 6 (1973): 1360–1380.

Grant, Adam. *Give and Take: A Revolutionary Approach to Success.* New York: Penguin, 2013.

Gruenfeld, Deborah H., M. Ena Inesi, Joe C. Magee, and Adam D. Galinsky. "Power and the Objectification of Social Targets." *Journal of Personality and Social Psychology* 95, no. 1 (2008): 111–127.

Haegele, Ingrid. "Talent Hoarding in Organizations." ArXiv, June 30, 2022. https://arxiv.org/abs/2206.15098.

Jazaieri, H., M. Logli Allison, B. Campos, R. C. Young, and D. Keltner. "Content, Structure, and Dynamics of Personal Reputation: The Role of Trust and Status Potential Within Social Networks." *Group Processes & Intergroup Relations* 22 no. 7 (2019): 964–983. https://doi.org/10.1177/1368430218806056.

Keller, J. R., and Kathryn Dlugos. "Advance 'Em to Attract 'Em: How Promotions Influence Applications in Internal Talent Markets." *Academy of Management Journal* 66, no. 6 (2023): 1831–1859.

McGinn, Kathleen L., and Nicole Tempest. "Heidi Roizen." Harvard Business School Case 800-228 (2000). www.hbs.edu/faculty/Pages/item.aspx?num=26880.

Peters, Kim, Jolanda Jetten, Dagmar Radova, and Kacie Austin. "Gossiping About Deviance: Evidence That Deviance Spurs the Gossip That Builds Bonds." *Psychological Science* 28, no. 11 (2017): 1610–1619.

Richeson, Jennifer A., and Nalini Ambady. "Effects of Situational Power on Automatic Racial Prejudice." *Journal of Experimental Social Psychology* 39, no. 2 (2003): 177–183.

Slavina, Vicki. "How to Be Remembered: A Q&A with Silicon Valley's Greatest Connector, Heidi Roizen." The Muse, January 16, 2013. www.themuse .com/advice/how-to-be-remembered-a-qa-with-silicon-valleys-greatest -connector-heidi-roizen.

Swaab, Neil. "Interview: Kyle T. Webster." *Business of Illustration* (November 3, 2014). http://businessofillustration.com/interview-kyle-t-webster/.

Webster, Kyle T. "Help Wanted." Accidental-Expert.com, September 14, 2023. https://accidental-expert.com/p/help-wanted.

CHAPTER 2: A MATTER OF TRUST

Allen, Tammy D., Lillian T. Eby, Mark L. Poteet, Elizabeth Lentz, and Lizzette Lima. "Career Benefits Associated with Mentoring for Protégés: A Meta-analysis." *Journal of Applied Psychology* 89, no. 1 (2004): 127–136.

Associated Press and Kyle Potter. "Couple's Arranged Marriage Turned into 19-Year 'Love Story.'" *Times Herald Online*, August 16, 2017. www .timesheraldonline.com/2017/08/16/couples-arranged-marriage-turned -into-19-year-love-story/.

Blau, Peter. *Exchange and Power in Social Life.* New York: Routledge, 2017.

Considine, Bob. "Still Together, 10 Years After Arranged Mall Marriage." Today .com, June 13, 2008. www.today.com/news/still-together-10-years-after -arranged-mall-marriage-wbna25121427.

Gruenfeld, Deborah H., M. Ena Inesi, Joe C. Magee, and Adam D. Galinsky. "Power and the Objectification of Social Targets." *Journal of Personality and Social Psychology* 95, no. 1 (2008): 111–127.

Hardy, Charlie L., and Mark Van Vugt. "Nice Guys Finish First: The Competitive Altruism Hypothesis." *Personality and Social Psychology Bulletin* 32, no. 10 (2006): 1402–1413.

Ibarra, Herminia, Nancy M. Carter, and Christine Silva. "Why Men Still Get More Promotions Than Women." *Harvard Business Review* (September 7, 2010). https://hbr.org/2010/09/why-men-still-get-more-promotions-than -women.

Moriarity, Michelle. "Student's Friends Will Pick His Bride." *Minnesota Daily*, June 4, 1998. https://mndaily.com/215631/uncategorized/students-friends -will-pick-his-bride/.

Murrell, Audrey J., Stacy Blake-Beard, and David M. Porter Jr. "The Importance of Peer Mentoring, Identity Work and Holding Environments: A Study of African American Leadership Development." *International Journal of Environmental Research and Public Health* 18, no. 9 (2021): 4920.

Murrell, Audrey J., and Jeannette E. South-Paul. "The Emerging Power of Peer Mentoring Within Academic Medicine." In *Mentoring Diverse Leaders*, edited by Audrey J. Murrell and Stacy Blake-Bear, 85–103. New York: Routledge, 2017.

Overbeck, Jennifer R., and Bernadette Park. "When Power Does Not Corrupt: Superior Individuation Processes Among Powerful Perceivers." *Journal of Personality and Social Psychology* 81, no. 4 (2001): 549–565.

Smith, Mary Lynn. "'Greatest Love Story' Began with Arranged Marriage at Mall of America, Ended Too Soon." *Minnesota Star Tribune*, May 22, 2018. www.startribune.com/david-weinlick-whose-buddies-picked-his-bride-at -mall-of-america-for-instant-wedding-dies/483342201/.

Smith, Sandra Susan. "'Don't Put My Name on It': Social Capital Activation and Job-Finding Assistance Among the Black Urban Poor." *American Journal of Sociology* 111, no. 1 (2005): 1–57.

Tost, Leigh Plunkett, and Hana Huang Johnson. "The Prosocial Side of Power: How Structural Power over Subordinates Can Promote Social Responsibility." *Organizational Behavior and Human Decision Processes* 152 (2019): 25–46.

CHAPTER 3: SMALL-TOWN LIVING IN A BIG CITY

Aiello, McKenna. "George Clooney Once Gave 14 of His Best Friends $1 Million Each, Rande Gerber Says." *E! Online*, December 13, 2017. www .eonline.com/news/899813/george-clooney-once-gave-14-of-his-best -friends-1-million-each-rande-gerber-says.

Apstein, Stephanie. "Her Journey to Become MLB's First Woman GM Is Just the Beginning." *Sports Illustrated*, March 23, 2021. www.si.com/mlb /2021/03/23/marlins-kim-ng-history-daily-cover.

Botelho, Tristan L., and Marina Gertsberg. "The Disciplining Effect of Status: Evaluator Status Awards and Observed Gender Bias in Evaluations." *Management Science* 68, no. 7 (2022): 5311–5329.

Burt, Ronald S. "The Network Structure of Social Capital." *Research in Organizational Behavior* 22 (2000): 345–423.

Burt, Ronald S., and Marc Knez. "Kinds of Third-Party Effects on Trust." *Rationality and Society* 7, no. 3 (1995): 255–292.

Cialdini, Robert B. *Influence: The Psychology of Persuasion*. Rev. ed. New York: HarperCollins, 2007.

Coleman, James S. "Social Capital in the Creation of Human Capital." *American Journal of Sociology* 94 (1988): 95–120.

Fahrenthold, David A., and Ryan Mac. "Elon Musk Has a Giant Charity. Its Money Stays Close to Home." *New York Times*, March 10, 2024. www.nytimes .com/2024/03/10/us/elon-musk-charity.html?searchResultPosition=1.

Feinsand, Mark. "Get to Know Kim Ng, the Marlins' 'Conductor.'" MLB.com, April 26, 2022. www.mlb.com/news/executive-access-conversation-with-marlins-general-manager-kim-ng.

Feld, Scott L. "Structural Embeddedness and Stability of Interpersonal Relations." *Social Networks* 19, no. 1 (1997): 91–95.

Gargiulo, Martin, and Mario Benassi. "Trapped in Your Own Net? Network Cohesion, Structural Holes, and the Adaptation of Social Capital." *Organization Science* 11, no. 2 (2000): 183–196. https://doi.org/10.1287/orsc.11.2.183.12514.

"George Clooney—The Enough Project." The Enough Project, 2017. https://enoughproject.org/upstanders/celebrity/george-clooney.

Gladwell, Malcolm. "In the Air." *New Yorker*, May 5, 2008. www.newyorker.com/magazine/2008/05/12/in-the-air.

Granovetter, Mark S. "The Strength of Weak Ties." *American Journal of Sociology* 78, no. 6 (1973): 1360–1380.

Johnson, Ted. "The Evolution of Celebrity Diplomacy." *Politico*, March 26, 2009. www.politico.com/story/2009/03/the-evolution-of-celebrity-diplomacy-020489.

Krisher, Tom, Michael Liedtke, and Adam Geller. "Elon Musk, an Erratic Visionary, Revels in Contradiction." Associated Press, May 11, 2022. https://apnews.com/article/elon-musk-spacex-technology-2e6b0f2c2f70fdd07f853169e3515e3b.

Mac, Ryan, Tiffany Hsu, and Benjamin Mullin. "Twitter's New Chief Eases into the Hot Seat." *New York Times*, June 29, 2023. www.nytimes.com/2023/06/29/technology/twitter-ceo-linda-yaccarino.html.

Malik, Tariq. "SpaceX's Elon Musk Donates $50 Million to Inspiration4 Spaceflight Fundraiser for St. Jude Children's Research Hospital." Space.com, September 19, 2021. www.space.com/elon-musk-inspiration4-st-jude-spacex-donation.

Masters, Kim. "Linda Yaccarino's Very Unmerry X Mess." *Hollywood Reporter*, November 29, 2023. www.hollywoodreporter.com/business/business-news/linda-yaccarino-elon-musk-x-advertisers-1235683997/.

Nguyen, Vi-An. "George Clooney Uses Nespresso Money for Satellite to Spy on Sudan Dictator." *Parade*, August 1, 2013. https://parade.com/59699/viannguyen/george-clooney-uses-nespresso-money-for-satellite-to-spy-on-sudan-dictator/.

Putnam, Robert D. *Bowling Alone: The Collapse and Revival of American Community.* New York: Simon and Schuster, 2000.

Thai, Xuan. "Miami Marlins GM Kim Ng's Journey to the Postseason." ESPN.com, October 3, 2023. www.espn.com/espn/print?id=38550785.

Wong, Sze-Sze, and Wai Fong Boh. "Leveraging the Ties of Others to Build a Reputation for Trustworthiness Among Peers." *Academy of Management Journal* 53, no. 1 (2010): 129–148.

CHAPTER 4: WE DON'T KNOW WHO WE DON'T KNOW

Anicich, Eric M., Jon M. Jachimowicz, Merrick R. Osborne, and L. Taylor Phillips. "Structuring Local Environments to Avoid Racial Diversity: Anxiety Drives Whites' Geographical and Institutional Self-Segregation Preferences." *Journal of Experimental Social Psychology* 95 (2021).

Brescoll, Victoria L. "Leading with Their Hearts? How Gender Stereotypes of Emotion Lead to Biased Evaluations of Female Leaders." *Leadership Quarterly* 27, no. 3 (2016): 415–428.

Collins, Hanne K., Serena F. Hagerty, Jordi Quoidbach, Michael I. Norton, and Alison Wood Brooks. "Relational Diversity in Social Portfolios Predicts Well-Being." *Proceedings of the National Academy of Sciences* 119, no. 43 (2022). https://doi.org/10.1073/pnas.2120668119.

Cox, Daniel, Juhem Navarro-Rivera, and Robert P. Jones. "Race, Religion, and Political Affiliation of Americans' Core Social Networks." PRRI, 2016. www.prri.org/research/poll-race-religion-politics-americans-social-networks/.

Epley, Nicholas, and Juliana Schroeder. "Mistakenly Seeking Solitude." *Journal of Experimental Psychology: General* 143, no. 5 (2014): 1980–1999.

Kossinets, Gueorgi, and Duncan J. Watts. "Origins of Homophily in an Evolving Social Network." *American Journal of Sociology* 115, no. 2 (2009): 405–450.

Marshburn, Christopher K., Kevin J. Cochran, Elinor Flynn, and Linda J. Levine. "Workplace Anger Costs Women Irrespective of Race." *Frontiers in Psychology* 11 (2020).

McPherson, Miller, Lynn Smith-Lovin, and James M. Cook. "Birds of a Feather: Homophily in Social Networks." *Annual Review of Sociology* 27, no. 1 (2001): 415–444.

Mollica, Kelly A., Barbara Gray, and Linda K. Treviño. "Racial Homophily and Its Persistence in Newcomers' Social Networks." *Organization Science* 14, no. 2 (2003): 123–136. https://doi.org/10.1287/orsc.14.2.123.14994.

Moody, James. "Race, School Integration, and Friendship Segregation in America." *American Journal of Sociology* 107, no. 3 (2001): 679–716.

Motro, Daphna, Jonathan B. Evans, Aleksander P. J. Ellis, and Lehman Benson III. "Race and Reactions to Women's Expressions of Anger at Work: Examining the Effects of the 'Angry Black Woman' Stereotype." *Journal of Applied Psychology* 107, no. 1 (2022): 142–152.

Obukhova, Elena, and Adam M. Kleinbaum. "Scouting and Schmoozing: A Gender Difference in Networking During Job Search." *Academy of Management Discoveries* 8, no. 2 (2022): 203–223.

Reagans, Ray. "Close Encounters: Analyzing How Social Similarity and Propinquity Contribute to Strong Network Connections." *Organization Science* 22, no. 4 (2011): 835–849. https://doi.org/10.1287/orsc.1100.0587.

Salerno, Jessica M., Liana C. Peter-Hagene, and Alexander C. V. Jay. "Women and African Americans Are Less Influential When They Express Anger During Group Decision Making." *Group Processes & Intergroup Relations* 22, no. 1 (2019): 57–79.

Santiago, Rawn, Nchopia Nwokoma, and Jasmin Crentsil. "Investigating the Implications of Code-Switching and Assimilating at Work for African American Professionals." *Journal of Business Diversity* 21, no. 4 (2021).

Schroeder, Juliana, Donald Lyons, and Nicholas Epley. "Hello, Stranger? Pleasant Conversations Are Preceded by Concerns About Starting One." *Journal of Experimental Psychology: General* 151, no. 5 (2022): 1141–1153.

Shelton, J. Nicole, and Jennifer A. Richeson. "Intergroup Contact and Pluralistic Ignorance." *Journal of Personality and Social Psychology* 88, no. 1 (2005): 91–107.

US Census Bureau. "2016–2020 American Community Survey 5-Year Estimates." American FactFinder.

———. "Current Population Survey, 1968 to 2023 Annual Social and Economic Supplements." American FactFinder.

Verbrugge, Lois M. "Multiplexity in Adult Friendships." *Social Forces* 57, no. 4 (1979): 1286–1309.

Yang, Yang, Nitesh V. Chawla, and Brian Uzzi. "A Network's Gender Composition and Communication Pattern Predict Women's Leadership Success." *Proceedings of the National Academy of Sciences* 116, no. 6 (2019): 2033–2038. https://doi.org/10.1073/pnas.1721438116.

Yoshino, Kenji. *Covering: The Hidden Assault on Our Civil Rights*. New York: Random House Trade Paperbacks, 2007.

Zou, Linda X., and Sapna Cheryan. "Diversifying Neighborhoods and Schools Engender Perceptions of Foreign Cultural Threat Among White Americans." *Journal of Experimental Psychology: General* 151, no. 5 (2022): 1115–1131.

CHAPTER 5: THE PROBLEM WITH MERIT

Benson, Alan, Danielle Li, and Kelly Shue. "Potential and the Gender Promotions Gap." SSRN, April 2, 2024. https://papers.ssrn.com/sol3/papers.cfm?abstract_id=4747175.

Biernat, Monica, and Melvin Manis. "Shifting Standards and Stereotype-Based Judgments." *Journal of Personality and Social Psychology* 66, no. 1 (1994): 5–20. https://doi.org/10.1037/0022-3514.66.1.5.

Biernat, Monica, and Theresa K. Vescio. "She Swings, She Hits, She's Great,

She's Benched: Implications of Gender-Based Shifting Standards for Judgment and Behavior." *Personality and Social Psychology Bulletin* 28, no. 1 (2002): 66–77. https://doi.org/10.1177/0146167202281006.

Brandon, D. P., and A. B. Hollingshead. "Transactive Memory Systems in Organizations: Matching Tasks, Expertise, and People." *Organization Science* 15, no. 6 (2004): 633–644.

Brener, Susan A., Willem E. Frankenhuis, Ethan S. Young, and Bruce J. Ellis. "Social Class, Sex, and the Ability to Recognize Emotions: The Main Effect Is in the Interaction." *Personality and Social Psychology Bulletin* (April 2023). https://doi.org/10.1177/01461672231159775.

Castilla, Emilio J., and Stephen Benard. "The Paradox of Meritocracy in Organizations." *Administrative Science Quarterly* 55, no. 4 (2010): 543–676. https://doi.org/10.2189/asqu.2010.55.4.543.

Castilla, Emilio J., and Aruna Ranganathan. "The Production of Merit: How Managers Understand and Apply Merit in the Workplace." *Organization Science* 31, no. 4 (2020). https://doi.org/10.1287/orsc.2019.1335.

Dobbin, Frank, and Alexandra Kalev. "Why Diversity Programs Fail." *Harvard Business Review* 94, no. 7 (2016).

Ginther, Donna K., and Kathy J. Hayes. "Gender Differences in Salary and Promotion in the Humanities." *American Economic Review* 89, no. 2 (1999): 397–402.

Jachimowicz, Jon M., Andreas Wihler, and Adam D. Galinsky. "My Boss' Passion Matters as Much as My Own: The Interpersonal Dynamics of Passion Are a Critical Driver of Performance Evaluations." *Journal of Organizational Behavior* 43, no. 9 (2022): 1496–1515.

Lord, Charles G., Lee Ross, and Mark R. Lepper. "Biased Assimilation and Attitude Polarization: The Effects of Prior Theories on Subsequently Considered Evidence." *Journal of Personality and Social Psychology* 37, no. 11 (1979): 2098–2109.

Moreland, Richard L., Linda Argote, and Ranjani Krishnan. "Socially Shared Cognition at Work: Transactive Memory and Group Performance." In *What's Social About Social Cognition? Research on Socially Shared Cognition in Small Groups*, edited by J. L. Nye and M. Brower, 57–84. Thousand Oaks, CA: Sage, 1996.

Rawls, John. *A Theory of Justice*. London: Belknap Press, 2005.

Rua-Gomez, Carla, Gianluca Carnabuci, and Martin C. Goossen. "Reaching for the Stars: How Gender Influences the Formation of High-Status Collaboration Ties." *Academy of Management Journal* 66, no. 5 (2023): 1501–1528.

"Tenure." AAUP.org, 2016. www.aaup.org/issues/tenure.

Wang, Ke, Erica R. Bailey, and Jon M. Jachimowicz. "The Passionate Pygmalion Effect: Passionate Employees Attain Better Outcomes in Part Because of More Preferential Treatment by Others." *Journal of Experimental Social Psychology* 101 (2022).

Woolley, Anita Williams, Christopher F. Chabris, Alex Pentland, Nada Hashmi, and Thomas W. Malone. "Evidence for a Collective Intelligence Factor in the Performance of Human Groups." *Science* 330, no. 6004 (2010): 686–688. https://doi.org/10.1126/science.1193147.

CHAPTER 6: WHAT IT MEANS TO SHARE

Aron, Arthur, Edward Melinat, Elaine N. Aron, Robert Darrin Vallone, and Renee J. Bator. "The Experimental Generation of Interpersonal Closeness: A Procedure and Some Preliminary Findings." *Personality and Social Psychology Bulletin* 23, no. 4 (1997): 363–377. https://doi.org/10.1177/0146167297234003.

Clawson, James G. "Active Listening." SSRN Electronic Journal (2006). https://doi.org/10.2139/ssrn.910376.

Echterhoff, Gerald, and Bjarne Schmalbach. "How Shared Reality Is Created in Interpersonal Communication." *Current Opinion in Psychology* 23 (October 2018): 57–61. https://doi.org/10.1016/j.copsyc.2017.12.005.

Fisher, R., and W. Ury. *Getting to Yes: Negotiating Agreement Without Giving In.* 2nd ed. Boston: Houghton Mifflin, 1991.

frozeneskimo02. "Today I Had One of the Best Conversations I've Ever Had." Reddit.com, May 29, 2022. www.reddit.com/r/CasualConversation/comments/v0166g/today_i_had_one_of_the_best_conversations_ive.

Good, Thomas L., Natasha Sterzinger, and Alyson Lavigne. "Expectation Effects: Pygmalion and the Initial 20 Years of Research." *Educational Research and Evaluation* 24, nos. 3–5 (2018): 99–123. https://doi.org/10.1080/13803611.2018.1548817.

Itzchakov, Guy, Kenneth G. DeMarree, Avraham N. Kluger, and Yaara Turjeman-Levi. "The Listener Sets the Tone: High-Quality Listening Increases Attitude Clarity and Behavior-Intention Consequences." *Personality and Social Psychology Bulletin* 44, no. 5 (2018): 762–778. https://doi.org/10.1177/0146167217747874.

Kluger, Avraham N., and Guy Itzchakov. "The Power of Listening at Work." *Annual Review of Organizational Psychology and Organizational Behavior* 9, no. 1 (2022): 121–146. https://doi.org/10.1146/annurev-orgpsych-012420-091013.

Mayer, Roger C., James H. Davis, and F. David Schoorman. "An Integrative Model of Organizational Trust." *Academy of Management Review* 20, no. 3 (1995): 709–734.

Reis, H. T., and B. C. Patrick. "Attachment and Intimacy: Component Processes." In *Social Psychology: Handbook of Basic Principles*, edited by E. T. Higgins and A. W. Kruglanski, 523–563. New York: Guilford Press, 1996.

Rosenthal, Robert, and Kermit L. Fode. "The Effect of Experimenter Bias on the Performance of the Albino Rat." *Behavioral Science* 8, no. 3 (1963): 183–189. https://doi.org/10.1002/bs.3830080302.

Rosenthal, Robert, and Lenore Jacobson. "Pygmalion in the Classroom." *Urban Review* 3, no. 1 (1968): 16–20.

Rossignac-Milon, Maya, Niall Bolger, Katherine S. Zee, Erica J. Boothby, and E. Tory Higgins. "Merged Minds: Generalized Shared Reality in Dyadic Relationships." *Journal of Personality and Social Psychology* (July 2020). https://doi.org/10.1037/pspi0000266.

Rousseau, Denise M., Sim B. Sitkin, Ronald S. Burt, and Colin Camerer. "Not So Different After All: A Cross-discipline View of Trust." *Academy of Management Review* 23, no. 3 (1998): 393–404.

Tamir, D. I., and J. P. Mitchell. "Disclosing Information About the Self Is Intrinsically Rewarding." *Proceedings of the National Academy of Sciences* 109, no. 21 (2012): 8038–8043. https://doi.org/10.1073/pnas.12021 29109.

Zander, Rosamund Stone. *The Art of Possibility: Transforming Professional and Personal Life*. Boston: Harvard Business School Press, 2014.

CHAPTER 7: THE DIFFERENT FORMS OF SPONSORSHIP

Anderson, Cameron, and Gavin J. Kilduff. "The Pursuit of Status in Social Groups." *Current Directions in Psychological Science* 18, no. 5 (2009): 295–298. https://doi.org/10.1111/j.1467-8721.2009.01655.x.

Anderson, Cameron, Sanjay Srivastava, Jennifer S. Beer, Sandra E. Spataro, and Jennifer A. Chatman. "Knowing Your Place: Self-Perceptions of Status in Face-to-Face Groups." *Journal of Personality and Social Psychology* 91, no. 6 (2006): 1094–1110. https://doi.org/10.1037/0022-3514.91.6.1094.

Babcock, Linda, Brenda Peyser, Lise Vesterlund, and Laurie Weingart. *The No Club: Putting a Stop to Women's Dead-End Work*. New York: Simon and Schuster, 2022.

Babcock, Linda, Maria P. Recalde, Lise Vesterlund, and Laurie Weingart. "Gender Differences in Accepting and Receiving Requests for Tasks with Low Promotability." *American Economic Review* 107, no. 3 (2017): 714–747.

Blake-Beard, Stacy, Melissa L. Bayne, Faye J. Crosby, and Carol B. Muller. "Matching by Race and Gender in Mentoring Relationships: Keeping Our Eyes on the Prize." *Journal of Social Issues* 67, no. 3 (2011): 622–643. https://doi.org/10.1111/j.1540-4560.2011.01717.x.

Bolino, Mark C., K. Michele Kacmar, William H. Turnley, and J. Bruce Gilstrap. "A Multi-level Review of Impression Management Motives and Behaviors." *Journal of Management* 34, no. 6 (2008): 1080–1109. https://doi.org/10.1177/0149206308324325.

Bolino, Mark, David Long, and William Turnley. "Impression Management in Organizations: Critical Questions, Answers, and Areas for Future Research." *Annual Review of Organizational Psychology and Organizational Behavior* 3, no. 1 (2016): 377–406. https://doi.org/10.1146/annurev-org psych-041015-062337.

Fischenich, Mark. "Eye on the World: Noted Journalist Thomas Friedman at Gustavus." *Mankato Free Press*, May 1, 2019. www.mankatofreepress.com /news/local_news/eye-on-the-world-noted-journalist-thomas-friedman-at -gustavus/article_18a0e3ba-6c65-11e9-a96c-2fce20e4b09d.html.

Flynn, Francis J., Ray E. Reagans, Emily T. Amanatullah, and Daniel R. Ames. "Helping One's Way to the Top: Self-Monitors Achieve Status by Helping Others and Knowing Who Helps Whom." *Journal of Personality and Social Psychology* 91, no. 6 (2006): 1123–1137. https://doi.org/10.1037/0022 -3514.91.6.1123.

Gallen, Yana, and Melanie Wasserman. "Does Information Affect Homophily?" *Journal of Public Economics* 222 (June 2023). https://doi.org/10.1016/j .jpubeco.2023.104876.

Kellermann, Kathy. "A Goal-Directed Approach to Gaining Compliance: Relating Differences Among Goals to Differences in Behaviors." *Communication Research* 31, no. 4 (2004): 397–445.

Owens, Jayanti. "Double Jeopardy: Teacher Biases, Racialized Organizations, and the Production of Racial/Ethnic Disparities in School Discipline." *American Sociological Review* 87, no. 6 (2022): 1007–1048.

Pedulla, David S., and Devah Pager. "Race and Networks in the Job Search Process." *American Sociological Review* 84, no. 6 (2019): 983–1012.

Press, Valerie G., Megan Huisingh-Scheetz, and Julie Oyler. "#SheForShe: Increasing Nominations Significantly Increased Institutional Awards for Deserving Academic Women." *Journal of General Internal Medicine* 36, no. 9 (2021): 2865–2866. https://doi.org/10.1007/s11606-020-06446-1.

Reeves, Arin. "Written in Black & White: Exploring Confirmation Bias in Racialized Perceptions of Writing Skills." Nextions, April 1, 2014. https: //nextions.com/insights/perspectives/written-in-black-white-exploring -confirmation-bias-in-racialized-perceptions-of-writing-skills/.

Rosenthal, Robert, and Lenore Jacobson. "Pygmalion in the Classroom." *Urban Review* 3, no. 1 (1968): 16–20.

"Thomas L. Friedman Official Biography." Thomas L. Friedman, n.d. www .thomaslfriedman.com/official-bio/.

CHAPTER 8: TO CREATE AND CONFIRM IS TO SHOW AND TELL

Ashoori, Minoo, Eric Schmidbauer, and Axel Stock. "Exclusivity as a Signal of Quality in a Market with Word-of-Mouth Communication." *Review of Marketing Science* 18, no. 1 (2020): 99–115. https://doi.org/10.1515/roms-2020-0022.

Bain, Kristin, Tamar A. Kreps, Nathan L. Meikle, and Elizabeth R. Tenney. "Amplifying Voice in Organizations." *Academy of Management Journal* 64, no. 4 (2021): 1288–1312. https://doi.org/10.5465/amj.2018.0621.

Boykin-Patterson, Eboni. "I'm Conan O'Brien's Assistant of 13 Years. I Nap on the Job, Expense Things I Shouldn't, and Talk Back—and I'll Probably Work for Him Forever." *Business Insider*, December 18, 2022. www.businessinsider.com/conan-obrien-assistant-sona-movsesian-family-job-podcast-2022-8.

Eilperin, Juliet. "White House Women Want to Be in the Room Where It Happens." *Washington Post*, September 13, 2016.

Elias, Naomi. "The Case for Meh Ambition." The Cut, July 19, 2022. www.thecut.com/2022/07/sona-movsesian-worlds-worst-assistant-conan-obrien.html.

"Khan Academy: Sal Khan." NPR, September 21, 2020. www.npr.org/2020/09/18/914394221/khan-academy-sal-khan.

McClean, Elizabeth J., Sean R. Martin, Kyle J. Emich, and Col Todd Woodruff. "The Social Consequences of Voice: An Examination of Voice Type and Gender on Status and Subsequent Leader Emergence." *Academy of Management Journal* 61, no. 5 (2018): 1869–1891.

Nothaft, Patrick. "Derek Jeter's 'The Captain' Documentary Part 1 Sheds Light on Good, Bad of Kalamazoo Upbringing." *Mlive*, July 20, 2022. www.mlive.com/sports/2022/07/derek-jeters-the-captain-documentary-part-1-sheds-light-on-good-bad-of-kalamazoo-upbringing.html.

Olney, Buster. "Derek Jeter: The Pride of Kalamazoo." *New York Times*, April 4, 1999. www.nytimes.com/1999/04/04/sports/1999-baseball-preview-derek-jeter-the-pride-of-kalamazoo.html.

Pfeffer, Jeffrey, Christina T. Fong, Robert B. Cialdini, and Rebecca R. Portnoy. "Overcoming the Self-Promotion Dilemma: Interpersonal Attraction and Extra Help as a Consequence of Who Sings One's Praises." *Personality and Social Psychology Bulletin* 32, no. 10 (2006): 1362–1374. https://doi.org/10.1177/0146167206290337.

Podolny, Joel M. "Networks as the Pipes and Prisms of the Market." *American Journal of Sociology* 107, no. 1 (2001): 33–60. https://doi.org/10.1086/323038.

Rashotte, Vivian. "Sona Movsesian Shares the Hilarious Realities of Being Conan O'Brien's Assistant." CBC, August 23, 2022. www.cbc.ca/radio/q/tuesday-aug-23-2022-sona-movsesian-matthew-mcconaughey-and-more-1.6558575/sona-movsesian-shares-the-hilarious-realities-of-being-conan-o-brien-s-assistant-1.6559464.

Rudman, Laurie A. "Self-Promotion as a Risk Factor for Women: The Costs and Benefits of Counterstereotypical Impression Management." *Journal*

of Personality and Social Psychology 74, no. 3 (1998): 629–645. https://doi
.org/10.1037/0022-3514.74.3.629.

Wayne, Sandy J., Jiaqing Sun, Donald H. Kluemper, Gordon W. Cheung, and
Adaora Ubaka. "The Cost of Managing Impressions for Black Employees:
An Expectancy Violation Theory Perspective." *Journal of Applied Psychology*
(August 2022). https://doi.org/10.1037/apl0001030.

CHAPTER 9: PROTECTING WITHOUT (RESORTING TO) POWER

Berger, Warren. "'Just Asking Questions': How Healthy Skepticism Morphed
into Toxic Denialism." Big Think, June 21, 2022. https://bigthink.com
/thinking/just-asking-questions/.

Bonaccio, Silvia, and Reeshad S. Dalal. "Advice Taking and Decision-Making:
An Integrative Literature Review, and Implications for the Organizational
Sciences." *Organizational Behavior and Human Decision Processes* 101, no. 2
(2006): 127–151. https://doi.org/10.1016/j.obhdp.2006.07.001.

Hildebrand, Laura K., Celine C. Jusuf, and Margo J. Monteith. "Ally Confron-
tations as Identity-Safety Cues for Marginalized Individuals." *European
Journal of Social Psychology* (June 2020). https://doi.org/10.1002/ejsp.2692.

Kotter, John P. *Leading Change.* Boston: Harvard Business School Press, 1996.

Nemeth, Charlan Jeanne, Joanie B. Connell, John D. Rogers, and Keith S. Brown.
"Improving Decision Making by Means of Dissent." *Journal of Applied
Social Psychology* 31, no. 1 (2001): 48–58. https://doi.org/10.1111/j.1559
-1816.2001.tb02481.x.

Nemeth, Charlan Jeanne, and Julianne L. Kwan. "Minority Influence, Divergent
Thinking and Detection of Correct Solutions." *Journal of Applied Social
Psychology* 17, no. 9 (1987): 788–799. https://doi.org/10.1111/j.1559
-1816.1987.tb00339.x.

Oc, Burak, Michael R. Bashshur, and Celia Moore. "Head Above the Parapet:
How Minority Subordinates Influence Group Outcomes and the Consequences They Face for Doing So." *Journal of Applied Psychology* 104, no. 7
(2019): 929–945. https://doi.org/10.1037/apl0000376.

Sniezek, Janet A., and Lyn M. Van Swol. "Trust, Confidence, and Expertise
in a Judge-Advisor System." *Organizational Behavior and Human Decision
Processes* 84, no. 2 (2001): 288–307. https://doi.org/10.1006/obhd.2000
.2926.

CHAPTER 10: TIME TO STRETCH

Cook, Alison, and Christy Glass. "Diversity Begets Diversity? The Effects of
Board Composition on the Appointment and Success of Women CEOs."
Social Science Research 53 (September 2015): 137–147. https://doi.org
/10.1016/j.ssresearch.2015.05.009.

DeNicola, Christina. "How Ng Built a Winning Culture in Miami." MLB .com, October 3, 2023. www.mlb.com/news/how-kim-ng-built-a-winning -culture-with-the-marlins.

Duguid, Michelle M., Denise Lewin Loyd, and Pamela S. Tolbert. "The Impact of Categorical Status, Numeric Representation, and Work Group Prestige on Preference for Demographically Similar Others: A Value Threat Approach." *Organization Science* 23, no. 2 (2012): 386–401. https://doi .org/10.1287/orsc.1100.0565.

Dwivedi, Priyanka, Aparna Joshi, and Vilmos F. Misangyi. "Gender-Inclusive Gatekeeping: How (Mostly Male) Predecessors Influence the Success of Female CEOs." *Academy of Management Journal* 61, no. 2 (2018): 379–404. https://doi.org/10.5465/amj.2015.1238.

Ghiroli, Brittany. "How Kim Ng Changed the Marlins: 'She's Relentless in Trying to Figure Out How to Improve.'" The Athletic, October 4, 2023, https://theathletic.com/4927865/2023/10/04/kim-ng-marlins-gm -playoffs/.

Glass, Christy, and Alison Cook. "Do Women Leaders Promote Positive Change? Analyzing the Effect of Gender on Business Practices and Diversity Initiatives." *Human Resource Management* 57, no. 4 (2017): 823–837. https: //doi.org/10.1002/hrm.21838.

Guldiken, Orhun, Mark R. Mallon, Stav Fainshmidt, and William Q. Judge. "Beyond Tokenism: How Strategic Leaders Influence More Meaningful Gender Diversity on Boards of Directors." *Strategic Management Journal* 40, no. 12 (2019). https://doi.org/10.1002/smj.3049.

Gupta, Vishal K., Seonghee Han, Sandra C. Mortal, Sabatino (Dino) Silveri, and Daniel B. Turban. "Do Women CEOs Face Greater Threat of Shareholder Activism Compared to Male CEOs? A Role Congruity Perspective." *Journal of Applied Psychology* 103, no. 2 (2018): 228–236. https://doi.org /10.1037/apl0000269.

Gupta, Vishal K., Sandra C. Mortal, Sabatino Silveri, Minxing Sun, and Daniel B. Turban. "You're Fired! Gender Disparities in CEO Dismissal." *Journal of Management* 46, no. 4 (2018): 560–582. https://doi.org/10.1177 /0149206318810415.

Hekman, David R., Stefanie K. Johnson, Maw-Der Foo, and Wei Yang. "Does Diversity-Valuing Behavior Result in Diminished Performance Ratings for Non-white and Female Leaders?" *Academy of Management Journal* 60, no. 2 (2017): 771–797. https://doi.org/10.5465/amj.2014.0538.

Henson, Steve. "Kim Ng, First Female General Manager, Leaves Marlins for Same Reason Derek Jeter Did." *Los Angeles Times*, October 16, 2023. www .latimes.com/sports/story/2023-10-16/kim-ng-leaves-marlins-general -manager-dodgers-yankees-red-sox-mets.

Kelly, Daniel. "Kim Ng Deserved Better from the Miami Marlins." *Sports Business Journal*, October 26, 2023. www.sportsbusinessjournal.com /Articles/2023/10/26/oped-26-kelly.

Vial, Andrea C., Jaime L. Napier, and Victoria L. Brescoll. "A Bed of Thorns: Female Leaders and the Self-Reinforcing Cycle of Illegitimacy." *Leadership Quarterly* 27, no. 3 (2016): 400–414. https://doi.org/10.1016/j.leaqua .2015.12.004.

INDEX

Christy Filkins

Dr. Rosalind Chow is an associate professor of organizational behavior and theory at Carnegie Mellon University. A social psychologist by training, Chow draws on both psychological and organizational behavior research to provide empirically validated insights on managerial practice. She has particular expertise on how members of dominant groups can contribute to the dismantling of systemic bias within organizations.

Chow is the founding faculty director for the Executive Leadership Academy (ELA), an executive leadership program aimed at addressing the challenges facing the advancement of Black leaders in Pittsburgh, Pennsylvania. She also serves as the faculty director for the CLIMB fellowship program, a partnership between Deloitte and Tepper Business School designed to increase the advancement of Black and Latino/Hispanic accountants.

Chow's research is published in top psychology and organizational behavior journals and featured in articles in the *Harvard Business Review* and the *MIT Sloan Management Review*. She is a consultant and speaker for a variety of organizations, such as Amazon Web Services, Genentech, Google Workspace, Kaiser Permanente, PNC Bank, and others. She lives in Pittsburgh with her husband, marketing professor Jeff Galak, and their two children.

PublicAffairs is a publishing house founded in 1997. It is a tribute to the standards, values, and flair of three persons who have served as mentors to countless reporters, writers, editors, and book people of all kinds, including me.

I. F. STONE, proprietor of *I. F. Stone's Weekly*, combined a commitment to the First Amendment with entrepreneurial zeal and reporting skill and became one of the great independent journalists in American history. At the age of eighty, Izzy published *The Trial of Socrates*, which was a national bestseller. He wrote the book after he taught himself ancient Greek.

BENJAMIN C. BRADLEE was for nearly thirty years the charismatic editorial leader of *The Washington Post*. It was Ben who gave the *Post* the range and courage to pursue such historic issues as Watergate. He supported his reporters with a tenacity that made them fearless and it is no accident that so many became authors of influential, best-selling books.

ROBERT L. BERNSTEIN, the chief executive of Random House for more than a quarter century, guided one of the nation's premier publishing houses. Bob was personally responsible for many books of political dissent and argument that challenged tyranny around the globe. He is also the founder and longtime chair of Human Rights Watch, one of the most respected human rights organizations in the world.

·　　·　　·

For fifty years, the banner of Public Affairs Press was carried by its owner Morris B. Schnapper, who published Gandhi, Nasser, Toynbee, Truman, and about 1,500 other authors. In 1983, Schnapper was described by *The Washington Post* as "a redoubtable gadfly." His legacy will endure in the books to come.

Peter Osnos, *Founder*